The Godly Image
Christ and Salvation in Catholic Thought from St Anselm to Aquinas

Romanus Cessario, O.P.

St. Bede's Publications
Petersham, MA 01366

St. Bede's Publications, Petersham, MA 01366

97 96 95 94 93 92 91 90   5 4 3 2 1

The following publishers have generously given permission to use extended quotations from copyrighted works: *Summa Theologiae* by Thomas Aquinas, edited by Gilby and O'Brien. Reprinted by permission of Eyre-Spottiswoode, Ltd. and McGraw-Hill.

Photo credit: frontispiece—Holy Trinity, Musée Th. Dobrée, Nantes (courtesy Rast-Foto, Switzerland).

Library of Congress Cataloging-in-Publication Data

Cessario, Romanus.
  The godly image : Christ & salvation in Catholic thought from St. Anselm to Aquinas / by Romanus Cessario.
    p. cm. — (Studies in historical theology : 6)
  Includes bibliographical references.
  ISBN 0-932506-74-7
  1. Satisfaction for sin—History of doctrines—Middle Ages, 600-1500.
2. Thomas, Aquinas, Saint, 1225/?/-1274—Contributions in doctrine of satisfaction for sin. I. Title. II. Series: Studies in historical theology (Still River, Mass.) : v. 6.

BT263.C48   1989   89-62742
232'.3'09022—dc20   CIP

For

The Faculty and Students

at the

Dominican House of Studies

1979 — 1989

Love, then, consists in this:
    not that we have loved God
    but that he has loved us
    and has sent his Son as an offering
        for our sins.

1 Jn 4,10

TABLE OF CONTENTS

ACKNOWLEDGEMENTS

In the first place, I wish to give credit to Mr. Edward Panico. Like most authors, I was happy to allow passing time to separate me from my doctoral dissertation, especially when I consider how much what I then thought counted as scholarship, in fact, influenced my academic style. For his own reasons, Dr. Panico, along with the good services of the Benedictine nuns at St. Bede's Publications, nonetheless persuaded me to produce this revised edition.

Accordingly, the present text represents some of what I have learned about the satisfaction of Christ during the past ten years. To the extent that these results exhibit an expanded ability to use the English language, I am indebted to Rev. John P. McIntyre, S.J. His patient efforts over the past several years assure me that the greater glory of God appears in ways that my Dominican upbringing failed to include. I count it a privilege, then, to be lately numbered among Fr. McIntyre's "old boys," who remain among the few really able to appreciate the power of the verb "to be." On the other hand, I could not have achieved the amount of revision I did without the technical support of Fathers Stephen Dominic Hayes, OP and Robert Twele, OFM Conv, who assisted me variously and variously at important stages of the revision. Their combined industry has brought this publication into the twenty-first century, where the wisdom of Aquinas finds as congenial a setting as in the thirteenth. Toward this achievement, Fr Robert showed more patience than even St Francis could have expected from one of his followers.

Although teaching assignments in other branches of theology, especially morals, during the past ten years has considerably broadened my reading of Aquinas, I have been fortunate also to continue several courses in the area of christology. The results of this program of study appears both in the revised text and, especially, in the expanded footnotes. These I have endeavored, moreover, to make reader-friendly in order to meet the needs of students coming to the study of christology or Aquinas for the first time. Mr Russell Shaw generously helped this entire project by his careful proofreading of the manuscript.

Finally, it gives me great pleasure to acknowledge the patience and good services of the students at the Dominican House of Studies during the years 1979-1989. More than any other, these men and women, friars and friends, both by their criticisms and their compliments, have encouraged me to present again this modest study on the meaning of Christ's love. I also recognize the substantive contribution given by my Dominican colleagues, especially Rev. Mark Heath, OP and Rev. Cyril Dettling, OP. As President of our Pontifical Faculty, the latter generously contributed toward the completion of this project. Despite its limitations, I still trust that the work contributes to the fulfillment of the Dominican charge to preach the truth about Jesus Christ -- *Praedicatio Jesu Christi.*

Washington, D.C.
7 March 1989

INTRODUCTION

The theological act remains an act of historical understanding in two respects. First of all, it bears upon a content that has been historically transmitted within the Christian tradition, beginning with the scriptural witness and proceeding thence through the intervening doctrinal and theological witnesses. Its objective, therefore, remains a set of claims about history which have themselves been historically mediated. At the same time, theological exercise is historical in another sense. For it queries the testimonial materials received from the past tradition in light of its present historical situation. Its retrieval of the past does not consist simply in an immediate attainment of past meanings and explanations. Rather, the encounter occurs within the perspective of concerns contemporary with the theological act itself. Such encounter is truly critical and measures up to the scientific charter of theological inquiry when the circuit is closed, as it were--i.e., when the perspective of the past and that of present theological inquiry are permitted to be mutually illumining.

The Christian claims about salvation and about the role of Jesus of Nazareth in God's final and definitive deed of saving humanity have been subject to a variety of understandings, explanations, and analogies over two millennia. Those claims and their various renderings possess a doctrinal and theological history. If one may be permitted a generalization about that received tradition, its operative perspectives seem to have been objectivist in large measure: for example, in the discussion of the incarnation, it uses the notion of "common nature assumed" as a central conceptual framework.

Presently, as theology attempts to penetrate and appropriate the received historical tradition, these are exactly the sort of perspectives which seem not to suit the contemporary situation. Whatever critical reservations one might have about it, the simple fact remains that quite different perspectives mark the contemporary situation of the theological act. The first of these, dominant since Descartes, regards the dynamism of the subject as in some measure creative of the meaning and value of his interactions with the world. Closely allied to this subjectivist interest and the personalist concerns which it generates is the emergence of historical understanding: the recognition that human being is not simply historical being, that what is distinctively human is present in those dimensions in which human being stands out from common nature and purely temporal succession.

This difference in perspectives provides the starting-point of any theological exercise directed toward recovering the Christian soteriological tradition. The practitioner of theological inquiry will enter upon this enterprise shaped to some extent by the contemporary perspective. And, due to this initial difference in perspectives between the past tradition and present inquiry, the initial encounter will be marked by a certain experience of the "foreignness" of the received tradition. The genius of the theological exercise remains, of course, to discover certain basic intelligibilities in the tradition without too facilely eliding the difference of perspectives.

St Thomas Aquinas's soteriological model of satisfaction provides the case at hand in this book.[1] Its basic perspective may appear alien at first, and any number of authors have taken up the challenge to explain why.[2] It further suffers from the baggage accumulated from the satisfaction theory of Anselm's *Cur Deus Homo?* and from its later conflation with substitutional theories of Christ's saving work.[3] As in all theological activity, the goal of this work will be to effect a merging of perspectives. This means respecting the distinctive perspective of St Thomas's account of the satisfactory character of Christ's work while seeking to recover and illumine its latent resonances with the contemporary situation of theological activity. For example, although the notion of "common nature assumed" has connotations alien to much of contemporary philosophy, in some respects it functions only as a preliminary element of explanation in St Thomas's account of Christ's satisfactory work. The human nature assumed by the Word is that whereby he is "homōousois hēmin," in the phrase of Chalcedon; it is a factor explaining our ontic accessibility and communion with Christ and other human beings insofar as all agree in possession of this nature. More importantly, however, this ontic communication is only the area for a mode of union based not simply upon the specific identity of natures, but rather preeminently personal in which both head and members are conjoined: fundamentally and hypostatically so in the case of the Word's union with his human nature, and intentionally so, by way of the personal activities of supernatural knowing and loving. What is salvifically significant is what transpires between the persons who are the subjects of a common nature.

The professional theological career of Aquinas spans some twenty years of preaching, teaching, and writing. During this period of time St Thomas produced some one hundred works.[4] Since the appearance of the *Index Thomisticus* in 1973, the student possesses a research tool which allows one to study the texts of St Thomas in a more thorough-going manner than was possible for previous generations of scholars.[5] Although primarily a tool for linguistic research of the middle ages, the *Index Thomisticus* also remains an invaluable tool for research in theology. The presently published sections of the *Index* provide the student of St Thomas immediate access to the some 1,200 places throughout the course of his writings where he uses some form of the Latin words "satisfactio" or "satisfacere."

The initial step in researching this work consisted in a careful examination of the passages in the Thomistic corpus where some form of the word "satisfaction" appeared. Setting aside those places where the word was used to denote something other than the satisfactory character of Christ's work or the penitential satisfactions of the members of Christ (as when the verb "satisfacere" denotes to satiate or to convince)[6], two basic areas of theological discussion emerged. The first concerns the salvific work of Christ, where St Thomas employs the model of satisfaction as a tool of theological explication for understanding the nature of God's saving deed in Christ. Closely allied to this first area of discussion is a second: the satisfaction accomplished by the members of Christ, that is, how the final and definitive salvation accomplished in Christ is mediated to those who by reason of their being a part of God's plan of salvation remain incorporated in some way into the person of Jesus Christ. The biblical image of head and members has been adopted in this study as a convenient metonymy for organizing the materials so as to reflect both the different contexts in which St Thomas discusses the notion of satisfaction and something of their intimate connection.[7]

As the second step followed in the preparation of this present work, we organized the materials in such a way as to acknowledge the chronology of St Thomas's works in and to take into account the fact of development in his thought. However, some departure from this basic procedure of presenting the works of St Thomas in chronological order is required because of the nature of the works themselves. For example, the commentaries on scripture seemed more appropriately treated in a single chapter at the beginning of the work, because of the difficulty in determining the exact chronology of certain works which, in some cases at least, were composed simultaneously. In general, though, the major systematic treatises are examined chronologically to the extent that the consistent application of this principle aids a coherent presentation of St Thomas's doctrine.

The third step involved the retrieval of the several controlling perspectives which marked St Thomas's theology of satisfaction as a distinctive and original contribution to the development of Christian soteriology. The elements of this perspective emerge gradually and with various imports, determined largely by the nature of the work in which satisfaction is discussed and the given work's relation to his mature thought, which, it becomes increasingly apparent, is clearly contained in the *Summa theologiae*. The principal aim of this book remains to demonstrate that St Thomas's contribution to the development of an adequate satisfaction-model for theological use in the discussion of the saving death of Jesus Christ remains a distinctive one. It should not be assumed that it is a simple restatement of St Anselm's satisfaction-theory, as Gustav Aulèn, for example, supposes, nor that it is easily drawn into service to support penal substitution theories.[8]

St Thomas's theological clarification of the satisfaction-model is marked by the same emphases found in his mature works, foremost among them a strong desire to accentuate the personal character of God-man relations as they are realized in the person of incarnate Word. Drawing upon the richness of the various testimonial witnesses available to him, St Thomas fashioned a satisfaction-model which derives both its explanatory elements and deepest meaning and vitality from a vision of the saving work of Jesus Christ as actualized in individual believers in order to move them forward on their journey to beatific fellowship. Central to this explanation is the notion of the reformation of the image of God in man which, with all of its dynamic resonances in St Thomas's account, is accomplished through the free exercise of satisfactory acts in the personal sin-marked histories of believers precisely as such acts are suffused with and undergirded by the eminent satisfaction of Christ. This scheme serves to highlight the unconditional priority of the divine action at the heart of the discussion, for it is God who is acting in Jesus to complete his plan for salvation.

In any discussion of a given part of St Thomas's theological synthesis, however, we must bear in mind how he understands the nature of the divine essence and how that shapes his conception of divine activity *ad extra*. God does not act in order to acquire some new perfection as an end or goal. Rather, as *ipsum esse subsistens*, his ontological transcendence is the root of the sheer liberality and graciousness of all his activities with respect to the non-divine. Thus the sole reason why God operates *ad extra* remains to be sought in the divine reality itself, that is, in the sheer communicative good that is his being.[9] Such operation is above all ordered to the bestowal of triune communion in that good upon the rational creature, who bears the image of that communion in his constitution and as his destiny. The achievement of this personal communion as a surpassing gift and in the face of human historical sin is the core-reality which St Thomas develops his satisfaction-model to explain and the meaning he fathoms in the words of St Paul, "in Christ God was reconciling the world to himself" (IICor 5:19).[10]

Satisfaction, therefore, is not something God requires of man, or even of Jesus, as a condition for accomplishing his saving plan. Rather it is the means whereby God in very fact accomplishes his plan to bring all men and women into loving union with himself. It is man and not God who is changed by satisfaction. For, on the one hand, the increment and restoration of perfection designated by the term "satisfaction" pertains entirely to the human creature; by contrast, the communication of that increment pertains with absolute priority to divine goodness and mercy penetrating the human creature with God's own love. It is, then, the individual, in the historical and social dimensions of his personhood, who in the progressive reformation of his God-like image (in the present order of things marred by the sin of Adam as well as by personal sin) is gradually changed into being what God intends his creature to be.[11]

In order to accomplish the purpose of this work the results of the research have been divided into six chapters. The first chapter is introductory in scope; in it the professional career of Thomas Aquinas is reviewed and the works in which he speaks of satisfaction are discussed as to purpose and general theme. The excellent study of the late James A. Weisheipl, O.P., *Friar Thomas d'Aquino*, has been adopted as a standard for both the biographical details of St Thomas's life and for establishing the authenticity and dating of his works.[12] It should be noted, however, that questions in either area which remain a subject of debate among scholars do not substantially affect the conclusions of this investigation.

The second chapter is devoted to St Thomas's commentaries, including the *reportationes*, on the sacred scriptures. As already noted, these have been collected into a single chapter without regard for their position in the chronological list of his works and has been placed at the beginning of the study. This was judged in the best interests of the work because the material concerning the satisfaction of Christ and of the members drawn from the scriptural commentaries could be better presented and more accurately analyzed in a global fashion, rather than introducing small snippets throughout the work. Such a manner of presentation also emphasizes the central role which commenting on the inspired texts played in the development of St Thomas as a theologian and, consequently, avoids the impression that the Bible was of peripheral or secondary importance to the theological task of systematization for a thirteenth-century *magister* such as St Thomas. In addition, the fact that the scriptural commentaries are among the most difficult of St Thomas's works to date precisely argued for this manner of presentation. Especially is this the case with the *Expositio et lectura super Epistolas Pauli Apostoli*, whose actual dates of composition remain the subject of considerable debate.

The third chapter concentrates exclusively upon the first theological synthesis of St Thomas, the *Scriptum super Sententias*. In this work St Thomas uses some form of the word "satisfaction" nearly 700 times in the course of commenting on the *Sentences* of Peter Lombard; thus a considerable amount of material had to be considered. Furthermore, the *Scriptum* remains the only systematic work in which one finds a detailed discussion of satisfaction as one of the principal parts of the sacrament of penance. The corresponding section of the *Summa theologiae* was not completed; in fact it was terminated at the brink of just such a discussion. For this reason, although the *Sciptum* is an earlier rendition of satisfaction-themes in St Thomas's theological enterprise which was subject to revision and to the introduction of new understandings as that enterprise advanced, the fact remains that the very wealth and variety of his treatment in the *Scriptum* affords it an important place in ascertaining what St Thomas taught. Hence the *Scriptum* is an important text for beginning a study of satisfaction, especially as it is related to the virtue of justice.

The fourth chapter considers works composed between the two major theological syntheses, the *Scriptum* and the *Summa theologiae*. In works such as the *De veritate*, the *Summa contra gentiles* and the *De rationibus fidei*, one finds a consideration of the notion of satisfaction which is guided and amplified by their distinctive intention (e.g., apologetic in the case of the latter two). In the *De veritate*, the notion is addressed more obliquely and by reference to certain closely allied notions such as the grace and merit of Christ as head. The works of this period exhibit some of the distinctive perspectives of St Thomas's theology that will shape the final contours of his satisfaction-model in the *Summa theologiae*. By way of preface to this exposition there is an examination of St Thomas's notion of sin viewed from the aspects of *poena* and *culpa* as he developed it in the *De malo*. The need for a more focused and extended treatment of the constituents of sin as St Thomas understands them was judged necessary because of its import for his satisfaction-model.

The final chapters, five and six, treat the *Summa theologiae*, the work of St Thomas's theological maturity. Within its restricted scope, the present study confirms the long-held belief that the most articulate expression of his thought is to be found within its pages. Concentration upon the *Summa*, however, has not always served the best interests of Thomistic studies. The emergence of an historically-minded approach to Aquinas's thought since the end of the last century has underlined the importance of studying St Thomas within his historical situation and in the context of possible development within his own thought.[13] Suffice it to observe the objectivist perspective for which Thomism is currently and frequently criticized--and which accounts for its initial appearance of "foreignness"--is often the result of having read St Thomas in an abstract and a-historical way rather than having adverted to the full dimensions and texture of his thought as it develops throughout his writing career. Nevertheless, given the systematic integrity of the *Summa theologiae* as a whole, no attempt will be made to discriminate between the various chronological periods of the extended composition of its parts; rather, the treatment will proceed as an ensemble.

The formally christological questions of the *tertia pars* are the subject of chapter five. They are introduced by material from the *prima secundae* in which a more fully developed notion of punishment as restorative is found and in which a marked personalistic development of these themes seems to prepare for St Thomas's development of satisfaction in the *tertia pars*. It is in the course of treating questions 46 through 55 of the *tertia pars* (devoted to the passion and death of Christ) that the argument is advanced that satisfaction is the guiding model or key-notion in St Thomas's theological explanation of the mystery of Christ's salvific death. Chapter six is intended to be a summary chapter in which the perspectives of St Thomas's theology of image-restoration accomplished through satisfaction are put into sharp relief. This is done by setting this doctrine into the concrete, historical dispensation of salvation-history as a history of both sinful rejection and overriding divine grace, a history ruled by a plan rendering satisfaction possible in a variety of historical modes, culminating in the Christian economy. As a last point of discussion, the sacraments of baptism and penance are examined as they are sign-actions mediating the satisfaction of Christ. However, at this point the primary focus is not analytical but synthetic, and so the final chapter should not be read as a minor treatise on Thomistic sacramental theology but, rather, as a summary of the entire treatment, stating how the satisfaction of Christ is a fulfillment of God's saving plan in the believer: "For in him all the fullness of God was pleased to dwell, and through him to reconcile to himself all things, whether on earth or in heaven, making peace by the blood of his cross" (Col 1:19-20).

NOTES

1. Research in Aquinas, of course, constitutes it own specialization. Terry L. Miethe and Vernon J. Bourke, *Thomistic Bibliography, 1940-78* (Westport, CT: Greenwood Press, 1980) provides a good start for materials since the Second World War. For earlier works, see Vernon J. Bourke, *Thomistic Bibliography: 1920-1940* (St. Louis: The Modern Schoolman, 1945) and Pierre Mandonnet and J. Destrez, *Bibliographie thomiste*, 2nd ed. by M.-D. Chenu (Paris: Bibliothèque thomiste, 1960). Currently, the *Rassegna di letteratura tomistica* (Naples, 1969-) continues the excellent work of the *Bulletin thomiste* (Bellevue, S.-et-O., 1924, then Le Saulchoir, S.-et-O, until 1968). For a specialized bibliography on the mysteries of Christ's life, see, I. Biffi, "Saggio bibliographico sui misteri della vita di Cristo in S. Tommaso d'Aquino," *La scuola cattolica* 99 (1971) *Suppl.*, 175*-238*. Also, see Bruner Gherardini, "La 'Satisfactio Vicaria' in San Tommaso," *Doctor Communis* 37 (1984), 103-22. For a different perspective, see John T. Noonan, "Agency, Bribery and Redemption in Thomas Aquinas," *Recherches de Théologie ancienne et médiévale* 49 (1982), 159-173.

2. For a representative reaction to this position, see Gerald O'Collins, S.J., *The Calvary Christ* (Philadelphia: Westminster, 1977), especially, 92 where he refers to the 19th-century American preacher Phillips Brooks and his uneasiness with the notion of satisfaction: "You say that it (sc. the death of Christ) appeased His (sc. God's wrath). I am not sure there may not be some meaning of those words which does not include the truth which they try to express, but in their natural sense which men gather from them out of their ordinary human uses, I do not believe they are true. This Reformation view perdures in the writings of the contemporary theologian Wolfhart Pannenberg, *Jesus-- God and Man*, trans. L.L. Wilkins and D.A. Priebe (Philadelphia: Westminster, 1968), especially, 277 ff. Pannenberg emphasizes the deficiencies of Anselm's theory, as he understands it, and underscores rather "the meaning that can be seen in the event of the cross within the context in which it happened in the light of Jesus' resurrection." Even Catholic theologians want to amend the notion, for example, Christian Duquoc, O.P., *Christologie: Le Messie* (Paris: Editions du Cerf, 1972), especially, 213-16: "Tel est le sens de la satisfaction: réintéger dans l'amour divin des actes qui furent des échecs à la gloire de Dieu.... La condition 'pénale,' le Christ, par sa lutte pour la justice et son amour de Dieu, la transforme de telle sorte que l'homme puisse y réécrire son histoire." On the other hand, liberationist theologians, for example, Juan Luis Segundo, S.J., *A Theology for Artisans of a New Humanity*, Vols. 1-5, trans. John Drury (New York: Orbis, 1974), leave the notion of satisfaction aside.

3. For a good example of penal substitution theories, see John Calvin, *Institutes of the Christian Religion* II, 16, trans. J. Allen (Grand Rapids: Erdemans, 1949), 553. Calvin recognizes that Christ has taken upon himself and suffered the punishment which by the righteous judgment of God impended over all sinners, and he also states that this expiation satisfies God the Father, appeasing his wrath. Even some contemporary authors so interpret the work of Christ, see, for example, Dorothee Sölle, *Christ the Representative*, trans. D. Lewis (Philadelphia: SCM Press, 1967), 150: "Christ took over God's role in the world, but in the process it was changed into the role of the helpless God. The absent God whom Christ represents is the God who is helpless in this world...." For a critique of penal substitution theories, see Philippe de la Trinité, OCD, *Rédemption par le sang* (Paris: Fayard, 1959).

4. For a complete list of Aquinas's work, see I. T. Eschmann, O.P., "A Catalogue of St. Thomas's Works" in Etienne Gilson, *The Christian Philosophy of St. Thomas Aquinas*, trans. L.K. Shook, CSB (New York: Random House, 1956), 381-439.

5. *Index thomisticus: Sancti Thomae Aquinatis operum omnium indices et concordantiae*, ed Robert Busa, S.J., *Indices distributionis*, 8 vols. (Stuttgart: Frommann-Holzboog, 1975-1976); Sectio II: *Concordantia prima*, 23 vols. (Stuttgart-Bad Cannstatt, 1974-1975). The *Index* studies principal terms found in some 179 Latin works written between the 9th and 16th-centuries. By far the most thorough index of Aquinas, the *Index* studies at least 100 of his authentic works. Prepared with the aid of computer technology, this work completes Peter of Bergamo's *Tabula aurea*. For a fuller description of the history and structure of the *Index*, see Walter Brugger, S.J., "Index Thomisticus," *Theologie und Philosophie* 52 (1977), 435-44.

6. For example, the following text appears in *ST* IIa-IIae q. 119, a. 2, ad 1: "Alii vero dicunt quod loquitur de cupiditate generali respectu cuiuscumque boni. Et sic manifestum est quod etiam prodigalitas ex cupiditate oritur: prodigus enim aliquod bonum temporale cupit consequi inordinate; vel placere aliis vel saltem *satisfacere* suae voluntati in dando." For obvious reasons, this study does not consider such meanings of the word "to satisfy."

7. Augustine, following the Johannine and Pauline writings, also likes to designate the Church as the whole Christ ("totus Christus"): "Therefore since he [Christ] is the head of the whole Church and the Church is his body, the head and the body make up the whole Christ" (*Sermo* 137, 1, 1, *PL* 38:754). Again, in his *Commentary on the Epistle of John (ad Parthos)* 10, 3 (*PL* 35:2055), he uses the beautiful phrase, "unus Christus amans seipsum," to express the intimate union between Christ and his members: "By loving one becomes himself a member, and through love he enters into the structure of the body of Christ, and

there will be one Christ loving himself. For when the members love one another, the body loves itself."

8. For instance, Gustav Aulèn argues that Aquinas simply represents a continuation of the Latin interpretation of vindicative justice first proposed by St Anselm. He contrasts this position unfavorably with the "classic" interpretation of redemption which he avers to find, for example, in the Eastern Fathers. See his *Christus Victor*, trans. A.G. Hebert (New York: Macmillan, 1969), 93. For a reply to those who continue to make this same assumption, see Jerry Bracken, C.P., "Thomas Aquinas and Anselm's Satisfaction Theory," *Angelicum* 62 (1985), 501-30.

9. St Thomas illustrates this prominent issue further in one of his disputed questions: "The ultimate end remains not the communication of goodness, but rather divine goodness itself. It is from his love of this goodness that God wills it to be communicated. In fact, when he acts because of his goodness, it is not as if he were pursuing something that he does not possess, but, as it were, willing to communicate what he does possess. For he does not act from desire for the end, but from love of the end" (*De potentia* q. 3, a. 15, ad 14).

10. Of course, Aquinas conserves the transcendence of God throughout his discussion of the incarnation and soteriology. For a reply to those theologians who argue that authentic reconciliation necessarily entails a "suffering God," see Jean-Hervé Nicolas, O.P., "Aimante et bienheureuse Trinité," *Revue Thomiste* 78 (1978), 271-92. St Thomas, on the other hand, places suffering and, therefore, change in the creature. For further refinement of this point, see Jean-Hervé, O.P., "La seconde mort du pécheur et la reconciliation," *Revue Thomiste* 79 (1979), 25-49.

11. For example, John A.T. Robinson, *Wrestling with Romans* (Philadelphia: Westminster, 1979), especially, 37-48, explains that the *hilasterion* principally affects human sinfulness which, the author affirms, both distorts and sours a person's relationship with God.

12. James A. Weisheipl, O.P., *Friar Thomas d'Aquino: His Life, thought, and Work* (New York: Doubleday, 1974), Second edition with *Corrigenda* and *Addenda* (Washington: The Catholic University of America Press, 1983).

13. In an important essay, Dom Odo Lottin, OSB delineates the correct historical method for reading Aquinas. See his "Pour un commentaire historiques de la morale de saint Thomas d'Aquin," in *Psychologie et morale au XIIe et XIIIe siècles*, 3/2 vol. (Paris: Gembloux, 1949), 579-601.

CHAPTER I

"A NEW LIGHT FROM GOD"

1252-1256: Sententiarius at Paris: *Scriptum Super Sententias*

Bernard Gui, one of Aquinas's earliest biographers, gives us a description of the success that St Thomas's early teaching achieved at the University of Paris.

> God graced his teaching so abundantly that it began to make a wonderful impression on the students. For it all seemed so novel--new arrangements of subject matter, new methods of proof, new arguments adduced for the conclusions. In short, no one who heard him could doubt that his mind was full of a new light from God.[1]

We can perhaps best describe the interval 1252-1256 in Aquinas's life as a period for graduate studies. During that time, he carried out the professional duties of an academic bachelor, especially the preparation of a "scriptum" based on the standard theological textbook of the day, the *Sentences* of Peter the Lombard.[2] Since the young scholastic theologian proved his skill and secured his professional standing in this way, medievalists rightly compare the production of such a "scriptum" to a modern Ph.D. thesis.[3]

Of course, the *Sentences* of Peter the Lombard mark an important development in the history of medieval theology. Furthermore, we discover commentaries on this work written as late as the 17th-century.[4] Suffice it to observe, however, that the text's popularity in the 13th-century owed much to the moderate course which this bishop-theologian steered between the ostensible rationalism (characteristic of the school of Abelard) and the method of textual analysis and criticism (characteristic of the approach used in the monastic schools). All in all, the Lombard took the collected sayings ("sententiae") of the authorities on a given topic and organized them. Taking his cue from St Augustine's teaching that theology concerns either "things" or "signs," Lombard arranged his material around four central articles of the Creed, namely, Trinity, incarnation, creation and sin, and the sacraments and four last things. The first three articles, he observed, belong to the category of "things" and the last one to that of "signs."[5] Thus, Lombard established a theological scheme for handling the testimonials of the tradition.

Aquinas changed that scheme. We find a good indication of the "new approach" of which Bernard Gui speaks in the way Thomas altered the Lombard's organization. In brief, he abandoned the Augustinian distinction between "things" and "signs" and, perhaps following a suggestion made by the Franciscan Alexander of Hales, divided the Lombard's book into roughly two equal sections, each containing two sub-divisions.[6] The first he designated the "exitus" (the coming forth of creatures from God) and the second, the "reditus" (the return of all things to God). This represented a conspicuous and innovative move on the part of a young bachelor. Why? Because he departed from the traditional approach, one hallowed by no less an authority than St Augustine himself, and opted instead to follow the lead of original thinkers, some of whom, like Plotinus, even stand outside of the Christian tradition.

Despite the freshness of outlook which characterized the teaching and the writing of the young "sententiarius," the *Scriptum super Sententias* remains only a commencement. In fact, shortly after Aquinas's death, we find concordances which point out the difference between what he teaches in the *Scriptum super Sententias* and how he later express himself in the *Summa theologiae*.[7] On the other hand, since the *Summa* remains an unfinished work, we do not find there every subject which Thomas had the opportunity to treat in the *Scriptum super Sententias*. As a result, certain subjects, including some attributes of satisfaction, find their only comprehensive and systematic treatment in the *Scriptum super Sententias*. The work, then, requires careful analysis for the present research.

Aquinas completed the work in the form in which we now have it around 1256.[8] More than just an edited set of notes used for classroom lecturing, the text is in fact a polished piece of writing. The author divides each of the four books into distinctions, questions, articles and sometimes even "quaestiuncula" or sub-questions. The topics which Aquinas discusses in these units do bear some relation to the corresponding text of the Lombard, but they also embody independent theological discussions which remain intelligible in themselves even when separated from the text of the original author. We can, thus, suitably refer to the work as a "scriptum" or a "writing" on the *Sentences*, rather than a proper commentary on the work of the Lombard.

Still, in order to understand Aquinas's theological mentality at this stage, we must also grasp the methodological principles employed in a work like the *Sentences* of Peter Lombard. In general, the work demonstrates the reverence in which medieval authors held traditional theological authorities, that is, the "approved sources." Broadly speaking, the medieval theologians esteemed what had gone before, especially during the patristic era. For them, the Fathers of East and West remained a benchmark for further investigation. The theological treatises of St Augustine and the biblical commentaries of St Jerome merited special regard, but even more recent works by authors such as Bernard of Clairvaux, Ivo of Chartres, Anselm of Canterbury also counted as sources for theology.[9] Not only might this consciousness of the past have proved restrictive, and consequently limited the development of theology by fostering a servile spirit towards authorities, this sometimes in fact happened, as the reaction to Aristotle's entry into the West testifies.[10] But it remains a sign of Thomas's genius that even from the start of his theological career, he was able to deal respectfully with the authorities and at the same time to exercise a creative kind of scholarship, which allowed him the freedom to develop a personal style. Even his earliest theological work shows a promise which will come to maturity in his later writings, especially the *Summa theologiae*.

At the same time, since it represents a systematic work, we will allot considerable space to the *Scriptum super Sententias*. In addition, a sustained look at St Thomas's teaching also allows us to make a comparison between his initial doctrine on satisfaction and subsequent developments. Since we can also presume growth in knowledge and understanding in one who, in fact, grew in grace, it remains a working hypothesis of this investigation that Aquinas's conception of Christian satisfaction did mature.

1256-1259 Regent Master in Theology at Paris: *De veritate; Quaestiones de quodlibet; Super Matthaeum; Super Isaiam; Contra impugnantes*

During the spring of 1256, Thomas left the ranks of the bachelors of theology at the University of Paris and received the title "master" in theology. Since the anti-mendicant controversy was at its height, this was an exciting period in the history of the University of Paris. In fact, shortly after his inception as a master Thomas was obliged to take time away from his formal classroom preparations in order to formulate a rejoinder to those University members who wished to restrict the number of religious on the teaching staff. As a testimony to that effort we have his work, *Contra impugnantes Dei cultum et religionem*, a long refutation directed against the vitriolic remarks of William of Saint-Armour in his *De periculis novissimorum temporum*.[11] William led the anti-mendicant forces. However, since it treats questions related to the apostolic activity of religious orders and their right to exercise certain apostolic functions within the Church, this work does not figure largely in the present study.

Once Thomas assumed the role of a master at the University of Paris, he performed the two indispensable duties of that office, namely, to lecture on the Bible and to determine or resolve in a scientific way the theological questions of his day. A third duty included the preaching of sermons at the University.[12] Although the place preaching held in the medieval method of instruction remains outside the scope of this work, we will examine Thomas's writings from the first Paris regency which represent the two academic functions of the master in theology.[13]

Among those texts which treat of christological satisfaction, the principal work dating from this period remains the disputed question, *De veritate*. In particular, we will focus upon those sections of the work (dating from Thomas's third year of teaching, 1258-59) which deal with the subject of Christ's human will and the effect on it of his habitual grace (qq. 21-29). Besides the ordinary academic disputations, we know that the masters undertook another kind of disputation. Held twice yearly during Advent and Lent, these special classes provided students and other members of the faculty of theology the opportunity to raise questions of all sorts. Since the students posed whatever questions they wished, these sessions were called "quodlibetal" disputations. Thomas's *Quaestiones de quodlibet*, then, cover a broad range of subjects, and sometimes even include questions which strike the modern reader as arcane. Even so, some important remarks do touch upon the notion of satisfaction, and these belong to Aquinas's first Paris regency.[14]

The obligation to read ("legere") and to comment upon the sacred scriptures was the foundation of magisterial teaching at the University of Paris during the 13th-century. By contrast, it remains a matter of dispute whether Aquinas ever actually taught the *Summa contra gentiles* or the *Summa theologiae*. The title *magister in sacra pagina*, as Weisheipl observes, remains the most ancient designation for a medieval theologian.[15] Besides, Thomas's scriptural commentaries include the most eloquent testimony to his spirituality as well as his theological competence. The dating of these commentaries, however, remains a subject of dispute among scholars, though it seems reasonably sure that *Lectura super Matthaeum*: *Reportatio* belongs to the period presently under discussion. Although the details of this particular work's publication seem complex, those sections of the *Lectura* pertinent to our study do not include passages of questionable authenticity.[16]

A second biblical commentary, the *Postilla super Isaiam*, also poses a difficulty as to its composition. Although Weisheipl assigns this work to the second period of Thomas's academic career in Paris, the Leonine editors argue, on the basis of a small autograph section, that it actually belongs to this first period.[17] The controversy, however, does not affect this study since the sole reference to christological satisfaction demonstrates Aquinas's synthetic approach to biblical commentary, but does not mark a shift in his thinking. Deliberate references to Aquinas's scriptural commentaries also illustrate the solid biblical foundation, the "underpinning of the rest," as the medieval author put it, which always undergirds even the most elaborate logical superstructure found in medieval theology.[18] As a result, these citations from the scriptural commentaries should give pause to those who like to characterize the theology of Thomas Aquinas as too analytic or, what is more misleading, methodologically dissociated from its revealed sources in the Christian faith.

1259-1268: In Service to the Church in Italy:
Summa contra gentiles; De rationibus fidei;
De rationibus fidei; In Job; De malo;
Summa theologiae, Prima pars

After his three-year term as master of theology, Aquinas left Paris and, as the custom of the Dominicans dictated, returned to Italy, where he had first entered the Friars Preachers. Scant documentation makes it difficult to establish an exact chronology of the next ten years of his life. We do know, however, that Thomas spent all of the time in Italy either in service to the Dominican Order or to the papal curia. The following chronology suggests where he served during his time in Italy.

Fall 1259	at Paris
1260 to fall 1261	at Naples
1261 to fall 1265	at Orvieto (papal curia)
1265 to summer 1267	at Rome
1267 to fall 1268	at Viterbo (papal curia)

Thus we see that Aquinas spent his time within the limits of the Papal States as established at that time. Since this provided him contact with the ecumenical Church, he was exposed to influences broader than those at Paris.

Even before completing his term at Paris, however, Thomas was asked to begin a new kind of apostolate of the pen. This kind of instruction he could continue even once he left the classroom. Dominican missionaries were working in Spain and North Africa with Moslems and Jews, many of whom had assimilated a great deal of the new Aristotelian learning. These missionaries needed help in responding to the objections posed by such "gentiles" in the course of evangelization. Tradition has it that the saintly Dominican Raymond of Peñafort asked his brother Thomas Aquinas to compose a work that would be serviceable to the missionaries. These latter encountered many difficulties from Islamic and Jewish converts interested in the truths of the Christian religion.[19] The *Summa contra gentiles* represents the fruit of this request. While primarily apologetic in purpose, the *Summa* embodies more than just a missionary manual. In fact, Père Chenu has written that this work "offers itself as a defense of the entire body of Christian thought, confronted with the scientific Greco-Arabic conception of the universe."[20] All in all, the work contains an apologetic theology. Although scholars agree that Thomas began this work in Paris, they speculate as to exactly how much of the manuscript was completed when he arrived in Italy.[21] We do know, however, that he completed the text while at Orvieto sometime during 1264.

Aquinas divided the *Summa contra gentiles* into two unequal parts, the first (Books I-III) dealing with truths about God that can be known by human reason alone, and the second (Book IV) with truths that are known only by revelation. The present study will have occasion to look at both parts, although our principal discussion, as one might expect, will concern Book IV where the author treats the incarnation. On the other hand, in Book III we also discover remarks about satisfaction, raised in the context of questions which inquire about our need for divine help in reaching beatitude. For one, Chenu refuses to make a philosophical *summa* out of Books I-III, and rather insists on a theological order for the entire *Summa contra gentiles*. Moreover, he cites Thomas himself in support of this argument: "After what has been said in Book I about God in Himself, there remains to continue with the things that come from Him."[22] Among those things which come from God, we, of course, principally include the incarnate Son in Book IV, but also the content of Books I and II. Retrospectively, then, Christ brings us to those truths which disclose the most hidden mysteries of the Christian faith, especially God, creation, and moral agency, even if in themselves they remain in some way accessible to reason alone.

A short time after Thomas had finished the *Summa contra gentiles*, another opportunity to render service to the Church's intellectual needs presented itself. A Christian missionary in Antioch requested his help in order to respond to certain objections raised against the faith claims by the Saracens, Greeks, and Armenians. Although Aquinas had recently finished a full treatment of such questions in the *Summa contra gentiles*, he nevertheless wrote a long reply to the still unidentified Cantor of Antioch. It has come down to us as the *De rationibus fidei contra Saracenos, Graecos et Armenos ad Cantorem Antiochiae*. Since one of the five questions posed by the Cantor deals directly with the question of satisfaction, we also give this text a careful examination.

First, Thomas prefaces this work with a standard caution concerning the impropriety of trying to demonstrate truths of the faith that remain beyond reason's ability to comprehend. Such an effort, he reminds the Cantor, can only result in bringing ridicule to the faith. On the other hand, the Christian missionary, aided by good theology, can show that nothing which Christians hold by faith contradicts right reason.[23] Next, Aquinas replies to the questions at hand. The relevant problem posed by the Cantor runs as follows: The Saracens say that Christ should not have died for the salvation of the world, for if he were divine and omnipotent he could have saved the human race by other ways or, preferably, have prevented us from sinning in the first place. First of all, Thomas indicates that we can only establish the suitability for whatever faith teaches concerning God's action in history. One cannot even begin to consider all the possible means God might have chosen or could have chosen to accomplish a goal. Indeed, good theological interpretation requires that we first consider how God actually ordained to accomplish his purposes. This holds true, furthermore, whether we consider something central to the faith, such as how he chose to save the world, or something incidental, such as how many stars he chose to put into the heavens. Since everyone who worships God, including a Saracen, reveres him as supremely good and providential, he or she should therefore look for reasons which explain why God's actual choice to do something epitomizes the best way. One should not seek to uncover hypothetical reasons why some other way would have been better. Aquinas, then, recapitulates a basic principle of the "via negativa": we know more about what God is not than we do about what he is. Apophatic theology made its mark on Aquinas, who never forgot that the "sacra doctrina" ultimately points to mystery.

Indeed, we could argue that this principle guides Aquinas's whole theological methodology. In the seventh chapter of the *De rationibus*, Thomas writes:

> If a man will devoutly consider the suitability of the passion and death of Christ, he will find there such an abyss of wisdom that more and greater things will continually reveal themselves to him. To such a man the truth of St Paul's words will be manifest, "but we preach Christ crucified, a stumbling block to Jews and folly to Gentiles, but to those who are called, both Jews and Greeks, Christ the power of God and the wisdom of God." And again--"For the foolishness of God is wiser than men" (*De rationibus fidei*, 7).

Since it reminds us of the premium Thomas puts on the role of meditation in the life of the theologian, this stance characterizes Aquinas's whole theological enterprise. The reasons ("rationes") which he gives for revealed truths of faith, only accessible under the "lumen fidei" of theological faith, come mainly from prayerful meditation and reflection on the very mysteries themselves. Elsewhere Aquinas points out the importance of the gifts of the Holy Spirit, especially understanding and knowledge, for the work of the theologian. No theological argument, then, replaces or uncovers a mystery of faith, although the substance of some mysteries, such as the existence of God and the immortality of the soul, do permit a kind of rational inquiry which other mysteries, such as the Trinity and the incarnation, do not.[24]

Let us turn to another text. During part of the time that Thomas was writing the *Summa contra gentiles*, he lived at the Dominican priory at Orvieto along side the curia of Pope Urban IV. As noted, Thomas aided Urban IV, especially in his efforts to heal the division between eastern and western Christianity. While in the papal service, Aquinas contributed to the intellectual efforts of the Dominican community in

Orvieto. The commentary *Expositio in Job ad litteram* represents one result of that service.

In fact, the *Constitutions* of the Dominican Order indicated that the "lector" of the convent, a post actually held by Thomas at the time, should regularly expose and comment upon the books of the Old and New Testaments. In this, the Dominicans demonstrated their singular concern for the revealed word of God. Since the actual text of the *Expositio in Job* is well-documented, scholars assume that it represents more than just a copy of Thomas's personal notes. Instead, Aquinas provides a polished and reworked text, the obvious fruit of assiduous study.[25] In the prologue of the *Expositio*, Thomas explains his intention: to comment on Job "secundum litteralem sensum." In other words, he will not attempt to develop still another spiritual exegesis. Why? According to his view, Gregory the Great, a patristic authority well-known to the medieval theologians, had already exhausted the potential for this kind of a biblical commentary in his *Magna Moralia*.[26]

Aquinas undoubtedly demonstrated his considerable teaching abilities to the satisfaction of all. For after this service, a provincial chapter of the Roman Province (1265) mandated that Thomas instruct young Dominican clerics who required special training for their evangelical work in the Church. In due course, he opened a small provincial "studium" (in fact, a sort of proto-seminary), located at the convent of Santa Sabina, the Dominican headquarters in Rome. Although scholars dispute this point, Weisheipl still argues that the *De malo* represents actual disputations held there during the academic year 1266-1267. In any event, certain articles of the disputed questions *De malo* contain important discussions about sin and evil--what the scholastic theologians called sin's "culpa" and "poena." These topics, of course, remain directly linked to the theological discussion of satisfaction, since the New Testament unquestionably presents Christ as one who saves us from our sins.

But the most important event during this Roman interlude remains the inauguration of the *Summa theologiae*. At this time, it appears, Aquinas conceived his major theological synthesis, the three-part *Summa theologiae*. It seems that, in the course of teaching theology to the young students at Rome, Thomas came to realize the critical shortcomings implicit in the *Sentences* of Peter Lombard. He saw, in other words, how inadequately this compilation served as standard textbook for beginners in the theological science. Thomas explains it this way:

> We have considered how newcomers to this teaching are greatly hindered by various writings on the subject, partly because of the swarm of pointless questions, articles, and arguments, partly because essential information is given according to the requirements of textual commentary or the occasions of academic debate, not to a sound educational method, partly

because repetitiousness has bred boredom and muddle in their thinking (*Summa Theologiae*, prologue).

Some suggest that he may have even thought of revising the *Scriptum super Sententias* in an effort to make the subject matter easier for his young charges to comprehend. But, in fact, he elaborated a plan for an entirely new "textbook for beginners," and sometime during the year 1266 he began work on the first questions of the *Summa theologiae*.

The question of the theoretical structure which controls the *Summa* remains a matter of interest even for contemporary scholars.[27] Although a complete exposé of the central conception behind Thomas's "chef d'oeuvre" remains outside the scope of this present work, one point merits special remark. The *Summa theologiae* of Thomas Aquinas embodies an organic unity, a sort of biological temper, which does not permit us to understand accurately the whole without a clear vision of the sum of its parts. In fact, Aquinas himself provides indications (in the form of prologues attached to the beginning of each major part of his work) which help the reader make the transition between one part of the work and another. Hence, an examination of these prologues provides us with a suitable introduction to a given section of the *Summa* and at the same time establishes the broader theological context within which Thomas speaks about a given topic, such as the satisfaction of Christ.

In the very beginning of the work, Aquinas writes: "The fundamental aim of holy teaching is to make God known, not only as he is in himself, but as the beginning and end of all things and of reasoning creatures especially" (*Summa theologiae* Ia, prologue). Accordingly, he announces his intention to treat three main topics, each of which corresponds to the three major divisions of the *Summa*.[28] Chenu, for instance, insists that Thomas's appeal to the neo-Platonic scheme of emanation and return remains a crucial element for an adequate understanding of what he intends to accomplish in the *Summa theologiae*. "Since theology is the science of God," Chenu writes, "all things will be studied in their relation to God whether in their production or in their final end, in their 'exitus et reditus'."[29] Of course, Aquinas had already employed this concept, at least inchoatively, in his original writings on the *Sentences* of Peter Lombard.

We know that the entire *prima pars* was written during Thomas's stay in Italy. Although the idea for writing the *Summa* was conceived in Rome, a good deal of the *prima pars*, at least the treatise on the rational creature, was actually written at Viterbo. At the request of still another provincial chapter, whose members undoubtedly remained intent on putting the most capable of the brethren close to the papal court, Thomas once again moved there during the summer of 1267. During his stay at Viterbo, moreover, Thomas profited from the company of Dominican William of Moerbeke, who was also in the curial service of the new pontiff.[30] In an effort to facilitate ecumenical dialogue between East and West, William was in the process of translating Greek theological and philosophical texts into Latin.

At Viterbo, Thomas came into close contact with byzantine theology, including the neo-Platonic theme of the "exitus-reditus." So, given the principal topics of the *prima pars*, we can understand Chenu's conviction that Thomas developed the "exitus" theme as a result of his increased exposure to classical thought. Thus, in the prologue, Thomas writes:

> The treatment of God will fall into three parts:
> first, his nature;
> secondly, the distinction of persons in God;
> thirdly, the coming forth from him of creatures.

On the other hand, we can also to cite other elements in the *prima pars*, e.g., the discussion of the beatific vision (q. 12) or on goodness (q. 5), which signal caution in applying Chenu's scheme too rigidly. Indeed, some even suggest that the explanation either gives an over-simplified explanation of Thomas's blueprint or misrepresents the plan of the *Summa* altogether. Thus, I propose a modified version of the "exitus-reditus" scheme which also takes into account other central issues in Aquinas's theological method.

Since the 12th-century and the progressive introduction of the works of Aristotle comprising the *logica nova* (above all, the two *Analytica*), the issue of theological methodology acquires new importance and self-consciousness.[31] The question was: in what respect does theology measure up to the Aristotelian canon of scientific knowing as that canon is expressed in the *Analytica Posteriora*? For scientific knowing involves universality and necessity; it is a knowledge of what cannot be other than the case and of the necessary connection between cause and effect.[32] Christian theology, by contrast, centers upon a God who is utterly free in his address to human freedom; it tries to render an account of the intersection and dialogue of divine and human freedoms, which is salvation-history. The methodological question for theology can be posed more precisely, therefore: how can there be a scientific account (one that corresponds to Aristotle's scientific ideal) about what is contingent, free, gracious, and historical?[33]

The genius of a solution to this question of theological methodology is to find a course between theology as "sacred history," where the intelligible connection between the mysteries is simply narrative chronology as in Hugh of St. Victor's *De sacramentis*, and theology as necessitarian emanationism as in Plotinus's *Enneads*. Aquinas himself confronted this issue in two ways: "in actu signato" in the methodological treatment of *Summa theologiae* I q.1, a.1 and "in actu exercito" in the structure of the *Summa theologiae* itself as he planned it. He adopted the "exitus-reditus" scheme from Dionysian neo-Platonism, but develops it, building the nuance of analogical understanding into the scheme. In fact, it is perhaps more accurate to view "exitus-reditus" in the pattern of the *Summa* not as a singular circular movement (thus, Chenu) but rather in terms of concentric circles, each possessed of its own degree of necessity. Thus, we can see in *Summa theologiae* I qq. 2-43 one cycle, an entirely intra-Trinitarian coming-forth in the Word and recoil in Personal Love; here the movement enjoys a certain necessity--i.e., that God cannot be other than a Father speaking a Word and together with that Word breathing forth the personal Bond of Love.

Broadly speaking, the material in the remainder of the *prima pars* and in the *secunda pars* is considered under the aspect of nature. The necessity here is hypothetical, i.e., given that God has freely chosen to create as he has. Nevertheless, given the divine will to create, there is a certain intelligibility and consistency, certain intrinsic requirements, to the natures that have been freely posited: man cannot be other than man, given that God has freely willed to create man for beatific communion. The final scheme of coming-forth and return would be represented in the *tertia pars*, which is expressive of the content of concrete history. Jesus comes forth and returns as the perfect and consummate historical agent in a personal history; he realizes human nature in its historically unsurpassable concrete shape; he enacts human nature as a perfect history.

The necessity here is even more tenuous, in one respect; for there is no necessity that God accomplish the consummation of human destiny and human salvation from sin by the incarnation of the Son. Nevertheless, God's election of this mode of accomplishing his loving design for human history and the excellence of a human history that is hypostatically that of the second Person of the blessed Trinity confer the necessity of an unsurpassable exemplar and final causality upon salvation-history as enacted in the personal history of Jesus of Nazareth. These necessities--that of salvation history, that of natures as constituted by God, and that of the divine triune reality itself--are interlocking: the former two being grafted on to and deriving consistency and intelligibility from the divine "necessity" that God be a Father uttering a Word with whom he breathes forth the force of loving recoil.

Aquinas, then, and with him the tradition of the Church, remains convinced that Christian revelation can furnish grounds for speculation concerning the purposes and works of God. Of course, the "sacra doctrina" possesses a sacred scripture which serves as the written record of that revelation. But as an artisan of the "sacra doctrina," Aquinas aims to combine into a single discipline both a study of salvation history itself as well as a speculative investigation of what that sacred history embodies.[34] Of course, the incarnation remains an event of salvation history and therefore a contingent and gratuitous revelation of the kindness of God. Yet it can enter into the pattern of the "exitus-reditus" even as a free act of God. Thomas envisioned nothing untoward in describing the ontological relations which exist between the created universe (especially the human nature of Christ, the human person, and the blessed Eucharist) and God prior to a direct reference to the actual way in which God chose to unfold historically his plan of salvation. On the contrary, he judged such a procedure both "a sound educational method" and an aid to teaching and understanding biblical revelation.

In accord with this mentality, Thomas therefore makes no apology for talking about the life of man uplifted in grace in the *secunda pars* before he presents Christ, the one mediator of that grace, in the *tertia pars*. He announces that man's destiny points to something infinitely above what our natural powers can achieve, nothing less than union with the triune God, and therefore argues that the creature requires a "gratia elevans" in order that human capacities can reach out for God. What remains significant, however, for the present investigation includes what Aquinas cannot directly treat in the *secunda pars*, namely, the satisfaction of Christ. Why? Satisfaction remains indisputably linked to the contingent, historical fact of Christ's passion and death on the Cross. "The incarnation was not absolutely necessary for the restoration of human nature," writes Thomas at the start of the *tertia pars*, "since by his infinite power God had many other ways to accomplish this end" (*Summa theologiae* IIIa q. 1, a. 2).[35] Thomas's study of philosophy helped him grasp the utter gratuity of the divine dispensation.

1269-1272: Second Parisian Regency:
Compendium theologiae; Pauline Commentaries; Super Johannem; De virtutibus; Quaestiones de quodlibet; De perfectione spiritualis vitae; Summa theologiae, secunda pars

In November of 1268, the Dominican Master General John of Vercelli instructed Thomas to return to the University of Paris in order to occupy the Dominican chair for a second term. Since reappointments were not the usual procedure, we may suppose that the renewed offensive of the anti-mendicant forces at the University played a major role in this decision. This time the camp found a leader in the archdeacon of Tournai, Gérard d'Abbeville.[36] Hence the Dominican Order judged it necessary to assign a competent friar to refute the charges and accusations leveled against all the mendicant orders by their opponents, thereby defending the newly-acquired rights and privileges of these religious threatened by the secular masters. In due course, Aquinas left Italy with some companions, arriving in Paris shortly after the beginning of the new year 1269. The fact that he reached Paris only after the academic year was well under way suggests a certain urgency associated with his reappointment.

Once arrived at Paris, he again assumed the professional duties of a regent master in theology. Scholars commonly number the three and one-half years which follow among the most productive years in Aquinas's life. Indeed, many also remain convinced that a significant development takes place in his thought during this period. Although one can easily observe the development, the causes for Aquinas's intellectual growth still remain obscure. For example, Gauthier observes that during this period Thomas mitigates his stress on things intellectual, a concern for the world of the mind which he had earlier displayed.[37] Weisheipl shares this view, adding that Thomas's return to the classroom and contact with young students and their needs also remains a factor in his development as a teacher and theologian.[38]

In any case, as a regent master in theology, Thomas was once again required to perform the threefold duties of that office, namely, to lecture on the Bible, to preside over public disputations (both ordinary as well as quodlibetal), and to preach sermons at the university. "He wrote on all the epistles of Paul, which he valued above all writings, the Gospels alone excepted; and while engaged on this work at Paris, he is said to have had a vision of the Apostle," wrote the chronicler William of Tocco in his *Hystoria beati Thomae*.[39] The commentaries on the Pauline corpus point to Aquinas's interest in the biblical doctrines of justification and divinization. Nevertheless, the *Expositio et lectura super Epistolas Pauli Apostoli* remains one of Thomas's works whose provenance, date, and manner of composition prove especially difficult to accurately determine. Noting the agreement of some contemporary witnesses on this point, Weisheipl also argue that Thomas lectured on these epistles at Paris.[40] Still, we can only say with certitude that the *Commentary on the Letter to the Romans* and part of the *Commentary on the First Letter to the Corinthians* were completed during the second Paris regency. This part of the "expositio" was corrected and edited by Thomas himself and, especially in Romans, manifests a style and precision of language which those sections of the work in "reportatio" lack. The edited text written or dictated by Aquinas includes the whole of Romans through I Cor 7:9. But from I Cor 7:10 until the end of the Pauline corpus (including, according to the custom of the times, the Letter to the Hebrews) the published text is the work of Reginald of Piperno, who recorded Aquinas's lectures.[41] Among all of Thomas's commentaries on Scripture, the "lecturae" on St Paul's writings, especially Romans, provide the primary biblical stimulus for the systematic development of satisfaction.

A second biblical commentary from this period also includes references to satisfaction, namely, *Lectura super Johannem: Reportatio*. We know that Thomas corrected the *reportatio* of his classroom lectures because of the interest and financial support of one of his students, a certain Adenulf of Anagni. Although this theological commentary on John does not offer a detailed treatment of satisfaction, it nevertheless does refer both to penitential and christological satisfaction at those places in the Vulgate text where the inspired author discloses these doctrines.

Next, the results of Thomas's academic disputations (held during his second regency) provide material for the present investigation. First, the ordinary academic disputation includes the *De anima* (which does not figure directly in our present investigation) as well as the short disputations collected under the title *De virtutibus* (*In communi, De caritate, De correctione fraterna, De spe, De virtutibus cardinalibus*). These latter parallel the discussions of the same subjects in the *secunda pars* of the *Summa theologiae*, which also fell among Thomas's express occupations at this time. In fact, the second and third disputations *De virtutibus* offer particular remarks on satisfaction which round out the longer systematic treatments in the *Summa theologiae*.

The *Quaestiones de quodlibet*, however, require further research in order to place them accurately in the chronology of Aquinas's works. For example, scholars commonly assign *Quaestiones* 1 - 6 and 12 to this period of Thomas's career.[42] Two texts relate to our topic: *Quaestio* 2 held at Christmas 1269 and *Quaestio* 3 held at Easter of the following year. On the other hand, *Quaestio* 12 represents a "reportatio" which in fact was discovered after Thomas's death and subsequently added to the collection; the single reference to satisfaction holds a marginal place in the present study.

The purpose for which Aquinas came to Paris explains the next work of interest to this study. The polemical *De perfectione spiritualis vitae*, published in the summer of 1269, represents the first work Aquinas completed upon his return to the City of Lights. It contains a response to Gérard d'Abbeville's *Contra adversarium perfectionis christianae*. We have already seen distinct reference to satisfaction in the *Contra impugnantes*, Thomas's response to Gérard's mentor, William of Saint-Amour. Now Aquinas presents a somewhat more developed doctrine. He points out not only the role that satisfaction plays in the life of an individual religious, but speculates as to how we can regard the religious life as a peerless satisfactory work for men and women. In addition, the text remains a clear example of development in the thought of Thomas, who now perceived, it appears, the important connection between the penitential character of satisfaction and Christian praxis.

By contrast, the date of composition for the *Compendium theologiae ad fratrem Reginaldum socium suum* remains difficult to fix exactly. Aquinas writes it for his devoted friend and "socius", friar Reginald of Piperno, who, among other tasks, transcribed Thomas's notes and lectures. It was Thomas's wish that Reginald have a summary of the principal teachings of the Christian doctrine at his disposal. Thus Thomas planned his "doctrina compendiosa" around the three theological virtues in which consists the highest perfection of the Christian life. The work, however, was never finished due (as an editor's note makes clear) to Thomas's death. The style of the *Compendium* as well as the purpose for which it was written gives the work a unique value. Even if it does not provide original contributions to the development of Thomas's theological teaching, we do find there succinct recapitulations of his thought which continue to serve as useful summaries of his teaching.

Although we know that Thomas began the *secunda pars* of his *Summa theologiae* at Viterbo (prior to his return to Paris), he nevertheless completed the major part of this section during the second Parisian regency. It has been said that the *secunda pars* represents Thomas's most original contribution to medieval theological literature.[43] As with the *prima pars*, the prologue to the *secunda pars* provides a good notion of the scope and general theme which Thomas envisioned for longest section of his *Summa theologiae*. Aquinas writes:

> Man is made to God's image, and since this implies, as Damascene tells us, that he is intelligent and free to judge and master of himself, so then, now that we have agreed that God is the exemplar cause of things and that they issue from his power through his will, we go on to look at this image, that is to say, at man, as the source of actions which are his own and fall under his responsibility and control (*Summa Theologiae* IIa prologue).

Gilby expresses the same idea concerning the *secunda pars* in another way, when he writes that this section "considers the returning home of human creatures to God by their own proper activities in the life of their grace-uplifted nature."[44]

Four topics make up the subject matter of the first part of the *secunda pars*. The first topic treats the final destiny of human life or the "returning home to God" (qq. 1-5). There Thomas clearly identifies human destiny and our ultimate happiness with the possession of beatific vision. "There can be no complete and final happiness for us," he writes in one of the opening questions of the *secunda pars*, "save in the vision of God" (*Summa theologiae* Ia-IIae q.3, a. 8). This unequivocal assertion about the universal call to holiness points to the fundamentally theological character of the *secunda pars*, which we can properly consider an essay on Christian anthropology. Still, "sacra doctrina" remains centered on God and loses nothing of its single mindedness when it also extends to his friends and creatures. Of course, God alone, already recognized in the *prima pars* as a Trinity of persons, remains the single goal whom all persons seek and in whom all alone find complete happiness.

Next, we turn to the image of God in the rational creature. This subject had already been introduced in the *prima pars* (q. 93) where Aquinas both describes our being created "ad imaginem et similitudinem Dei" and analyzes the theological implications of this patristic theme. Now he turns to explore the nature of human acts (qq. 6-21) and the emotional life of man (qq. 22-48). The theological axiom, "man is made to God's image," enjoys a solid foundation both in the New Testament authors, who recognize the implications of the doctrine for both creation and salvation, as well as in the patristic writers, who develop the theological conclusions for both soteriology and anthropology.[45] For our purposes, however, the restoration of the image of God, marred by sin in a fallen human race, remains a way of describing salvation and the work of satisfaction. And Thomas will make abundantly rich use of this specific analogy in order to explain the results of Christ's satisfaction in the Church. Furthermore, his reference at the very beginning of the *secunda pars* to man as created in God's image indicates that the economy of salvation remains a guiding principle for his discussion of the moral life.

The third topic comprises a discussion of the virtues and vices in general (qq. 49-70) as well as specific details on sin (qq. 71-89). Man remains the "source of actions which are his own and fall under his responsibility." And although Aquinas distinguishes the freedom of specification from the freedom of exercise, he nonetheless recognizes that radical freedom characterizes the moral life of the believer, allowing one to choose between the good and evil. Thus God does not force our ultimate happiness upon us; rather, we choose it freely by our own proper activity. Aquinas develops a moral theory which centers both on the end of human existence and the means to reach that end. His treatment of the virtues and vices then represents a major contribution to the development of Christian ethics, which otherwise frequently turns on rewards and punishments, sins and commandments.

The major fourth topic found in the first half of the *secunda pars* includes Aquinas's celebrated discussion of the new law of grace and freedom. The closing questions treat the law of the old and of the new dispensations (qq. 90-108) as well as the life of "grace-uplifted nature" (qq. 109-114). Thomas's purpose in placing this discussion of grace at this particular turn of the *Summa*'s development represents an important methodological decision. It is interesting to contrast his mode of presentation and that which we find in the Scriptures. Of course, both *Summa* and New Testament concern themselves with our happiness and salvation. But the *Summa* speaks first of all about the work of grace which conforms man to the trinitarian life of the God. This conformity, begun here on earth, reaches its perfection in a union which we designate as the beatific vision. Only then does the *Summa* consider the person of Jesus Christ, the sole mediator of our saving grace, through whose causality we receive the grace of God. This, of course, reverses the order of the biblical narration. There Christ comes as the one who discloses the very reality of created grace and the possibility of our union with the Father.

The second part of the *secunda pars* develops a more specific and detailed presentation of the virtues and vices. "Having set out the general theory on vices, virtues and other topics related to morals,"

Thomas writes at the beginning, "we must turn to specific details about each" (*Summa Theologiae* IIa-IIae, prologue). We should point out that Thomas was working on the *secunda pars* at the same time that he was reading Aristotle's *Nicomachean Ethics*. The Philosopher, as Aquinas calls him, helps Aquinas explicate his moral scheme.[46] In addition to a shared teleological perspective, Aquinas also develops a moral theology centered on character and virtue, especially the cardinal virtues. But Thomas's concept of the Christian life surpasses Aristotle's humanism, for Aquinas's moral theology points to a progressive development from grace to glory as much as human flourishing, to living out the beatitudes as much as following the norms of "recta ratio." The Gospel, not philosophy, principally accounts for Thomas's decision to elaborate the moral life in terms of the virtues; and this explains his inclusion of the gifts of the Holy Spirit and the beatitudes.[47]

In the *secunda-secundae*, the largest number of questions concerns the virtues which touch the lives of every man and woman (qq. 1-179) and a smaller number treat the virtues which pertain only to those men and women who seek ecclesiastical offices or who pronounce the vows of religion (qq. 180-189). As I have said, along with each virtue, Aquinas treats the corresponding gift, the opposed vices, and the applicable affirmative or negative precept. Although we customarily refer to the *secunda pars* as Aquinas's moral theology, such a distinction remains foreign to his conception of theology, since the entire *Summa theologiae* embodies a single theological essay about the "sacra doctrina." Moreover, to interpret the *secunda pars* in this way also isolates morals from their christological context in the *Summa*. Such a misreading also dislocates the theology of satisfaction, since the discussion of sin and its consequences in the *secunda pars* comes before the *tertia pars* and its presentation of Christ and the sacraments. Finally, we note several references to penitential satisfaction in the *secunda pars* such as the traditional forms of satisfaction, prayer, fasting, and almsgiving.

1272-1273: Regent at Naples:
Summa theologiae, Tertia pars;
Super Psalmos; Sermons

Sometime after Easter of 1272, Thomas with his companion Reginald of Piperno left Paris. He had assisted at the installation of his successor in the master's chair, a certain Dominican named Romanus of Rome. Aquinas once again returned to Italy, and among his effects were some questions of the *tertia pars* of his yet incomplete *Summa*. Once at Naples he took up residence at the Convent of San Domenico where for the next year and a half he would continue his university duties on a smaller scale. He did not, however, diminish his efforts, as testimony from his canonization process indicates, for he was "always studying, lecturing or writing for the good of his fellow Christians."[48]

Obviously, the main object of Thomas's writing during this period was the *tertia pars* of the *Summa theologiae*. Still, some other writings dating from this period do make incidental reference to satisfaction. Foremost among them remains the commentary which Thomas began on the Psalter. Fundamentally, the work is a "reportatio" made by Reginald. Prior to 1880, the series consisted of the commentaries on Psalms 1 to 51. But in that year a researcher discovered the commentaries for Psalms 52-54.[49] On the basis of a copyist's note, scholars speculate that Thomas abruptly terminated this work at the same time that circumstances forced him to discontinue work on the *Summa theologiae*.

In addition, a second group of writings exhibit minor interest for a theology of satisfaction. Although frequently cited as opuscula, they in fact represent "reportationes" of sermons that Thomas delivered in the Church of San Domenico during the Lent of 1273. The present scholastic form of these sermons discloses something of their original style, but not much. We know, for example, that they were preached in the vernacular and recorded in Latin notes from which the text as we have it composed. In particular, we have three texts, the *Collationes super Credo in Deum*, the *Collationes super Pater Noster*, and the *Collationes de decem praeceptis*.

All in all, the outstanding accomplishment of this final period of Thomas's academic career remains the completed work on the *tertia pars* of the *Summa theologiae*. The story of his experience before the crucifix in St Nicholas's chapel of San Domenico provides us with a context for interpreting the mind of Aquinas as he drew closer to the experience of the mystery of Christ. Whatever the cause of his outburst, the immediate effect of this experience found its way into the permanent history of St Thomas's life: "Reginald," he said, "I cannot write any more, because all that I have written seems like straw to me."[50] The *Summa theologiae* stops with q. 90, a. 4 which occurs in the course of a discussion on penance (unfortunately prior to his projected discussion of penitential satisfaction). Nonetheless Thomas did complete the properly christological questions (qq. 1-59) and some of the treatises on the sacraments. Editors later provided a *Supplementum* from earlier works to round out the whole treatise.

Again, the prologue to the *tertia pars* clearly outlines Thomas's vision for the final section of his work. There he introduces his discussion of the person of the incarnate Son and the saving mysteries of Christ's life.

> Our Savior, the Lord Jesus Christ, as he was according to the angel's witness, saving his people from their sins, showed in his own Person that way of truth which, in rising again, we can follow to the blessedness of eternal life. This means that after

our study of the final goal of human life and of the virtues and vices, we must bring the entire theological discourse to completion by considering the Saviour himself and his benefits to the human race (*Summa Theologiae* IIIa, prologue).

We have already remarked on Thomas's wish to introduce an "ordo disciplinae" into sacred history and his employment in the *Summa* of the Platonic "exitus-reditus" theme, although modified to give full account of the several kinds of necessity operative with respect to God's action towards creatures. The *tertia pars* completes that design with a discussion of the actual way in which God chose to accomplish the return of the human creature to himself. The same "ordo disciplinae" now seeks to find suitable reasons for what revelation discloses about the person and work of Jesus Christ. One may call these arguments reasons of convenience or refer, as Lafont does, to "the economic necessity of the incarnation."[51] This method,of course, does not seek to penetrate the divine mysteries further than the sacred scriptures allow, for Aquinas always observes the norms of "theologia negativa," as bequeathed to western theology by the Christian tradition of the East.

The mystery of the Incarnation includes both the mystery of Jesus Christ as well as the benefits of his life-giving resurrection. Thus, in the prologue Thomas also suggests that a complete consideration of the economy of salvation unfolds under three principal headings.

First, the Saviour himself;
secondly, his sacraments, through which we attain salvation;
thirdly, the goal of life without end that we attain
  through Christ by our resurrection
                    (*Summa Theologiae* IIIa, prologue).

More specifically, we notice that Aquinas divides the first principal section into two main parts: on the mystery of the incarnation, whereby God became a man for our salvation (qq. 1-26) and on what was done and suffered by our Saviour (qq. 27-59). This expresses his approach to functional christology. It is because Christ is both the divine Word and man that what he accomplishes possesses significance for us. Hence attempts to articulate a purely functional christology always remain inadequate to the extent that such christologies content themselves with the activities of Christ's life. Aquinas, rather, seeks first to understand Christ's distinctive personal structure, that is, how God assumes to himself an individual human nature in the person of the Logos. Only then does he proceed to examine the meaning of Christ's human actions. This procedure, moreover, honors the pattern established in the great christological debates which surrounded the council of Chalcedon (451).

In question 26 (devoted to the office of Christ as Mediator), we reach a pivotal point in the text. The fact that it is among the briefest in the *Summa* "would appear absurdly out of proportion if it were not understood that the whole remaining part of the work, dealing with Christ's mysteries and the Church of faith and of the sacraments, is an examination of Christ's actual mediation."[52] In the prologue to the *tertia pars*, Thomas introduces the Savior Jesus Christ as one who shows to man "a way of truth" which we "can follow to the blessedness of eternal life." This way of truth which Christ shows to us constitutes a sort of "reditus," the route that leads the creature back to the triune God. The metaphor of "way" remains a dynamic one, for it emphasizes growth in Christ as a means of making positive advance towards the promised goal of perfect union with God.

To sum up: Christ summons a fallen humanity, itself blocked from attaining such an elevated goal because of human sin, to the blessedness of eternal life which remains coincident with the vision of the blessed Trinity (already treated both at the very beginning of the *Summa* itself and at the beginning of the *secunda pars*). Significantly, then, does Thomas choose his introductory words from the 14th-chapter of John's Gospel, where Christ speaks of himself as "the way, and the truth, and the life" (Jn 14:12). In short, Christ represents the way along which we march to our final goal of eternal life; Christ embodies the way in which the created image of God, marred but not effaced by Adam's sin, achieves restoration to its original condition. Indeed, the Johannine metaphor controls the theological development of Aquinas's christology.

By the same token, the actual order of salvation remains one of redemption. Hence, Thomas's employment of the Gospel of St Matthew in the prologue to the *tertia pars* points to this equally significant theme of his christology. "Joseph, son of David, do not fear to take Mary your wife, for that which is conceived in her is of the Holy Spirit; she will bear a Son, and you shall call his name Jesus, for he will save his people from their sins" (Mt 2:20-22). Indeed, this theme of the *tertia pars* provides an important focus for what follows. For the actual way by which we return to God always entails the way of the cross, a way of satisfaction for sin accomplished first and preeminently by Christ the head. Throughout the *tertia pars*, Aquinas will endeavor to establish the theological basis for incorporating the members of the body of Christ into the perfect satisfaction achieved by the incarnate Son of God.

NOTES

1. Bernard Gui, *Legenda Sancti Thomae Aquinatis* in *S. Thomae Aquinatis Vitae Fontes Praecipuae*, ed Angelico Ferrua, O.P. (Alba: Edizione Domenicane, 1968), 142: "Erat enim in legendo novos articulos adinveniens novumque modum determinandi inveniens et novas producens in determinationibus rationes, ut nemo audiens ipsum dubitaret quin ipsum Deus novi luminis radiis illustrasset."

2. Peter the Lombard (d. 1160), known to medieval theology as the "Magister Sententiarum," wrote one of the most influential text books in the history of theology, the *Libri Quattuor Sententiarum*. For a good introduction to his life and works, see Peter the Lombard, *Sententiae in IV libris distinctae*, 3rd ed., 2 vols. (Grottaferrata [Rome]: Collegium S. Bonaventurae Ad Claras Aquas, 1971,1981).

3. Thus, Weisheipl, 70. For a popular description of the efforts currently underway to provide a critical edition of this and other works of Aquinas, see Cullen Murphy, "All the Pope's Men. Putting Aquinas together again," *Harper's Review* (June, 1979), 45-64. The *Opera omnia Leonina* (Leonine edition, named for Pope Leo XIII), Rome, 1880 - is still in progress.

4. The commentaries at first stayed close to the text, but as the centuries went on, the original discussion of the Lombard was often only the occasion for discussing issues of contemporary relevance. For example, see the work of Juan Martinez de Ripalda, S.J. (1594-1648), *Brevis Expositio Magistri Sententiarum* (Madrid, 1635).

5. See *Sententiae* I, d. 1, c. 1, [55]: "Ut enim egregius doctor Augustinus ait in libro *De doctrina christiana* I, c. 2, n. 2, 'omnis doctrina vel rerum est vel signorum. Sed res etiam per signa discuntur. Proprie autem hic res apellatur, quae non ad significandum aliquid adhibetur; signa vero, quorum usu est in significando.'" See M.-M. Labourdette, O.P., "Histoire de la pensée médiévale," *Revue thomiste* 73 (1973), 146-47.

6. The Franciscan Alexander of Hales (c. 1186-1245), teaching in Paris in the 1220's, first introduced the Lombard's *Sentences* as a text in the classroom. The "Doctor Irrefragabilis" suggests the "exitus-reditus" distinction in *Glossa in quattour libros Sententiarum* I, ed PP. Collegii S. Bonaventurae (Quaracchi: Bibliotheca Franciscanum Scholastica, 1951), 4: "Sed quaeri potest quare ordine praepostero in praedicta auctoritate librorum fit distinctio. Respondeo: duplex est ordo. Este ordo rerum prout exeunt a Creatore vel Recreatore vel Reparatore, et sic proceditur in hoc opere. Et est ordo rerum prout reducuntur ad Creatorem...."

7. For example, see work of the 15th-century Dominincan Petrus a

Bergomo (d. 1482), *Concordantiae Textuum discordantium Divi Thomae Aquinatis*, ed. I. Colosio (Florence: Libreria Editrice Fiorentina, 1982).

8. We have this on the explicit authority of Tolomeo di Lucca, *Historia ecclesiastica nova* in *Vitae Fontes*, 356-7: "XXV autem annorum erat, cum primo Parisius venit, ubi infra XXX annum Sententias legit, et conventum in theologia, sive licentiam recepit. Infra autem magisterium quattuor libros fecit super Sententias, videlicet primum, secundum, tertium et quartum."

9. For a study of this topic, see E.A. Synan, "Brother Thomas, the Master, and the Masters" in *St. Thomas Aquinas, 1274-1974*, ed. A. Maurer et al., 2 vols. (Toronto: Pontifical Institute of Mediaeval Studies, 1974), 2:219-42.

10. For a study of negative reactions to secular learning in theology, see J.F. Wippel, "The Condemnations of 1270 and 1277 at Paris," *Journal of Medieval and Renaissance Studies* 7 (1977), 169-201.

11. Although Alexander IV's "Quasi lignum vitae" (1255) confirmed the privileges of the mendicants at Paris, strong reaction nonetheless continued, *viz.*, Louis IX had to dispatch the royal archers to protect the Dominincan master Florent of Hesdin at his inaugural lecture. For further details, see D.L. Douie, *The Conflict Between the Seculars and the Mendicants at the University of Paris in the Thirteenth Century* (London: Aquinas Papers, n. 23, Blackfriars, 1954).

12. For a contemporary description of the threefold function of a regent-master, see Peter the Cantor, *Verbum abbreviatum*, c.1: "In tribus igitur consistit exercitium sacrae Scripturae: circa lectionem, disputationem et praedicationem .... Praedicatio vero, cui subserviunt priora, quasi tectum est tegens fideles ab aestu, et a turbine vitiorum. Post lectionem igitur sacrae Scripturae, et dubitabilium, per disputationem, inquisitionem, et non prius, praedicandus est."

13. For a fuller report on educational methods in theology, see Palémon Glorieux, "L'enseignement au Moyen Age. Techniques et méthodes en usage à la Faculté de théologie de Paris au XIIIe siècle," *Archives d'histoire doctrinale et littéraire du Moyen Age* 43 (1968), 65-185. Although originally published in 1923, C.H. Haskins, *The Rise of Universities* (Ithaca: Cornell University Press, 1957) contains an updated bibliography. Still, Hastings Rashdall, *The Universities of Europe in the Middle Ages*, a new edition in 3 volumes by F.M. Powicke and A.B. Emden (Oxford: Clarendon Press, 1936) remains the classical study.

14. For the variety of questions treated in the quodlibetal literature, see Leonard E. Boyle, O.P., "The Quodlibets of St. Thomas and Pastoral Care," *The Thomist* 38 (1974), 232-56.

15. See Weisheipl, 110. For a study of the intimate relationship between biblical and systematic theology in certain 13th-century theologians, see M.-D. Chenu, O.P., *La Théologie comme Science au XIIIe siècle* (Paris: J. Vrin, 1957).

16. For details of this matter, see Weisheipl, 371-2. The commentary on Mt 5:11-6:8 and 6:14-19 found in some printed editions represents a spurious work, possibly written by the Dominican Pietro de Scala.

17. For the particulars of this debate, see St Thomas Aquinas, *Opera Omnia*, cura et studio Fratrum Praedicatorum, vol. 28, *Expositio super Isaiam ad litteram* (Rome: Editori di San Tommaso, 1974), 20*. But also, see Weisheipl, 120-1.

18. Again, the phrase comes from Peter the Cantor, *Verbum*, c. 1: "Lectio autem est quasi fundamentum, et substratorium sequentium...."

19. For the origin of this tradition, see Peter Marsilio, *Chronicle of the King of Aragon, James II* as cited in Weisheipl, 130-1. However, Peter Marc offers another explanation in his "Introduction" to the *Liber de Veritate Catholicae Fidei* (Toronto: Marietti, 1967).

20. M.-D. Chenu, O.P., *Toward Understanding Saint Thomas*, trans. A.-M. Landry and D. Hughes (Chicago: Henry Regnery Company, 1964), 292.

21. For the details of this discussion, see Weisheipl, 130-4; 144-5. During this period, moreover, all of Aquinas's writings should probably be seen as an act of apostolic service to the intellectual needs of the Church and to the needs of men seeking the truth. As the medieval chronicler, Tolomeo of Lucca, remarked after Thomas had left Paris he came to Italy where he wrote "many useful works."

22. Chenu, *Understanding*, 294. In support of his view, Chenu cites the text of Aquinas itself: "... post ea quae de Deo in se in primo libero sunt dicta, de his quae ab ipso sunt restat prosequendum" (*Summa contra gentiles* II c.4, n.6).

23. See *De rationibus fidei*, 2 for this testimonial to Aquinas's understanding of theology's task.

24. The scholastics distinguished between a supernatural truth "quoad modum substantiae" and "quoad modum revelationis." Although this way of putting it strikes the modern reader as a bit wooden, the distinction nonetheless shows that the hierarchy of revealed truths relates to human reason in diverse ways. This nuance, however, remains lost in theologies which confuse the orders of creation and grace.

25. For the details of this discussion, see the "Prefatio" in *Expositio super Job ad litteram*, vol. 26 (Rome: Leonine edition, 1965), especially, 25*-26*.

26. For further information on Gregory the Great as biblicist, see Beryl Smalley, *The Study of the Bible in the Middle Ages*, third edition (Oxford: Blackwell, 1983), especially, 1-27.

27. See especially Chenu, *Understanding*. But also, André Hayen, S.J., *Saint Thomas d'Aquin et la vie de l'Egilise* (Paris-Louvain: Desclée de Brouwer, 1952); Per Erik Persson, *Sacra Doctrina: Reason and Revelation in Aquinas*, trans J.A.R. Mackenzie (Philadelphia: Fortress Press, 1970); Ghislain Lafont, OSB, *Structures et Méthodes dans la Somme théologique de saint Thomas d'Aquin* (Paris-Louvain: Desclée de Brouwer, 1961); Michel Corbin, *Le Chemin de la Théologie chez Thomas d'Aquin* (Paris: Beauchesne, 1974), especially, c. 4.

28. Hence, Aquinas divides his principal theological synthesis into three parts: (1) concerning God; (2) concerning the return of the rational creature to God; (3) concerning Christ, in whose humanity we discover the way towards God.

29. Chenu, *Understanding*, 304. Also, see T.F. O'Meara, O.P., "Grace as a Theological Structure in the *Summa theologiae* of Thomas Aquinas," *Recherches de Théologie ancienne et médiévale* 55 (1988), 130-53. Although the author argues that "grace" serves as a controlling conceptuality for the whole *Summa* ("Grace under various terms is present in the entire *Summa theologiae*"), at the same time he elides major distinctions which Aquinas emphasizes between God's general presence to his creation and that special mode of presence which constitutes personal communion with the blessed Trinity. For a balanced critique of this direction in Thomist studies, see William J. Hill, O.P., "Uncreated Grace--A Critique of Karl Rahner," *The Thomist* 27 (1963), 333-56.

30. William of Moerbeke (c.1215-86), Dominican translator of Greek philosophical and scientific texts and, later, Archbishop of Thebes, provided Aquinas with many new sources for theology. See D.A. Callus, O.P., "Les Sources de Saint Thomas. Etat de la question" in P. Moreaux et al., *Aristote et Saint Thomas d'Aquin* (Journées d'études internationales: Chaire Cardinal Mercier, 1957), 93-174.

31. Aristotle, in his "first entry" into western medieval thought, had been known for his grammatical works, the *Categories* and *Peri hermeneias*. In the later 12th-century, the "second entry" introduced his *Prior* and *Posterior Analytics*, the *Topics*, and the *Sophistic Refutations*, which provided the theologians with a theory of knowledge and demonstration.

32. See Aquinas's own commentary, *In I Analytica Posteriora*, lect. 4, 5 for his explanation of this canon.

33. For a contemporary perspective on this characteristic feature of Aquinas's method in the *Summa*, see H.-M. Féret, "Christologie

médiévale de saint Thomas et Christologie concrète et historique pour aujourd'hui," *Memorie Domenicane* 6 (1975), 107-41.

34. Thus, Thomas C. O'Brien, "'Sacra Doctrina' Revisited: The Context of Medieval Education," *The Thomist* 41 (1977), 475-509 takes exception to the position of James A. Weisheipl, O.P. in "The Meaning of *Sacra Doctrina* in the *Summa Theologiae* I, q.1," *The Thomist* 38 (1974, 49-80 which tends to devalue the speculative aspect of the *sacra doctrina*.

35. This consideration explains why we find the majority of texts on both penitential and christological satisfaction in the *tertia pars*.

36. The secular master Gérard d'Abbeville, a lifelong friend of William of Saint-Amour, and his followers, called Geraldini, took advantage of the three year "sede vacante" after the death of Clement IV in 1268 to prolong old hostilities against the mendicant professors. Both Franciscans and Dominicans cooperated in defending their newly acquired papal privileges.

37. For more information, see R.A. Gauthier, O.P., "La date du Commentaire de Saint Thomas sur l'Ethique à Nicomaque," *Recherches de théologie ancienne et médiévale* 18 (1951), 103, n. 91.

38. Weisheipl, 245. Also, see Dominique Dubarle, O.P., "L'ontologie du mystère chrétien chez saint Thomas d'Aquin," *Angelicum* 52 (1975), 277-301; 485-521; 53 (1976), 277-68.

39. See William of Tocco, *Hystoria beati Thomae de Aquino* in Ferrua, *Vitae Fontes*, 56: "Scripsit super Epistolas Pauli omnes, quarum Scripturam partes Evangelicam super omnes commendabat, in quarum expositione Parisius visionem praefati Apostoli dicitur habuisse."

40. See Weisheipl, 247-9; 372-3.

41. Reginald of Piperno (c. 1230-90) Dominican priest and companion of Aquinas, especially during the last fifteen years of his life, served as principal secretary and confessor to St Thomas. See A. Dondaine, *Secretaires de saint Thomas* (Rome, 1956), especially, 198-202.

42. Weisheipl, 246-7.

43. For a defense of the pastoral motives behind the composition of the *Summa theologiae*, see Leonard E. Boyle, O.P., "The Setting of the *Summa theologiae* of Saint Thomas," The Etienne Gilson Series 5 (Toronto: Pontifical Institute of Mediaeval Studies, 1982). Observing the number of independent manuscripts of the *secunda pars* which remain extant, Boyle argues that pastoral concerns actually moved Aquinas to write a moral theology textbook for which he then subsequently provided a theological context, namely, the *prima* and *tertia partes*.

44. Thomas Gilby, O.P., *Purpose and Happiness* (1a2ae. 1-5), Vol. 16 (New York: McGraw-Hill, 1969), xiii. In general, Gilby presents a balanced account of Aquinas's teleological ethics throughout his commentary, appendices, and notes in the several volumes of the Blackfriars edition of the *Summa theologiae* which he edited.

45. For the historical background to this central doctrine, see Jaroslav Pelikan, "*Imago Dei*: An Explication of *Summa theologiae*, Part 1, Question 93," *Calgary Aquinas Studies*, ed Anthony Parel (Toronto: Pontifical Institute of Mediaeval Studies, 1978), 27-48.

46. See Gauthier, especially 66-105. But for the limits of Aquinas's dealings with the Aristotle, see F. van Steenberghen, *Thomas Aquinas and Radical Aristotelianism* (Washington, D.C: Catholic University of America Press, 1980).

47. Alasdair MacIntyre, *Whose Justice? Which Rationality?* (Notre Dame, IN: University of Notre Dame Press, 1988), especially, 164-208 provides one example of renewed interest in virtue theory.

48. See the "Processus canonizationis sancti Thomae Aquinatis, Neapoli," n. 77 in Ferrua, *Vitae Fontes*, 314.

49. The texts for psalms 52-54 were discovered by Uccelli in the Regio Archivo (Naples), n. 25. He later published them at Rome in 1880. For further information see, Palémon Glorieux, "Essais sur les commentaires scriptuaires de Saint Thomas et leur chronologie," *Recherches de théologie ancienne et médiévale* 17 (1950), 237-66.

50. The report actually comes to us from a certain Bartholomew of Capua who undoubtedly received the story firsthand from Reginald himself, "Processus," n.79 in Ferrua, *Vitae Fontes*, 319.

51. Lafont, 305-309.

52. Colman E. O'Neill, O.P., *The One Mediator* (3a. 16-26), Vol. 50 (New York: McGraw-Hill, 1965), xxiv.

CHAPTER II

"FIGURES OF OTHER REALITIES"

Principles of Thomas's Biblical Interpretation

Since Leo XIII's *Aeterni Patris* at the end of the 19th-century, Thomism has especially championed the systematic works of Aquinas, *viz.*, the *summae* and *quaestiones disputatae*. No such revival, however, has yet attracted similar attention to his scriptural commentaries. Nonetheless, it remains an historical fact that for a 13th-century master of theology like Thomas Aquinas teaching the Bible was his principal professional responsibility.[1] As a result, one could argue that an examination of his lectures on the Old and New Testaments is an indispensable introduction to the study of his systematic works. Were such a procedure faithfully observed, moreover, the novice reader of Thomas would never risk taking away the impression that his theology is divorced from its living sources in the Word of God. Nor, for that matter, do the scriptures secure mere ornamental status in the *Summa theologiae*. On the contrary, biblical scholarship actually informs and directs every aspect of Aquinas's systematic theology.

Still, Thomas's exegesis poses a difficulty. Do his medieval methods of biblical interpretation invalidate the Thomistic theological enterprise? Although this question also falls outside our present scope, one Thomist proposes a distinction which, for me, correctly evaluates Aquinas's methods of biblical interpretation and at the same time allows students of Thomas to use his scriptural commentaries with profit. Edmund Hill addresses the doubt concerning the value of Thomas's theology that might occur, for example, to a student educated in scientific exegesis while reading q. 102 of the *prima pars* where Aquinas treats the Garden of Eden. Hill argues that the validity of Thomas's theology is vindicated against this sort of doubt if one grants that, while his interpretation of scripture uses techniques that are indeed obsolete, his method nonetheless is controlled by principles that remain true to the essence of the Catholic tradition in scriptural exegesis. As a result, Aquinas produces work that is essentially valid.[2] On the other hand, Hill remarks that Origen, to cite but one instance, illustrates the case of a theologian of genius and devotion whose work nevertheless is essentially invalidated by wrong principles of interpretation introduced, moreover, from outside the Catholic possession of scripture.

Hill's distinction between Thomas's "principles" and "techniques," of course, requires further clarification and discussion. Obviously, the techniques of a 13th-century exegete do remain largely obsolete, especially after nearly a century of progress in the development of textual and historical research. The judgment of presumed obsolescence, however, did not await the significant advances made in this century by schools of scriptural higher criticism. Even Erasmus depreciated the value of Thomas's theology on the comparatively simple grounds that he was ignorant of the biblical languages![3] Of course, a certain historical anachronism enters into the debate at this point. We need to recall which tools were wanting to Thomas and his contemporaries--critical editions of the biblical texts, first hand knowledge (in Thomas's case, at least) of the biblical languages, handbooks, dictionaries on ancient civilizations and culture, etc.

On the other hand, Aquinas's principles for reading the scriptures still retain their validity today. His exegetical techniques, although different from those used by modern exegetes, nonetheless sufficed to disclose the meaning of the "sacra pagina." We see a good example of one such principle in a certain quodlibetal question where Thomas clearly describes his sensitivity to the contents of sacred scriptures.

> The scriptures are meant especially to show us the truths which are necessary for salvation. The manifestation or the expression of these truths is able to be accomplished either by means of words or by means of things; the words, in effect, designate the things, and these things themselves are able to be figures of other realities. The Author of all things has the power not only to use words to designate things, but also to use things in a way that they signify other things. It follows that in the scriptures, the truth manifests itself in a double fashion: first, the words yield certain realities--that is the literal sense; and second, these realities become figures of other realities--that is the spiritual sense (*Quodlibetal* VII, q.6, a.1).

He expresses the same principle in the *De potentia*. If there is a truth, he writes, which seems suitably expressed by a passage of scripture but which the author of the text did not understand, we can nevertheless rest assured that it was understood by the Holy Spirit, who remains the principal author of the Bible.[4]

In other words, Thomas's conviction concerning the revelational intention of the divine author disclosed both in the literal sense and in the spiritual senses guides his approach to the reading of the Bible. Applications of a spiritual sense to various texts of scripture need not cause disquiet for the realist theologian, who fears that symbolic meanings can be difficult to control. "There is nothing hidden in any text of the sacred scriptures," Aquinas assures us, "that is not manifestly expounded elsewhere in them; whence expositions of the spiritual sense ought always to have a foundation in some other literal exposition of the scriptures, and thus one guards against error" (*Quodlibetal* VII, q. 6, a. 1, ad 3). In other words, Aquinas recognizes the fundamental value of the literal meaning of the scriptures.

Historians of medieval exegesis, in fact, underscore that Thomas's approach to the Bible exhibits a sobriety regarding the use of the spiritual sense. In his *Esquisse d'une Histoire de l'Exégèse Latine au Moyen Age*, C. Spicq, for instance, calls Thomas a "revolutionary figure."[5]

St Thomas insisted less than the better part of his predecessors on the spiritual senses. Thanks to his analysis of the modes of signification of the signifying words, and of the things signifying and signified, he gave to literal exegesis its full value, and reduced considerably the interest in mystical interpretations during the high middle ages.

Above all, this attitude of respect for the literal sense of the scriptures expresses the basic principle of Aquinas's method. Since he remained faithful to Catholic principles, Aquinas continues to serve as a trustworthy interpreter of the Bible. Although the hubris of our age sometimes insinuates the contrary, it would be absurd for a Christian believer who understood the opening lines of Hebrews 1:2--"but in these last days he has spoken to us by a Son"--to imagine that God would have hidden for nearly nineteen centuries the tools required to explore the true meaning of his Word.

The Satisfaction of Christ the Head

Postilla super Isaiam: A Biblical Christology

Scholastic exegesis slips almost imperceptibly from exegesis into systematic theology. Thus, although the bulk of the *Postilla super Isaiam* remains devoted to the division and explanation of the text "ad litteram"--for such was the basic scholastic method of reading the scriptures to the students (each of whom did not possess a personal copy of the Bible)--we still find theological digressions periodically written into the text.[6] A good example of this is found in the ninth chapter of the commentary where Thomas discusses Isaiah 9:6: "For to us a Child is born, to us a Son is given; and the government will be upon his shoulder." Three theological notes are given to explain the phrases "a Child is born" ("Parvulus natus est"); "to us . . . is given" ("datus est nobis"); and "upon his shoulder" ("super humerum eius"). Each of the notes, as we shall see, actually embodies a brief essay on biblical christology.

The first note describes the abasement of Christ involved in the Incarnation ("kenosis"). Granted Aquinas does not refer to the great christological text in Philippians 2:5-11, we know that Thomas nonetheless has grasped the gist of St Paul's thought. The incarnation signifies a voluntary humiliation on the part of the eternal Son whose human existence observes the principle of credibility.

> With respect to the words "Parvulus natus est," it should be noted that Christ is called a little one first as regards his birth because of his age: "And going into the house they saw the Child with Mary his Mother" (Mt 2:11); second, as regards his possessions, since he was poor: "For you know the grace of Our Lord Jesus Christ, that though he was rich, yet for your sake he became poor" (II Cor 8:9); third, as regards his heart, since he was humble: "Learn from Me; for I am gentle and lowly in heart" (Mt 11:29); fourth, as regards his vile death: "Let us condemn him to a shameful death" (Wis 2:20) (*Super Isaiam* c. 9, l. 1).

Christ remains the incarnate Son of God whose human life takes on the poverty of human existence for our salvation.

Next, the second note suggests nine ways in which Christ can be thought of as "for us." We observe in this section the movement to include the concerns of functional christologies.

> Noting the phrase "datus est nobis," it can be said that Christ is given to us first as a brother: "O that you were like a brother to me, that nursed at my mother's breast!" (Song of Solomon 8:1); second, as a doctor: "Be glad, O sons of Zion, and rejoice in the Lord, your God; for he has given you a doctor of justice" (Joel 2:23); third, as a watchman: "Son of man, I have made you a watchman for the house of Israel" (Ezekiel 3); fourth, as a defender: "He will send them a saviour and will defend and deliver them" (Isaiah 19:20); fifth, as a shepherd: "And I will set up over them one shepherd. . . . and he shall feed them" (Ezekiel 34:23); sixth, as an example for our activities: "For I have given you an example, that you also should do as I have done to you" (Jn 13:15); seventh, as food for wayfarers: "The bread which I shall give for the life of the world is my flesh" (John 6:52); eighth, as a price of redemption: "The Son of man came not to be served but to serve, and to give his life as a ransom for many" (Mt 20:28); ninth, as a price of remuneration: "To him who conquers I will give some of the hidden manna" (Rev 2:17). (*Super Isaiam* c.9, l.1).

Christ remains the true teacher and example of God's wisdom. He establishes an order in the world which opens up to communion with the blessed Trinity.

Finally, having described the ways in which Christ "emptied himself" and having listed several more ways in which the mission of

Christ is directed toward mankind, Thomas turns his attention to the final phrase--"super humerum eius." Here he can speak about the roles given to Christ in salvation history, especially, as the priest who satisfies and the victor who is glorified. One recognizes here a trace of another Pauline antithesis (besides the "kenosis" found in Philippians 2:5-11). In this excerpt, we can identify Christ's own "exitus-reditus" which corresponds to his abasement and exaltation.

> Similarly it should be observed concerning the words "super humerum eius" that God placed upon the shoulders of Christ first sins, as upon one who satisfies, as Isaiah says: "And the Lord has laid on him the iniquity of us all" (Isaiah 53:6); second, a key, as upon a priest: "And I will place on his shoulder the key of the house of David; he shall open, and none shall shut" (Isaiah 22:2); third, principality, as upon a conqueror: "And the government will be upon his shoulder" (Isaiah 9:6); fourth, glory, as upon one who triumphs: "And they will hang upon him the whole weight of his Father's house" (Isaiah 22:24) (*Super Isaiam*, c. 9, l. 1).

Christ, then, exercises his ministry of reconciliation in a way which conforms to the requirements of the human condition, especially the estrangement from divine worship in which sin results.

The sample from the commentary on Isaiah strikingly displays not only Aquinas's scriptural methods but also the grounds for his theological reflection and synthesis. Of course, the text of the Latin Vulgate offers him the opportunity to develop this synthesis. To be sure, certain terms found in the Vulgate text disappear in subsequent translations of the scriptures. For example, the term "doctor" in the verse from Joel appears elsewhere as "rain".[7] But semitics does not constitute a sure science. Even if newer translations do not always conform to the very appropriations used by Thomas, his exegetical skill nonetheless points to his familiarity with the standard version of his day. Granted the limitations which the state of 13th-century biblical scholarship imposes, we can still recognize even in this small excerpt from an Old Testament commentary a teacher of sacred doctrine thoroughly informed of the inspired source of his science. If we take into consideration the opinion of the Leonine editors that this work represents very first of Thomas's theological endeavors, we cannot but wonder at the appreciation for the sacred scriptures which the passage demonstrates.[8]

The Commentaries on the Gospels of Matthew and John:
The Allegorical Sense of the Scripture: Christ and the New Adam

To be sure, texts from the commentaries on the Gospels will deal with the satisfaction of Christ.[9] At the same time, they also serve as good examples of what Thomas calls the spiritual sense of scripture. In the first question of the *Summa theologiae*, he explains that in addition to the literal sense of the scriptures there exists a spiritual sense which is sometimes called the mystical sense.[10] This spiritual sense does not abide directly in the significance of the words as happens in the literal sense, but in the figures to which the words point. The medievals distinguished three kinds of spiritual senses, the allegorical, the anagogical, and the moral.[11] We will find examples of all three varieties used by Aquinas to illustrate Christian satisfaction. First, however, we consider the allegorical spiritual sense where old law incidents signify the messianic realities in the new law.

Each of the following texts, then, touches upon some circumstance of Christ's passion, for example, the instrument of his death, the time of his suffering, or the place where he suffered. Each also employs some allegorical interpretation of an Old Testament passage to illumine the soteriological significance implicit in the event as recorded in the New Testament. For instance, in *Super Matthaeum* c. 27, l. 2, Thomas comments on Matthew 27:35: "And when they had crucified him." There he observes that death by crucifixion was a fitting way for Christ to have satisfied for the sin of Adam, who had sinned "in ligno," that is, by eating of the fruit of the tree ("de ligno") of the knowledge of good and evil. Often a third text mediates the significance of the Old Testament text for the new dispensation. For instance, Thomas quotes Wisdom 14:7: "For blessed is the wood by which righteousness comes." Thus, in accord with a tradition in Christian piety, Thomas affirms that Christ's desire to suffer "in ligno" and thereby to satisfy for the sin of Adam points to an element of the biblical account of original sin. Next, the time of Adam's sin gives rise to another spiritual interpretation. Thomas asserts that the sin of Adam must have taken place in the afternoon since it is written in Genesis 3:8 that, having sinned, Adam and Eve "heard the sound of the Lord God. . . in the cool of the day." Christ's passion and death likewise took place in the afternoon as well, as the words of Matthew 27:45 indicate: "Now from the sixth hour there was darkness over all the land until the ninth hour." A third detail of the passion which Thomas discovers in the Genesis account of original sin deals with the circumstance of place. In the *Lectura super Johannem* c. 19, l. 6, (n.4) he recalls that the sin of the first man was committed in a garden--"paradise" being interpreted as a "garden of delights" ("in paradiso voluptatis"). It is significant that in satisfying for such a sin "Christ was captured in a garden, suffered in a garden, and finally buried in a garden." Allegory, then, presents a coherent picture of divine revelation by using figures and images from both Testaments to illuminate major themes concerning Christian salvation.

Another variety of the spiritual sense of scripture includes the anagogical, "when the things that lie ahead in eternal glory are signified."[12] Aquinas continues the garden theme. Since we sometimes refer to the Church as an enclosed garden, Thomas sees the Church as spiritually signified even by the olive garden where Christ's passion and our glorification began. In another example of eschatological interpretation, heaven itself is signified by the image of a garden. Since by his passion Christ leads mankind to its destiny, Aquinas recognizes paradise as a garden of delights. Thus, Luke 23:43 says, "Today you will be with me in Paradise."[13] The anagogical sense always points, then, to the eschatological dimension of the Christian life.

Although they illustrate a style of biblical interpretation favored by medieval theologians, these examples of Thomas's spiritual exegesis also point to the theological development of satisfaction found in his other biblical commentaries, especially those on the Pauline writings. Likewise we can discern there the beginnings of a systematic theology. "The 'magister in sacra pagina,'" explains Chenu, "begets the 'magister in theologia' or, for the medieval experience, exegesis brings about scholasticism."[14]   Moreover, we can recognize several features of Thomas's christology in these texts. First, the satisfaction made by Christ on the cross derives its urgency both from the sin of Adam and all subsequent sins which reduce the human race to a condition of bondage.   In *Super Matthaeum* c. 26, a. 5, Thomas comments on Matthew 26:38--"Then he said to them, 'My soul is very sorrowful, even to death'"--and says that Christ added "even to death" to indicate that by his death he would satisfy for the present crime of his betrayal as well as for all other sins. Second, the satisfaction accomplished by Christ makes it possible for us to reach our supernatural end.   So when Thomas speaks about the Church as a community "consecrated" by the blood of Christ, the community of the Elect, he elaborates an eschatological construction; thus the Church as an "enclosed garden" points to an anagogical interpretation of the Scriptures. In any event, the unity of the "sacra doctrina" remains evident throughout Aquinas's scriptural studies.

The Commentaries on the Letters of Saint Paul and on Hebrews

Christ as "Propitiatio" for our sins

When Thomas repeatedly refers to the satisfaction of Christ as something necessary on account of the sins of mankind, he points, in fact, to one of the principal elements of the primitive gospel preaching. As C. H. Dodd points out, St Paul gave authenticity to his teaching simply by reminding his audience of the gospel which underlay it.[15] For example, in I Corinthians 15:1-3 he writes: "Now I would remind you, brethren, in what terms I preached to you the gospel, which you received." Paul then continues, "For I delivered to you as of first importance what I also received, that Christ died for our sins in accordance with the scriptures." Aquinas draws inspiration from this central tenet of the Pauline "gospel" and, as the following texts from his commentaries demonstrate, queries the tradition as to the correct meaning of Christ's expiation for sins.

First, Thomas's commentary on Romans 3:23-26 provides the occasion to treat the expiatory character of Christ's satisfaction.[16] There St Paul writes: "They are justified by his grace as a gift, through the redemption which is in Christ Jesus, whom God put forward as an expiation" (Rom 3:24). In his commentary, Thomas first explains the need for the satisfaction made by Christ. Commenting on the phrase, "through the redemption which is in Christ Jesus" he writes:

> It is as if someone, having committed some fault, became indebted to the king and was obliged to pay a fine. One who paid the fine for him would be said to have redeemed him. Such a debt was owed by the whole human race because of the sin of the first parents. So it was that no other one apart from Christ was able to satisfy for the sin of the whole human race, since he alone was free of every sin (*Super ad Romanos*, c. 3, 1. 3).

Although inserted into the biblical *lectura*, an interpretive gloss such as this identifies a given New Testament locus as seminal for the theological topic at hand. So, in this particular excerpt, Thomas cites the sinlessness of Christ as the reason why the satisfaction which he accomplished remains an efficacious one for the human race.

Similarly, continuing his commentary, Thomas affirms that Christ alone is our redemption "whom God put forward as an expiation ("propitiationem")." First, Thomas attributes the efficacy of our justification to God's hidden plan, which includes the predestination of Christ: "Because God had ordained him for this according to his own counsel who accomplishes all things according to the counsel of his will" (*Super ad Romanos* c. 3, 1. 3). Of course, the reference to Ephesians 1:9-11 does recall the mystery of God's purposes in the world, culminating in the universal call to holiness for all men and women who participate in the fruits of Christ's redemptive work. But the term "propitiatio" of Thomas's Latin Vulgate Bible provides the definitive clue for interpreting this and other texts concerning satisfaction: "Christ satisfies for us" means that he makes amends for or propitiates for our sins. Aquinas repeats this in several different contexts. For example, when the Psalmist cries: "Propitius esto peccatis nostris," "Forgive our sins!," Aquinas understands him to cry out for the satisfaction accomplished by Christ.   Or when the I John 2:2 refers to Christ as "the expiation ("propitiatio") for our sins," Aquinas explains that Christ has satisfied for us.   Again, employing the principles of spiritual exegesis, Aquinas points to the instruction contained in Exodus 25:17, namely, to put the mercy seat ("propitiatorium") over the ark, and interprets the text to refer to Christ our expiation being placed over the new ark of the covenant, the holy Church.   As in the Bible itself, redemption and sin remain correlatives throughout Aquinas's theology.

In the Pauline literature, furthermore, the expiatory value of Christ's death remains closely associated with the liturgy of sacrifice.   For instance, L. Cerfaux refers to Romans 3:23-26 as a particularly important text for this theme.   There St Paul refers to Christ as he "whom God put forward as an expiation by his blood."   And Thomas adds: "It is only through the Blood of Christ that both the sins of the present as well as those of the past are able to be forgiven" (*in loco*). Although the blood of Christ possesses an objective efficacy, the believer realizes its power to nullify the power of sin only to the extent that he or she maintains faith in the power ("virtus") of his blood for redemption.   Thus, Thomas comments on Romans 3:25, "to be received by faith:"

> This death of Christ is applied to us by faith, by which we believe that the world has been redeemed by his death--Galatians 2:20: "I live by faith in the Son of God, who loved me."   For even among men, satisfaction by one for another is without worth, unless such confidence is present (*Super ad Romanos* c. 3, l. 3).

In his commentary on Hebrews, Thomas further develops the theological ramifications of the sacrifice implicated in Christ's satisfaction.   For instance, at Hebrews 1:1-4, we read that Christ makes "purification for sins."   Thomas comments that on the altar of the cross Christ satisfied for the punishment ("reatus poenae") incumbent upon the human race due to sin.   Again, commenting on the fifth chapter of Hebrews, where the author sets forth the majestic theme of Christ's high priesthood, Thomas argues that Christ himself perfectly embodies the priest since, according to the command of Leviticus 4:26, he carries out sin offerings.   The commentary continues that since "every high priest is appointed to offer gifts and sacrifices, it is necessary for this priest to have something to offer."   But in the new dispensation, Christ himself incarnates that offering since he alone can fulfill the Old Testament requirement that the offering be without spot or blemish.   In addition, the role of Christ as high priest allows an individual member of the race to satisfy for the sins of the same race.   Thus, Christ offers himself in satisfaction for the sins of his brothers and sisters.   And such an efficacious sacrifice remains the reason, according to Thomas, why the sacrifices of the old law, which, in fact, only sinners offered, could not "perfect the conscience of the worshipper" nor symbolize true satisfactory worship. By contrast, the sacrifice offered by Christ, who alone remains sinless, instantiates an acceptable offering and accomplishes true satisfaction.

The theme of death also intrigues Aquinas. For instance, in his commentary on II Timothy 1:10, he explicitly identifies the death of Christ with satisfaction for sin. But Thomas also distinguishes the way in which the devil might have a power concerning death. And although he remains careful to dissociate himself from early medieval "rights of the devil" theories, he does advert to the patristic theme that Christ's death rent the power of Satan in the world. So he suggests some analogies to explain this fundamentally mythological viewpoint. For example, a judge can be said to have dominion over death when he commands a capital punishment. Or, a thief can also have a certain dominion over death but only in the sense that he has merited it by his crimes, as when we say that someone has a "right" to death. Aquinas prefers the latter explanation, since it explains the commonly held view that the devil led man to death, without granting the devil a positive claim on mankind. But Christ's redemptive death destroys even the devil's supposed right concerning death. Even if the devil presumes to extend this effect of sin to include Christ himself, still the power of the sinless Christ easily conquers the power of the devil, thereby freeing us from the devil's bondage which remains a metaphor for the servitude of sin.

The same theme occurs elsewhere, for instance in Aquinas's commentary on the "kenosis" hymn in Philippians 2. There Thomas makes another comparison between the roles played by the devil in seducing man away from God and the role played by Christ in leading man back to God. Commenting upon Philippians 2:6 ("though he was in the form of God, Christ did not count equality with God a thing to be grasped ["rapinam"]"), Thomas remarks that one can contrast the humility of the Logos who sought to lower himself with the audacity of man who, being filled with pride, sought to grasp ("rapina") at divinity. Of course, Christ was entitled to such a holding on to divinity since he knew well his personal identity, but the human creature possessed no grounds for such a rapine. Hence, the sin of pride (for which Christ satisfied) explains the words of the psalmist: "What I did not steal ("non rapui"), must I now restore?" Again, we discern Aquinas's preference for organizing his theological materials around key-words and phrases in the biblical text.

The commentary on Ephesians 1:7-8 enlarges on the meaning of expiation ("remotio peccati") as an interpretation for the satisfaction of Christ: "In him we have redemption through his blood, the forgiveness of our trespasses, according to the riches of his grace which he lavished upon us." Thomas notes that there are two things which separate fallen man from God: one is sin itself ("macula peccati") and the other is a debt of punishment ("noxa poenae"). Christ's satisfaction remains sufficient to remove both obstacles which impede our union with God. "In him we have our redemption," writes St Paul, and that redemption, according to Thomas's interpretation, clearly means liberation from the stain of sin. Human sin remains then the "terminus a quo" of Christian salvation. Still this salvation "according to the riches of his [God's] grace," means that God bestows gratuitously on an unworthy people redemption and sanctification accomplished by the satisfaction of his Son. Indeed, Thomas does not hesitate to call this grace a superabundant one ("ex superabundanti gratia") because God was willing to safeguard the honor of the human race at the price of his Son, whose death, after the fashion of justice ("quasi per justitiam"), liberated us from the servitude of sin.

On the other hand, liberation from sin remains only one aspect of Christ's redemptive work. God also turns the human creature toward himself and effectively reunites the whole of creation with himself. It is this aspect of satisfaction that Thomas speaks about in commenting on Ephesians 2:16 where St Paul talks about redemption as "bringing the hostility to an end." There Thomas simply observes: "Christ sufficiently satisfied for our sins and since the price was paid, it follows that reconciliation should occur"(*in loco*). Of course, the biblical metaphor of price strains the personalist interpretation Aquinas will later put onto such texts, but even here he shows that Christian satisfaction remains ordered to reconciliation. So we now turn to this important theme for theology.

Christ is our "Reconciliatio"

Up to this point, Thomas has emphasized Christ's subjective state, especially his sinlessness, as a chief reason for the efficacy of the satisfaction which he accomplished. But in commenting on the words of St Paul in Romans 5:8ff, "But God shows his love for us in that while we were yet sinners Christ died for us," he offers another reason for this efficacy. The satisfaction of Christ constitutes not only the shedding of his sinless blood but also the love with which these sufferings, especially death, were borne. Of course, this shift of emphasis to the charity of Christ continues the theme of the sinless Christ. For the principal sign of Christ's love for us remains the sufferings he bore and the death he died while we were still at odds ("inimici") with God. "The very death of Christ itself shows God's love for us, because he gave his Son that he might die in order to satisfy for us," writes Aquinas in *Super ad Romanos* c. 5, l. 2. Hence Christ's love, Thomas continues, gives his death the salvific value that it actually enjoys.

To be sure, the death of Christ as a mere natural phenomenon sets forth nothing acceptable to a God who "does not delight in the death of the living." However, if we consider Christ's loving and obedient acceptance of death, then we identify the elements which valorize this otherwise cruel action.

> From this was the death of Christ meritorious and satisfactory for our sins, and as such acceptable to God, adequate for the reconciliation of all men, even of those killing Christ, some of whom were saved by his very prayer, when he said: "Forgive them, for they know not what they do" (*Super ad Romanos*, c. 5, l. 2).

Here we arrive at the heart of the matter of salvation. The will of Christ formed by love and obedience gives his death saving significance for the world.

Thus, reconciliation follows. "For if while we were enemies we were reconciled to God by the death of his Son, much more, now that we are reconciled, shall we be saved by his life" (Romans 5:10). The fruit of satisfaction accomplished by love remains reconciliation between God and man, a reconciliation made possible both by the removal of the offense and the satisfaction of punishment. Thomas has recourse to an argument from human experience, suggested by the Pauline text itself, to further explain his point. The unique character of Christ's love is shown when we consider that in human affairs a person remains less disposed to do good to an enemy until some form of reconciliation takes place. Christ, however, died for a sinful race. When Thomas writes that "even now we are joined to God through faith and charity" (*Super ad Romanos* c. 5, l. 3), he expresses the full impact of the reconciliation which the death of the sinless Christ accomplishes. The scriptures, moreover, insist that reconciliation amounts to more than the removal of some obstacle which previously separated two parties. Because the satisfaction made by Christ results in our being given a full share in his (risen) life, it constitutes something positive.

There remains another side to the doctrine of satisfaction which also appears in the biblical commentaries. Since one person can make satisfaction for another, the actuality of the mystical body also figures in Aquinas's doctrine on satisfaction. Although a full discussion of this important issue occurs only in the systematic works, we find grounds for the validity of vicarious satisfaction, for example, in St Paul's injunction, "Bear one another's burdens, and so fulfill the law of Christ" (Galatians 6:2). In his commentary on this text, Thomas spells out three ways in which one might carry out such an instruction. The third points to mutual support among Christian believers, namely, satisfaction for the punishment owed another through prayers and good deeds. He next cites Proverbs 18:19, "A brother helped is like a strong city," in support of this argument. Aquinas's personalism is (happily) also a call for us to turn to persons-as-agents engaged in satisfactory practices as well as persons-as-subjects expressing themselves.

The satisfaction accomplished by Christ in excelling love and through a frightful passion results in our reconciliation and harmony with God. In the commentary on Romans, Thomas affirms such reconciliation at verse 5:11, "we also rejoice in God through whom we have now received our reconciliation" (*in loco*). And the commentary on II Corinthians 5:18 provides another occasion for Thomas to elaborate on reconciliation, "All this is from God, who through Christ reconciled us to himself and gave us the ministry of reconciliation." Here Thomas outlines two benefits which result from the work of Christ, the one a general benefit for all of us and the other a special benefit given only to the Apostles. The general benefit includes the fact of reconciliation itself: "For men were enemies of God because of sin; Christ, however, took away this enmity from their midst by satisfying for sin" (*Super ad II Cor* c. 5, l. 5). In the commentary on Hebrews 8:2-6, moreover, Thomas describes our reconciliation as a union when he writes that all those for whom Christ's expiatory sacrifice was offered are united to God. At the same time, there exists a special benefit which derives from reconciliation and which God gives to the Apostles. It is the ministry of reconciliation for others: the Apostles remain the instruments through which the effects of Christ's satisfaction reach out to the world. Aquinas recognizes, then, the patristic doctrine that in the end Christ delivers all things to the Father. All in all, the Adam-Christ typology inspires Thomas's talk about satisfaction. In brief, sin and death for all followed upon Adam's pride and disobedience; satisfaction and reconciliation, on the contrary, result from Christ's love and obedient suffering for all. But this wonderful exchange runs deeper than the level of actions, even those which flow from the capital actions of Christ. Because Christ satisfies on the cross, all men and women can reach the beatific destiny intended for us by God. This means nothing less than a radical revolution in the very order of creation. In the final analysis, then, this fundamental conception of Christian salvation, as the New Testament itself repeatedly points out, guides Thomas's systematic treatment of Christ's satisfaction.

The Satisfaction of the Members

Expositio in Job "ad litteram":
Penitential Satisfaction and the Moral Sense of Scripture

In the prologue to his commentary on Job, Thomas explains his intention to comment on Job "secundum litteralem sensum."[17] Six centuries earlier, of course, Gregory the Great had already exhausted the spiritual meaning in his *Moralia*. But Thomas also separates himself from the mentality of other contemporary commentaries on Job.

For example, the writer of the anonymous Victorine letter (an instruction to a young monk about to begin his theological education in the monastic tradition) roundly denied that the book of Job had any useful literal significance and counseled that one should read it only as an image of Christ and his Church.[18] In a clear break with this tradition, Thomas identifies the book's literal theme or purpose: "to demonstrate through probable reasons that human affairs are subject to divine providence." As one author observes, "Thanks to his 'compendious' treatment, the 'purpose' never disappears behind the exposition of isolated texts."[19] And although Thomas acknowledges that one who undertakes a commentary on Job will be bound to explain how the sufferings and afflictions of the just one can be reconciled with the existence of a loving Providence, the theme of patience traditionally associated with the book does not figure largely in his commentary.

On the other hand, Thomas's intention to follow the literal meaning of the text of Job does not imply that he will avoid all spiritual interpretation in his commentary. Rather, he will refrain from offering the kinds of accommodated interpretations and forced explanations of the texts already provided by others. Chenu explains this balance :

> His reaction was a significant one, for it brought out the fact that theology was putting up a safety-catch against the multiplying of figures and allegories without criterion or limits. It remains that, *de facto*, St Thomas did practice on his own, in his running interpretation of the texts, that classical type of interpretation wherein utilization of the Bible for spiritual purposes oversteps the explanation of the word of God.[20]

The references to satisfaction contained in the *Expositio in Job* do not refer directly to the satisfaction of Christ. Instead, since it is the relationship of divine providence to human affairs that is the subject of Job, Aquinas looks at what the members of Christ's body accomplish by their sufferings. Even when he employs the spiritual senses of scripture, Thomas includes neither the allegorical (messianic) spiritual sense nor the anagogical (eschatological) spiritual sense. Rather, he uses the moral sense, a third variety of spiritual interpretation. Elsewhere he writes of the moral sense: it is brought into play "when the things done in Christ and in those who prefigure him are signs of what we should carry out" (*Summa Theologiae* Ia q. 1, a. 10). In his commentary on Job he consequently discusses the penitential satisfaction "we should carry out."

The first mention of satisfaction comes at the start of the commentary. In the biblical narrative, Job offers sacrifices for his sons, after they had completed their cycle of feasting. Commenting on the line, "burnt offerings according to the number of them all (i.e., his sons)" (Job 1:5), Thomas notes the correspondence between the number of the sacrifices and the number of Job's sons. "Each sin," he writes, "should be expiated by a corresponding satisfaction" (*Super Job* c. 1 [185]). A second reference to satisfaction is found in the commentary on the seventh chapter, where Job laments his state--"If I sin, what do I do to thee, thou watcher of men?" (Job 7:20). This cry of human infirmity moves Thomas to suggest reasons why, given human weakness, God should forgive our sins. "Man is unable to do anything condign by way of recompense for the offense which he has committed against God" (*Super Job* c. 7 [449]). If God keeps so close a watch over our actions, surely he must realize that by human effort alone we are unable to win forgiveness for sins. Finally, commenting on the eighth chapter, Thomas speaks about satisfaction, emphasizing the role of prayer as a proper satisfaction for sin. It is Job's friend, Bildad, who addresses him in the biblical text: "If you will seek God and make supplication to the Almighty" (Job 8:5). This inspires Thomas to comment that "among the works of satisfaction prayer seems to be foremost" (*Super Job* c. 8 [97-99]). Of course, it is the Latin word for supplication ("deprecatus") in the Vulgate text which again suggests the satisfactory work of prayer ("deprecare," to pray). Actually, this forms the second stage of a three-step plan offered by Bildad whereby Job might win pardon and relief from his sufferings. Briefly put, the plan includes: to rise quickly from sin, to make satisfaction, and to avoid falling back into sin.

The last two passages which speak of satisfaction are found in the final chapter of the commentary. There Thomas reflects on Job's admission that he now understands the practical import of God's actions, interpreting this as a sign that Job now is aware of his sinfulness. Thomas comments: "The more a man considers the justice of God, the more he will be aware of his own faults" (*Super Job* c. 42 [41-44]). Still, mere knowledge of one's sinfulness is never enough, since full repentance always includes satisfaction. Job, moved by this recognition of the fragility of human nature, acknowledges this when he says, "[t]herefore I despise myself and repent in dust and ashes" (Job 42:6). Thomas comments on the fittingness of this conclusion, remarking that "a humble satisfaction is appropriate to expiate for the pride of man's thoughts" (*Super Job* c.42 [44-49]). This relationship between a humble spirit and the personal desire to make satisfaction remains an important theological point for the theology of satisfaction.

We also find a similar observation in the single reference to satisfaction contained in a minor work of Thomas, the *De regno*,[21] written for a King of Cyprus who apparently died before he had a chance to receive Thomas's good counsels on governance. Here we discover Aquinas's explanation of why a bad king or tyrant is incapable of making satisfaction. He says: "Such tyrants, bloated as they are with pride, are rarely sorry for their sins and are rightly deserted by God; steeped in a desire for human adulation, they even more rarely are able to make suitable satisfaction" (*De regno* 1, c. 11).

Thus we learn the importance of personal dispositions in the life of the Christian.

In a final passage in Job, we have a text which remotely points to christological satisfaction. Although it does not directly deal with the person of Jesus Christ, it does consider the intercession of a holy man for others. The remark occurs in relation to what the contemporary editors call Job's epilogue, that is, the section in which the ancient folktale (which has served as a setting for the biblical account) reappears abruptly within the inspired text.[22] The friends of Job have not spoken well of God and, in Aquinas's view, have sinned with malice, since their actions represent a conscious error in doctrine regarding God's providence. Thus, in the biblical account they are asked to offer up a sacrifice of seven bulls and seven rams. But first the Lord instructs them to "go to my servant Job and offer up for yourself a burnt offering; and my servant Job shall pray for you, and I will accept his prayer not to deal with you according to your folly" (42:8). Thomas sees in this command a two-fold significance which bears upon satisfaction. First, God affirms the principle that the one who sins must also perform the satisfaction. So Job's three friends themselves are ordered actually to "offer up for yourselves" the required sacrifice. Second, the friends are asked to go to Job for his intercession. In Thomas's opinion, this indicates that the sacrifice of sinners requires the help of a holy man--"but your satisfaction needs the intercession of a faithful man" (*Super Job* 42 [71-83]). Since Job's prayers are added to the satisfaction undertaken by the guilty friends, they will escape the full punishment they deserve. This teaching, moreover, adumbrates the relationship which Thomas describes between the perfect satisfaction of Christ and the various penitential satisfactions undertaken by his members.

Commentaries on the New Testament: Satisfaction in the Context of Baptism and Penance

The relationship between the satisfaction of Christ the head and the satisfaction of the members, especially with respect to satisfactory works within the Church's sacramental system, is a subject developed by Aquinas chiefly in his systematic works. Nonetheless, there are a group of New Testament texts that offer Thomas the occasion to speak, even according to the principles of spiritual interpretation, about penitential satisfactions in connection with the sacraments of baptism and penance. First, in a commentary on Romans 11:29, "The gifts and call of God are irrevocable," Thomas observes a difference in the Church's sacramental practice (*Super ad Romanos*, c. 11, l. 4). He notes that baptism, because it draws on the regenerative power of Christ's passion, works "per modum cuiusdam generationis." This means that baptism, which constitutes a real birth in Christ, completely removes whatever there is of the "poena" or the result of sin in those who receive it. The sacrament of penance, on the contrary, works per "modum sanationis." This means that the healing process involved in this sacrament allows the effects of sin to remain so that the believer can undergo a progressive conformity through works of penance. Thus, in the sacrament, the satisfactions enjoined by the priest as a penance are meant to draw the penitent into a process of integral healing. (Aquinas, it should be noted, always orders his discussions of doctrine to the practice of the Church.)

Next, commenting on II Corinthians 7:10, "For godly grief produces a repentance that leads to salvation and brings no regret, but worldly grief produces death," Thomas speaks about the traditional threefold division of the sacrament of penance, "contritio cordis, confessio oris, satisfactio operis" (*Super II ad Corinthios* c. 7, l. 2).[23]   Godly grief, Aquinas writes, leads to lasting salvation ("in salutem stabilem," as the Vulgate reads) because it moves us to initiate the other two parts of sacramental penance. Again, he speak sbout the three parts of penance in a gloss on I Corinthians 11:27--"Whoever, therefore, eats the bread or drinks the cup of the Lord in an unworthy manner will be guilty of profaning the body and blood of the Lord" (*Super I ad Corinthios* c.11, l.7). First, Thomas lists three ways in which a person might approach the Eucharist in an unworthy manner. Then he asks, should one who has committed a mortal sin approach the Eucharist? Like St Paul, he replies that such a one would be guilty of profaning the body and blood of the Lord.   Still, it might happen that under certain circumstances an individual could not approach the sacrament of penance and perform a satisfaction for his sins before receiving communion. In that case, a simple act of contrition would suffice since such an expression of sorrow removes the determination to sin. While Thomas acknowledges that such a preparation should not serve as the regular ("regulariter") preparation for the Eucharist, it nonetheless remains, in his view, an adequate one.

In this discussion, we learn that Aquinas distinguishes two effects which every morally bad act necessarily entails, namely the stain of sin ("macula peccati") and the punishment due to sin ("reatus poenae").[24] In his commentary on Psalm 50, for instance, Thomas writes that when David asked to regain the innocence he had lost by turning away from God, he sought "first that the evil or sin be removed and second that the effect of sin be removed" (*In psalmos* 50, 1.6 [1-6]).[25] The essential act of conversion always consists in a renewed act of charity. Sin turns the sinner away from God, with the result that only charity can reverse this estrangement; therefore theologians point to the alienation of sin, the "macula peccati." But sin also makes the sinner liable to punishment.   Thus, sacramental penance looks to the whole phenomenology of sin, including the "reatus poenae" within a certain juridical framework which includes the imposition of penances. Even so, Aquinas shows no hesitation about allowing a sinner who has turned to God in charity to receive the Eucharist, despite the fact that (due to circumstances beyond the individual's control) he has not had the chance to express this sorrow within the sacramental forum and to perform the required satisfaction.

Beyond the merely juridical aspects of the sacrament, however, Aquinas recognizes that satisfaction also plays an important role in reforming the image of God in the believer. We find him discussing the restorative powers of the sacrament in, for instance, the commentaries on Matthew and John. Commenting on the cure of the paralytic in Matthew 9:1-8, Thomas writes:

> There were three things about the sick man: he was lying on his bed, he was carried by others, he was unable to walk. Because he was lying down Christ said "Rise"; because he was carried in, Christ commanded that he take something up--"Take up your bed"; because he was unable to walk, Christ said "Rise and walk" (*Super Matthaeum* c. 9, 1. 1).

Then Thomas gives his spiritual interpretation of the episode and its moral meaning for the Christian who has sinned: "Likewise to the sinner lying in sin [Christ] says: 'Rise' from your sin by contrition; 'Take up your bed' by satisfaction; 'And go home' into the house of eternity, or with a clean conscience" (*in loco*).

A commentary on a healing miracle in John 5:1-9 also examines the role of satisfaction in rehabilitating persons from the effects of sin. The verse refers to the man at the pool of Bethzatha: "Jesus said to him, 'Rise, take up your pallet and walk'" (Jn 5:8). First, the Lord commands the sick man to rise from sin ("recedendo a peccato"). Second, Christ instructs the sick man to take up his pallet as a means of satisfying for his sins. "For the pallet, on which a man lies, signifies sin. When a man picks up his pallet he is carrying the burden of penance imposed on him for his sins" (*Super Johannem* c. 5, 1.5), as we read in Micah 7:9: "I will bear ("portabo") the indignation of the Lord because I have sinned against Him." But Thomas interprets the final command to mean that the one who has confessed his sins and performed the appointed satisfaction must now continue to advance in goodness ("proficiendo in bono"). Again we see his interest in the practical application of the scriptural message.

Next, Thomas turns to St Augustine's interpretation of this same gospel story. Although the details of their allegorizations differ, the two theologians agree that the command of Christ to the paralytic points to the principal motive for the incarnation. Christ liberates us from sin so that we can once again advance toward our proper human destiny, which remains personal union with the triune God. This remark merits attention since it puts Christian satisfaction immediately within its larger theological framework. Neither forgiveness of sin nor satisfaction for sin remains an end in itself; rather both constitute indispensable steps in the process by which a fallen race returns to God. The healing that satisfaction effects rectifies the personal disorders caused by sin, even those occurring after conversion. In short, satisfaction redirects our efforts toward the final goal of beatitude.

Postilla super Psalmos: Satisfaction Produces a Joyful Spirit

In Aquinas's commentary on the psalms, especially Psalm 50, ("Miserere"), we discover new dimensions in his teaching on forgiveness. This psalm, frequently employed in the liturgical and para-liturgical life of the medieval Dominican priory, contains David's moving expression of remorse for sin. The title (in Thomas's Vulgate text) indicates the occasion for its composition: "A psalm of David, when Nathan the prophet came to him, after he had gone into Bathsheba." First, Aquinas notes that even the number of the psalm (in the Vulgate enumeration) appropriately corresponds to that jubilee year when, according to the precepts of Leviticus, all debts were forgiven.[26] So the "Miserere," speaks about the full cycle of Christian sorrow and reconciliation. In the prologue, Thomas writes that Psalm 50 also assigns a fourth element or effect to penance, viz., "how penitence restores us to a perfect state. Therefore among all the other psalms this one is most frequently used by the Church" (*In psalmos* (50) [22-27]). Here, too, he expresses the intention of following a principle of St Jerome, "who in his commentary on Ezekiel gave us," Aquinas writes, "a rule which we will follow in our exposition on the psalms, namely, that the happenings recounted in the psalms should be interpreted as saying something either of Christ or of the Church" (*in loco*).

The "Miserere" represents David's prayer for mercy. Aquinas identifies this mercy which David seeks with the divine goodness itself. Thus, when David prays to be washed thoroughly from his iniquity, Thomas understands that he asks to be cleansed from both the stain of sin ("macula peccati") and its punishment ("reatus poenae"). In effect, then, David prays, "I ask that you grant me a reprieve from punishment, but also that you cleanse me of the stain of sin" (*In psalmos* (50), 1). Aquinas even uses David as a warning to us. If King David, he writes, who was blessed with such a special relationship with God, could turn and sin against him, then we must be on our guard against falling into sin. In a similar vein, he writes of Psalm 37:5, "My wounds grow foul and fester," that the danger of recidivism remains a real one, just as scar tissue remains prone to infection. But satisfaction, he continues, provides a means of healing the wounds of sin because it strengthens us against future temptation (cf. *In psalmos* (37), 2). Again, we recognize the pastoral concern Aquinas exhibits in his biblical commentaries.

But we also detect Aquinas the psychologist. For instance, at the verse of psalm 50, "Behold, thou desirest truth in the inward being," Thomas writes with special perception about the relationship between the willingness of a sinner to make satisfaction and his acquiescence to the truth concerning his sinful condition. Aquinas puts it this way:

"Ecce enim veritatem dilexisti." The one who wants to satisfy must love that which God loves. God however loves the truth of the faith: John 18:37, "Everyone who is of the truth hears My voice." Likewise God loves justice: Psalm 88:15, "Steadfast love and faithfulness ("veritas") go before thee." Such love of truth and justice is required in a penitent in order that one might be punished in those very things in which one has failed (*In psalmos* (50), 3).

Even hyssop can serve as a symbol for Thomas of the humility required for an authentic act of repentance. In brief, he notes that the hyssop plant grows close to the ground and thus fittingly symbolizes a faith accompanied by humility. This provides an essential disposition for the performance of satisfaction.

The sprinkling with the hyssop branch points further to the sprinkling of the blood of Christ in I Peter 1:2, "sanctified by the Spirit for obedience to Jesus Christ and for sprinkling with his Blood." Such an effective cleansing gives the Psalmist hope of full restoration. David then awaits the return of his prophetic gifts as well as the joy that comes from a clear conscience. The theme of joy being given back to the repentant sinner predominates in Aquinas's theology. In his commentary on the Beatitudes, for example, he interprets "Blessed are those who mourn, for they shall be comforted" (Mt 5:4) as the consolation of joy that comes to one who mourns for personal sins (*Super Matthaeum* c. 5, l. 2). Again in Psalm 50, commenting at "let the bones which Thou has broken rejoice," he can write: "Through the sadness of repentance the heart of man is broken: and therefore when men are happy it means that the bones that were broken themselves share in the joy" (*In psalmos* (50), 5). The disordered delight that accompanied David's sexual congress with Bathsheba can not compare with the joy which the Gospel promises. So Thomas explains:

This kind of joy the Psalmist had lost and therefore he asks that it be restored to him, when he says, "Redde mihi laetitiam"--not carnal joy, but the joy "Salutaris tui," that is, of your salvation. Another text has "laetitiam Jesu," namely the joy of the Savior, through whom the remission of sins is accomplished (*In psalmos* (50), 6).

Aquinas insistently represents the Christian life as a positive experience of human fulfillment.

In the prologue to this book, Thomas explained that the subject of the psalms is "all the works of the Lord" (*in loco*). Now he principally interprets the "right sacrifices" of the "Miserere" as referring to the sacrifice of Christ on the cross. Only Christ's satisfaction gives joy to the repentant sinner. A final text from the commentary on Psalm 50 looks forward to the eschatological completion of Christ's work. There Aquinas suggests that the joy of salvation given to the penitent David anticipates the beatific vision. Thus, David recognizes God's plan to bring all men and women to himself. The human person remains the only creature on earth God has willed for himself and our call to holiness terminates in nothing less than the beatific contemplation of the triune God ("speculatio veritatis ad beatam contemplationem"). As a Dominican, Aquinas valued the psalms. We see this, for example, again in the prologue where he tells us that the psalms "so clearly treat everything which pertains to the purpose ("ad finem") of the incarnation that it might almost be considered a gospel instead of a prophecy" (*in loco*).

Conclusion

To sum up: the scriptural commentaries emphasize three important features of Aquinas's theology. There we find expressed his concern for an integral christology, one which considers every aspect of the incarnate Son's human history as relevant to the final and definitive sacrifice which Christ offers on the cross. Next, we discover the importance Aquinas assigns to Christ's human psychology as a constitutive part of authentic soteriology. Finally, where Christ the head has trod, so also his members follow. Satisfaction forms an indispensable part of the Christian life.

First, we remark the many explicit references to the satisfaction of Christ which appear throughout his commentaries on both the Old and the New Testaments. For example, the long text from the *Postilla super Isaiam* places Christ's satisfaction within the broader framework of a biblical christology which seeks to account for both the person and the work of the Savior. In this descriptive presentation we see Aquinas treat the titles of Christ, his manner of life, his relationship to God, and the effects of his saving activity, thereby putting his later systematic analysis of Christ's death and resurrection into a fully biblical perspective. We therefore find no reason to suppose that Thomas depends exclusively on the expiatory characteristics of Christian redemption for his soteriology.[27]

Second, we see the importance Aquinas puts on the scriptural passages which indicate the state of Christ's human subjectivity during the passion. All in all, Christ's love, obedience, and humility gives value to his blood-shedding and other physical sufferings. As a result, the death of the sinless Christ breaks the cycle of sin caused by Adam, making it possible for those united to him also to perform satisfactory works. Aquinas recognized the importance of the pre-Chalcedonian disputes about the human soul of Christ and he gives Christ's psychic activities a principal place in his soteriology. For Aquinas, the human soul of Christ clearly achieves the status of a complete theological factor in the redemption; he eschews all forms of cryptic monophysitism.

Third, the same dispositions of love and obedience in the member of Christ can transform any burdensome work into an act of satisfaction. Moreover, satisfaction points to the risen life of Christ himself. Aquinas recognized that the satisfactions performed by the members of Christ, especially within the sacramental ministry of the Church, contribute to the gradual reformation of the image of God in each one. Thus, we recognize the same reciprocal relationship between the subjective dispositions of the believer and the external works of satisfaction as exist in Christ. Humility, in addition to obedience and love, also moves the member to recognize the need for satisfactory acts since the performance of satisfaction increases our awareness of sin. In this description of the Christain life, Aquinas fathoms the meaning of St Paul's teaching that every believer makes up what remains lacking in the sufferings of Christ. "Now I rejoice in my sufferings for your sake," Paul writes, "and in my flesh I complete what is lacking in Christ's afflictions for the sake of his body, that is, the Church" (Col 1:24).

It is impossible to over-state the importance of Aquinas's scriptural commentaries, since in these works he sets the conceptual issues in the context of the images and teachings of God's revealed word. By locating Aquinas's claims about satisfaction in contexts which range from exegesis to sacraments, especially baptism, penance, and Eucharist, from our virtues to specific activities (particularly almsgiving, fasting, and prayer), Aquinas suggests the inseparability of conceptual and other kinds of practical issues when dealing with Christian satisfaction. In fact, insights like these tell us more about the context for Aquinas's claims about satisfaction than many technical analyses of "satisfactio."

NOTES

1. For more information see, H. Denifle, "Quel livre servait de base à l'enseignement des maîtres en théologie dans l'Université de Paris," *Revue Thomiste* 2 (1899), 149-61. Also see Ceslas Spicq, O.P., *Esquisse d'une histoire de l'exégèse latine au moyen age* (Paris: J. Vrin, 1944).

2. See Edmund Hill, O.P., *Man Made to God's Image* (Ia. 90-102), Vol. 13 (New York: McGraw-Hill, 1964), especially, xxviii.

3. Of course, chronological proximity kept the humanists from appreciating the Middle Ages. See Erasmus, *Annotationes in Novum Testamentum* (1515), Basileae, fol. 228 v: "Et quid aliud potuisset Thomas, alioqui vir bono ingenio, qui ea temporum natus est, in quibus bonae litterae omnes et Latinae et Graecae et Hebraicae tamquam sepultae et emortuae ignotae jacebant. . . ."

4. See *De potentia* q.4, a.1: "Unde si etiam aliqua vera ab expositoribus sacrae Scripturae litterae aptentur, quae auctor non intelligit, non est dubium quin Spiritus sanctus intellexerit, qui est principalis auctor divinae Scripturae. Unde omnis veritas quae, salva litterae circumstantia, potest divinae Scripturae aptari, est eius sensus." For further commentary on Aquinas and the literal sense of scripture, see Smalley, especially, 269-70. She credits Aristotelian realism as the inspiration behind this approach.

5. See Spicq, 288. All in all, the author discusses Aquinas's use of the literal sense in seven chapters of this major study.

6. Edition used: *Postilla super Isaiam ad litteram*, Leonine edition, vol. 28 (Rome, 1974).

7. The correct reading of the Hebrew text remains a matter of dispute among scholars. Modern commentators, however, prefer to read "rain" instead of "doctor" in Joel 2:23. For further discussion, see *Les petits prophètes*, trans and commentary by A. Deissler and M. Delcor, *La Sainte Bible*, tome VIII, 1ère partie (Paris: Letouzey, 1961), 165, n. 23.

8. The chronology is unsure, though earlier dates have more plausibility. The commentary on cc. 1-11 is magisterial, replete with theological development, whereas cc. 12 to the end are literal and cursory. The two parts, then, probably come from different times.

9. Editions used: *Lectura super Matthaeum. Reportatio*, ed. R. Cai (Turin: Marietti, 1951) and *Lectura super Johannem. Reportatio*, ed. R. Cai (Turin: Marietti, 1952) [ET: *Commentary on the Gospel of St. John*, cc. 1-7, trans. J.A. Weisheipl, O.P. and F.R. Larcher (Albany, NY: Magi, 1980).

10. See *Summma Theologiae* Ia q. 1, aa. 9,10. For a detailed study on medieval exegesis, see Henri de Lubac, S.J., *Exégèse médiévale; les quatre sens de l'Ecriture*. 4 Vols. (Paris: Aubier, 1959-64).

11. The threefold division of the spiritual sense goes back at least as far as the Venerable Bede. The allegorical and messianic sense is the typifying and prefiguring of the new covenant by the old; the moral sense exemplifies how we should live and act by grace; and the anagogical or eschatological sense is the foreshadowing of the state of eternal life.

12. See *Summma Theologiae* Ia q. 1, a. 10, where Aquinas defines the anagogical sense as concerned with things which pertain to eternal glory. Again, in *Quodlibetal* VII q. 6, a. 2, he describes the figure as pointing towards the Church triumphant.

13. For the complete setting and interpretation of this anagogical interpretation, see *Super Johannem* c. 18, l. 1 [n.1].

14. See Chenu, 253. But, in the *Expositio super librum Boethii De trinitate*, q, 2, a. 3, ad 5: "Theological argument should not fasten on figures of speech, remarks Peter Lombard. And Dionysius says that symbolic theology is not scientific--it certainly is not when it is not expository.

15. For further details, see C.H. Dodd, *The Apostolic Preaching and its Development* (New York: Harper & Row, 1964), especially, 10ff.

16. Edition used: *Expositio et lectura super Epistolas Pauli Apostoli*, ed. R. Cai, 2 vols. (Turin: Marietti, 1953) [Four English translations have so far appeared, *viz. Galatians*, trans. F.R. Archer, 1966; *Ephesians*, trans. M.L. Lamb, 1966; *I Thessalonians* and *Philippians*, trans. F. R. Archer and M. Duffy, 1969, from Magi, Albany, NY.] Renewed interest in the commentary on Romans accounts for works such as T. Domanyi, *Der Römerbriefkommentar des Thomas von Aquin: Ein Beitrag zur Frage des Intellektualismus bei Thomas von Aquin* (Fribourg, Switzerland, 1979).

17. Edition used: *Expositio super Job ad litteram*, Leonine edition, vol. 26 (Rome, 1965).

18. For further details, see the *Epistola anonymi ad Hugonem amicum*, ed. Martène and Durand, in *Thesaurum Novum Anecdotum* I, 487-88.

19. See Smalley, 236. "This particular book," she continues, "will serve as a measure for the distance between the Victorines, Hugh of St. Cher, St. Albert, and St. Thomas."

20. Chenu, 257.

21. Edition used: *De regno ad regem Cypri*, (Turin: Marietti, 1954). [ET: *On Kingship to the King of Cyprus*, trans. G.B. Phelan and I.T. Eschmann (Toronto: Pontifical Institute of Mediaeval Studies, 1949).]

22. Scholars point out that the style, language, and situation of the folk narrative apparent in Job 1:1-2:13 reappears at the end of the book in 42:7-17. For more information see, N.M. Sarna, "Epic substratum in the Prose of Job," *Journal of Biblical Literature* 76 (1957), 13-25.

23. The medieval theologians recognized three essential elements in the sacrament of penance, contrition of the heart, confession from the lips, and satisfaction through works. See Colman O'Neill, O.P., *Sacramental Realism. A General Theory of the Sacraments* (Wilmington: Michael Glazier, Inc., 1983), especially, 164-184. For an historical study of rites of reconciliation in the Church, see Joseph A. Favazza, *The Order of Penitents* (Collegeville, MN: The Liturgical Press, 1988).

24. For further information on this important topic for Christian anthropology and sacramental practice, see T.C. O'Brien, *Effects of Sin, Stain and Guilt* (1a2ae 86-89), Vol. 27 (New York: McGraw-Hill, 1974), especially, 99-133.

25. Edition used: *Postilla super Psalmos*, Parma edition (1863), reprinted vol. 14 (New York: Musurgia, 1949), 148-353.

26. "The year of the ram's horn," as it is called in Hebrew, marked the fiftieth year in a cycle of Sabbatical Years observed in ancient Israel, when land that had been leased by families to avert poverty reverted to its original owners, and indentured Israelite servants were set free. The sounding of the ram's horn throughout the land inaugurated the Year of Jubilee, which began on the Day of Atonement, the tenth day of the seventh month, Ethanim (Sept.-Oct.).

27. Aulèn, 93 partially recognizes this feature of Aquinas's work. He writes: "In Thomas, also, certain of the characteristic points of the classic view ("Christus Victor") appear, such as deliverance of men from the power of the devil, which he seeks to reconcile with the idea of satisfaction (Latin view)." On the other hand, the author finally classifies Aquinas and the medieval theologians in general as exponents of the deficient Latin view of salvation, which Aulèn mistakenly characterizes as mainly consisting in the payment of a debt.

CHAPTER III

"A RELATIVELY INFINITE CHARACTER"

Scriptum super Sententias, Book Four:
A Dialectic Between Two Classical Definitions of Satisfaction

We now consider the first of Aquinas's systematic works. In the *Scriptum super Sententias* we possess his initial effort to set forth the "sacra doctrina" in a thematic way.[1] We know, for instance, that Aquinas chose the "exitus-reditus" theme both for the *Summa theologiae* (where it remains implicit) and for his commentary on the *Sentences* of Peter Lombard (where he actually refers to it). Still, critical differences remain between the elaborated structure of Thomas's first effort at systematic theology and the mature work of his professional career.[2]

In brief, we can suppose that Aquinas's intellectual and spiritual development during the more than ten years between the completion of the *Scriptum super Sententias* and the beginning of the *Summa theologiae* accounts for this theological advance. Even so, during roughly the first two centuries of Thomism, the followers of Aquinas still read the *Scriptum super Sententias*, as John Capreolus's *Defensiones* indicate.[3] In addition, the *Scriptum super Sententias*, as I have said, also provides the chief systematic discussions of those subjects Aquinas did not treat in the *Summa*.

This particular alone gives the work a certain value in its own right. For example, we find a complete treatment of the sacrament of penance only in the *Scriptum* IV, dd. 14-22. Even there, however, Aquinas observes a different ordering in the treatment of penance and so sketches a different theological perspective from the comparable treatment in the *Summa*. As the Lombard himself does, Thomas puts the sacrament of penance within the context of justification, thereby emphasizing the role played by the sacraments in conversion. This setting also points to a theological stress on the concrete, historical economy of salvation in the Church.[4] In the *Summa theologiae*, however, we find the question of justification separated from the general christological and sacramental discussions in the *tertia pars*. Thomas instead discusses justification as part of the treatise on our rebirth in grace. This displacement of the treatise on justification indicates Thomas's preference for the "ordo disciplinae" in the *Summa theologiae* (where the discussion of grace and justification comes after that on original sin) over the order of sacred history which still controls his commentary on the *Sentences*. Likewise, the "ordo disciplinae" allows Aquinas to emphasize better the work of divinization which grace accomplishes. On the other hand, in the *Scriptum* he only points toward this goal.

In any event, the sacrament of penance remains "ordained to the removal of evil, which comes about as a result of the things we do in this life;" moreover, it provides the setting for Aquinas's first talks on satisfaction (IV, d. 14, "divisio textus"). The discussion of satisfaction begins in Book Four, distinction 15. In the introduction to this distinction, Aquinas writes: "Here one should inquire about satisfaction and its parts; whence there are four things that are discussed, the first of which is satisfaction itself" (IV, d. 15, q. 1, a. 1). In order to define satisfaction, Aquinas first examines two definitions which had become standard within the schools.

The Definitions of the *Liber ecclesiasticorum dogmatum* and of *Cur Deus homo?*

Since the *Sentences* of Peter Lombard contain a compilation of important theological texts from the medieval and patristic tradition, Thomas develops his first approach to satisfaction by commenting upon two definitions that had become commonplace within the theological tradition. The first definition comes from a work called the *Liber ecclesiasticorum dogmatum*. Although this work was generally attributed to Augustine by all of Thomas's contemporaries, he at least supposed that it came from another source. In fact, the book was written by Gennadius of Marseille (c. 470). Since the source, however, remained anonymous for Thomas, he always refers to the *Liber* without citing an author. (The reference in Quodlibet 12,10, "Sed ille liber non est Augustini, sed Gennadii" obviously represents a marginal gloss.[5]) In any event, as a result of its supposed Augustinian authorship, the definition was highly regarded in the Middle Ages. It states: "Satisfactio est peccatorum causas excidere, et eorum suggestionibus aditum non indulgere."[6] In other terms, satisfaction aims at cutting out the root causes of sin and at strengthening one against its enticements in the future. This penitential definition of satisfaction constitutes the first step of Aquinas's dialectic.

Next, we find another element of the tradition on satisfaction in the definition of Anselm in the *Cur Deus homo?*: "Satisfactio est honorem Deo impendere."[7] Initially, Anselm defines satisfaction as giving God due honor. This points, of course, to the transcendent side of satisfaction, namely, the healing of our relationship to God. As I have said, Thomas develops a dialectic between these two definitions which serves as his general understanding of satisfaction in the *Scriptum*. Given the sacramental context of the discussion, Aquinas unfolds this early notion in the context of penitential satisfaction and its three traditional expressions, almsgiving, fasting, and prayer. In particular, we consider three questions in d. 15, q. 1, a. 1, *quaes.*, 1-3: (1) whether satisfaction is a virtue or an act of virtue; (2) whether satisfaction is related to the virtue of justice; and (3) whether the pseudo-Augustine's definition of satisfaction adequately serves the tradition.

In response to the first question, Aquinas clearly establishes satisfaction as an act of virtue. What reason does he give? In short, satisfaction fulfills the essential requirement of a moral virtue, namely, that it establishes a mean between two extremes. "And because equality is a mean," says Thomas, "which is implied in the very term 'satisfaction' (for one does not speak of something as satisfactory except insofar as it possesses some proportioned equality to something else), it is obvious that satisfaction, formally speaking, is an act of virtue" (IV, d. 15, q. 1, a. 1, *quaes.*, 1). Even if satisfaction does not always concern something freely chosen or at times can even be enjoined on one just then quite ill-disposed to accept a penance, its virtuous character endures only if one freely consents to fulfill the obligation. In this case, however, the one who imposes the penance, at least, should ordinarily act freely. Anyway, satisfaction realizes a compensation in the moral order.

But if satisfaction is an act of virtue, to what virtue does it belong? Perhaps, Aquinas speculates, it belongs to charity, since the reconciliation which it produces remains related to love. Or, again, it may belong to prudence which entails foresight, since the one who makes satisfaction for some past offense will be suitably reminded about similar failure in the future. Finally, however, Aquinas rejects these proposals, and turns to something fundamental in the very notion of satisfaction itself, namely, the fact that it relates to something due another. To prove this, he refers to Anselm's definition, "Satisfactio honorem debitum Deo impendit." Since satisfaction gives to God an honor due him, and justice remains the moral virtue which governs things due another, Aquinas associates satisfaction with the virtue of justice.

The response to d. 15, q. 1, a. 1, *quaes.*, 2 explains further why satisfaction belongs to justice. Referring to Aristotle's discussion of rectificatory justice in Book Five of the *Nicomachean Ethics*, Thomas notes that the adverb "satis," (from which the term "satisfaction" derives) means "enough." This he refers to that proportioned equality which constitutes the mean of justice. "This, then, is what the just is," writes Aristotle, "the proportional; the unjust is what violates the proportion."[8] When applied to satisfaction, this proportioned equality establishes in the one performing the satisfactory deed a kind of balance or equilibrium in relationships with others. Thus, Thomas includes satisfaction as part of that justice which exists between one individual and another. The scholastic tradition calls this commutative or rectificatory justice.

Strictly speaking, however, satisfaction reestablishes an equilibrium which is disturbed not so much by taking away another's goods but by hurtful actions, those which upset the right inter-personal relations that should exist between members of a commonweal. Satisfaction presupposes that something has gone wrong in the past and, further, that some offense has upset an established equilibrium. Reference to past inequalities leads Aquinas to conclude that grounds exist to relate satisfaction to the virtue of penitence. Since it implies the restoration of a due equilibrium, satisfaction also forms part of the virtue of justice in another way, namely, the virtue of justice which is called penitence. Some past offense causes the one satisfying to make amends.

This allows Aquinas to formulate a more complete description of satisfaction by putting together two definitions received from the tradition. Anselm's definition insists that satisfaction include the rectification of a personal injury. But can satisfaction so defined, Aquinas inquires, fit the definition given by the *Liber ecclesiasticorum dogmatum*? In the fifth objection of d. 15, q. 1, a. 1, *quaes.*, 3, Thomas, in fact, asks whether the Anselmian definition, i.e., satisfaction gives to God an honor that is due him, does correspond with that of the *Liber*, i.e., satisfaction aims at cutting out the root causes of sin and strengthening one against its enticements in the future. Although the context of the discussion alone would have led him to lean towards the "moral" definition of the *Liber*, Aquinas also favors the augustinian heritage over that of the more recent St Anselm. For in the hierarchy of authorities current at Thomas's time, even a pseudo-Augustine ranked higher than St Anselm. The former was numbered among the "ancient, saintly Fathers," while the latter was still young enough to be counted among the "modern masters"--a group who from the beginning of the 12th-century nonetheless came to be regarded as having some limited authority in determining theological discussions.[9]

In any event, Thomas begins by deliberating the twofold end accomplished by satisfaction. First, he observes the fundamental discrepancy between the *Liber*'s definition and that of Anselm: the former speaks of satisfaction in relation to the causes and effects of sin, but the latter speaks about it as redressing an injury. The *Liber* defines satisfaction as aiming to cut out the root causes of sin and to strengthen one against enticements to similar sin in the future, but Anselm speaks of it as restoring to God the honor denied him by some deed in the past. Aiming to resolve the supposed discrepancy, Thomas turns to Aristotle, who, in the *Nicomachean Ethics*, writes: "if the virtues are concerned with actions and passions, and every passion and every action is accompanied by pleasure and pain, for this reason also virtue will be concerned with pleasures and pains. This is indicated also by the fact that punishment is inflicted by these means; for it is a kind of cure, and it is the nature of cures to be effected by contraries."[10] Aristotle, then, indicates a second purpose for satisfaction. Not only does satisfaction aim at re-establishing an equilibrium upset by some prior offense, it also concerns guarding against repeating the same offense in the future. "Satisfaction, an act of that virtue of justice concerned with penalties," writes Aquinas, "is a medicine: it cures past sins and guards against future ones" (IV, d. 15, q. 1, a. 1, *quaes.*, 3).

At this point, Aquinas recognizes the anthropological effects of satisfaction, but he clearly does not yet recognize how the divine agency functions in this work. Nevertheless, both curative and preventative aspects of satisfaction remain important parts of his subsequent theology of satisfaction.

With Aristotle's help, Thomas now can reconcile the two traditional definitions. Again, the metaphor of the medicine which both cures and prevents serves as a key image in the resolution. Thomas writes:

> Satisfaction can be defined in two ways. One way is with respect to past faults, which it heals ("curat") by recompense; thus it is said that satisfaction is a recompense for injury according to justice's measure. This is also expressed in Anselm's definition that satisfaction gives to God an honor due him, due because of a fault committed. Satisfaction can also be defined with regard to future faults, from which one is preserved ("praeservat") by satisfaction (IV d. 15, q. 1, a. 1, *quaes.*, 3).

Of course, the metaphor of medicine, like all limping analogies, requires a qualification to take full account of the differences between healing the body and healing the whole human person. Although one can cure physical disease by eliminating its causes, spiritual "disease" or sin touches deeper roots of the personality. Our free will cannot be forced. So we should interpret pseudo-Augustine's "peccatorum causas excidere" as eliminating or shunning the cause of previous sins and "eorum suggestionibus aditum non indulgere" as the tempering of free will with respect to future temptations. Aquinas nevertheless does manage to reconcile the two classical definitions, bringing out from each one important features of Christian satisfaction.

In the replies of d. 15, q. 1, a. 1, *quaes.*, 3, Aquinas clarifies some further issues. For example, since satisfaction does not nullify original sin, it can not eliminate the remote causes of sin or "fomes peccati." Rather, satisfactory penances touch the concupiscence of the flesh, aroused for instance by past actual sins as well as by the occasions of sin. In another response, Thomas throws some further light on the reciprocal relationship between redressing a previous injury and preventing its repetition. He says:

> Being careful about the future is a kind of recompense for the past since one is dealing with the same thing, sin, only in different ways. In being mindful of our past we detest the causes of sin because of the sins we have committed; our aversion is motivated by sin itself. Whereas in being careful about the future our aversion is directed to the causes of sin, so that when they have been removed we might more easily avoid the sin itself (IV d. 15, q. 1, a. 1, *quaes.*, 3, ad 4).

Aquinas recognizes the importance of satisfaction as an instrument for Christian life and perfection.

In the *Scriptum super Sententias*, distinction 15, question 1 remains fundamental for Thomas's understanding of satisfaction. First, he locates satisfaction as a good act of virtue. Next, since it deals with redressing past faults, he locates satisfaction as that part of the virtue of commutative justice which we call penitence. He then examines the two traditional definitions and develops an understanding of satisfaction which takes account of them both. However, the metaphor of medicine, as shedding light on the sacraments themselves, controls the discussion. This leaves us to consider next the difference between satisfaction and restitution, in order more clearly to define the concept of satisfaction.

More Than Restitution

Thomas begins d. 15, q. 1, a. 5, *quaes.*, 1 by asking whether restitution forms a part of satisfaction. For example, since satisfaction reconciles a person both to God and to one's neighbor and since restitution likewise reconciles one person with another, it would appear that they are identical. Again, we perform satisfaction by doing something contrary to the sin committed (e.g., one satisfies for gluttony by fasting), but restitution also involves a contrary since it is opposed to taking something which does not belong to one; therefore both deal with the same matter. Furthermore, St Ambrose is credited with saying that true penance is to stop sinning, and restitution is a kind of cessation of sin since one stops holding onto that to which another has the right; therefore both have the same effect. Accordingly, both restitution and satisfaction form parts of the virtue of penitence.

But Thomas again cites St Anselm, who claims that we can make satisfaction to God but restitution only to our neighbor. Therefore, restitution does not form a part of satisfaction. Why? Restitution chiefly deals with restoring external goods that have been unjustly taken; it deals with restoring equilibrium somehow disrupted, e.g., by the theft of property. Satisfaction, on the other hand, deals not just with external goods but with the actual actions and attitudes wherewith one perpetrates an injustice. Thus, Thomas envisions the possibility that one can exist without the other, as when someone, unable to make full restitution, nonetheless humbles himself before a neighbor hurt by some contumacious word or deed. We can envision the opposite case when, for example, someone who has robbed his neighbor makes restitution by restoring the ill-gotten goods but refuses to satisfy for the personal hurt caused by the violent act of robbing.

Thus, restitution remains a narrower concept than satisfaction, even if ordinarily it forms a preliminary step. Thomas further observes that one who restores something justly owed to another does not achieve reconciliation simply by doing so. Full reconciliation requires satisfaction. The remaining *quaestiunculae* of d. 15, q. 1, a. 5 treat allied questions such as to whom, by whom, and how restitution should be made. In sum, Thomas shows that satisfaction involves more than simply re-establishing the balance of justice or regaining a status quo. Restitution does that. But satisfaction always remains a question of redressing a personal offense, especially when the offended ones includes God himself.

Qualified Satisfaction to God

Only adumbrated in the earlier discussion, Aquinas treats the question of satisfactions's relatively infinite character explicitly in d. 15, q. 1, a. 2. There he examines how a creature can makes satisfaction to the Creator. Of course, the initial considerations suggest that such a satisfaction remains impossible. If we accept that the amplitude of an offense is judged according to the dignity of the one offended, sin has a sort of infinite character to it. Yet a creature, of course, can do nothing infinite. Furthermore, being God's servants, we already owe him everything. How then could we make satisfaction to him? Already, all our time is owed to God's service, so that we simply have no opportunity to satisfy. Finally, when one considers that an incarnate God was necessary to satisfy for original sin, how could a mere creature hope to satisfy for grave, actual sins which possess a greater malice than original sin? In fact, most of these arguments represent aspects of St Anselm's discussion in *Cur Deus homo?*

Yet there must be some way in which the creature can make satisfaction to God since God himself requires it, for example, in Luke 3:8, "Bear fruits that befit penance." God would not ask us to do something impossible. Indeed, we are obliged to pay a twofold kind of debt: we owe thanksgiving and worship, first, for the good things which we have received from God while, second, we owe satisfaction for the sins which we have committed. Of course, even pagans knew that when it came to thanking either one's parents or the gods, no strict equivalence could be imagined. But friendship does not demand equivalency except as it is possible, says Aquinas. Thus, when speaking about making satisfaction to God, one must understand that the "satis," the "enough," is not reckoned according to a strict quantitative measure but according to a certain proportion. This distinction, moreover, applies to the definitions of both justice and satisfaction.

Finally, Aquinas replies to the above-mentioned arguments, thereby completing the discussion. Three replies treat the ways in which we, who already owe everything to God, can even think of offering something extra in order to satisfy for an offense. Thomas's approach remains balanced and practical: although one may have wasted time in the past by sinning, there remains other free time--time not owed to God by precept--for satisfying in the future. While it is true that we already owe everything to God, this does not mean that we are therefore obliged to do everything that we can do. In fact, in this life, since one is bound by so many different obligations, one should first fulfill those things that are commanded, while leaving the things not commanded as supererogatory works and thereby potentially satisfactory as well. Next, although it is true that the creature always remains God's servant, we nonetheless are servants endowed with freedom. This freedom provides occasions for making satisfaction in the same way human autonomy disposed us to sin in the first place. In short, Aquinas makes distinctions which qualify the rigidity of the arguments in *Cur Deus homo?*.

In the response to the first objection, however, Thomas further explains how we can hope to compensate for an offense which nonetheless possesses a kind of infinite character. He argues: "Just as an offense has a certain infinity because of the infinite character of the divine majesty, so also the satisfaction takes on a certain infinity because of the infinite character of the divine mercy" (IV d. 15, q. 1, a. 2, ad 1). Of course, this kind of satisfaction embodies a work of grace. Moreover, the discussion of whether we can adequately make satisfaction to God touches a larger theological context, namely, the relationship between the creature's satisfying God and the mediation of Christ. God is willing to accept a modified kind of equality, an equality proportioned to what we can do, in place of what strict justice would entail. This tempering of justice's demands for satisfaction made to God remains an act of the divine mercy. Thomas flatly rejects the opinion that man could satisfy God without the aid of grace. On the contrary, he endorses the opinion that human satisfaction for sin only has value because of the merit of Christ, although in this early period he still maintains that if grace were bestowed in some way other than through Christ, it too would be equally effective for giving a sinner's satisfaction an infinite dimension.

As an Expression of Friendship

The first three *quaestiunculae* of d. 15, q. 1, a. 3 treat the same issue from a different perspective. How does charity, the love of friendship, relate to satisfaction? The first question asks whether a person can satisfy for one sin while at the same time withholding satisfaction for another; the second, whether one who has confessed certain sins but then fallen into new ones can still continue to satisfy for the sins he has confessed; and the third, whether it is possible to reactivate the satisfaction made while outside charity after one has returned to the state of charity. Although the conjectural and obscure tone of the questions seems distant from our experience, they do provide Aquinas with an entree into an important issue. In each instance, he can underline the importance of friendship in making satisfaction.

We consider each question in turn. Because making satisfaction is not a mechanical act but the restoration of a personal relationship that has been broken by offense, the answer to the first query is negative. "The removal of something offensive," says Thomas, "constitutes a restitution of friendship; therefore if there is something which impedes friendship, even among men, satisfaction is not possible" (d. 15, q. 1, a. 3, *quaes.*, 1). Sin, however, breaks the love of friendship which should exist between God and his creatures, and thus it is impossible for us to satisfy for one sin and not for another. Furthermore, when we sin, we break the equality of justice which is a ground for friendship. Since the equality of justice with regard to God is less a matter of equivalency than of his accepting whatever proportional equality we can restore, it would be preposterous to think that God would continue to accept a deficient redress once that bond of friendship has been broken by a subsequent sin. Again, without love there can be no satisfaction. Finally, satisfaction is based upon the supposition that one is pleasing to God and thus deeds done outside the bond of friendship with him cannot qualify as satisfactory, even retroactively, since they originally did not proceed from love. The same argument is used to show why good deeds done outside charity merit nothing worthwhile of either temporal or eternal value, although Thomas will allow them a role in leading us to seek again the state of friendship with God. In short, the acts of satisfaction which we make to God are not isolated, unit exchanges with an intrinsic value all their own. Rather, satisfaction finds its worth within a broader context, as part of the relationship that exists between God and man which is the love of friendship or charity. For an individual's satisfaction to possess any value or goal, the broader relationship must remain an active one.

Although satisfaction is achieved only within this broader relationship of love, it does not follow that one must unceasingly make satisfaction. In this respect satisfaction differs from contrition, or sorrow, for sin. Since he still writes in the context of justification, Thomas asks whether the whole of this life ought to be a time for contrition. In d. 17, q. 2, a. 4 he recalls that contrition, like satisfaction, is a part of penance. But if one is not always obliged to make satisfaction, then neither should one remain always contrite for past sins. Thomas replies that, although it is true that one need only accomplish the satisfaction given for a particular sin, nonetheless one still remains obliged to remain consistently contrite for this same sin. Why? Unlike satisfaction, contrition expresses a radical attitude of soul. Satisfaction, on the other hand, points to transient actions. This somewhat unqualified position reflects more the juridical mentality which predominates in the *Scriptum*.

If satisfaction requires the charity of Christ, we can inquire further about the sacraments of the old law and their efficacy. The argument of d. 1, q.1, a.5 runs like this: If it is impossible to satisfy without grace, then how did the sacraments prescribed for various sins in the old dispensation have their value? Did they confer grace? Thomas replies in the negative, but still tries to explain how one might nonetheless regard the sacrifices of the old law as satisfactory. Indeed, the sacraments and sacrifices of the old law did nothing to take away the stain of sin ("culpa") because at the time that they were offered no bond of friendship between God and the world existed. Since they were burdensome, however, Aquinas does allow them some salvific value, namely, that they were able to satisfy in part for the punishment ("poena") of sin. Thomas also appreciates, of course, that in addition to being performed within the broader context of love and friendship, authentic satisfaction must impose some burden on the individual.

Satisfaction: Burdensome Task

Thomas begins this discussion in d. 15, q. 1, a. 4, *quaes.*, 1,2 by referring to the familiar definition of Anselm's *Cur Deus homo?*, "satisfaction gives to God an honor that is due him." If this be the case, writes Aquinas, it does not seem likely that satisfaction should require a painful or burdensome activity, since to give honor to someone does not usually imply suffering. Moreover, we read that God does not delight in our sufferings; so it is unlikely that he would be honored by painful or burdensome deeds. Furthermore, how can one offer to God something owed him when, strictly speaking, nothing can be taken from God in the first place? The objections again serve as so many foils for Aquinas's replies.

Thomas writes that satisfaction both looks back to healing a past sin and forward to preserving one from a similar fall. Both of these medicinal functions demand painful or burdensome actions. Redress or recompense always involves the restoration of a certain balance or equilibrium; thus it remains the burden of the one who has offended to make this restoration. In human affairs this restoration occurs simply by taking from one who has more than is just and giving to one from whom something has been unjustly taken. Since, however, it is impossible for any creature to take something away from God, the restoration which satisfaction makes is of a different kind. Still, Thomas does cite the authority of St Anselm and *Cur Deus homo?*, which teaches that the sinner takes away from God due honor. On the other hand, such would not have been the case had the sinner followed the way of justice and rectitude. For this reason a sinner remains bound to satisfy. But recompense in this case can proceed no further than by taking something away from the sinner, for God can acquire nothing even when we offer honor to him.

Of course, a good act in itself would offer honor to God but not take anything away from the sinner; on the contrary it would rather perfect the sinner. On the other hand, a painful act in itself would subtract something from the sinner but not offer honor to God. Hence, in order for a true satisfaction to be made to God the act must be both good and painful. It must be good so that God will be honored and painful so that something will be taken away from the sinner. Aquinas concludes that these two features remain indispensable for Christian satisfaction. At the same time, he recalls that painful actions do have a preventative character ("poenae medicinae sunt"). Thus, we have in place the principal requirements for defining an authentically satisfactory work.

Next, Thomas admits that although punishment as such does not please God, nevertheless punishment which is just does please him, not because it is painful but because it is just. But Anselm's definition of satisfaction seems to allow merely good works to be satisfactory. Thomas clarifies: "What is owed ("debitum") for sin is a redress of an offense which cannot be accomplished without punishment; and it is of such a debt that Anselm was speaking" (d. 15, q. 1, a. 4, quaes., 1, ad 3). Then he turns to the question of "flagella," that is, the punishments which God allows to befall us but which we do not choose. His response follows St Augustine in the De Civitate Dei, which says that in the same affliction bad folk blaspheme God whereas the just praise and beseech him.[11] Thomas explains that if we accept punishments which are outside of our control in a spirit of patience and penance, they can be means of satisfaction for our sins. On the other hand, if one does not accept them in such a spirit, they serve simply as instruments of vindication, as when one is required to make recompense either by the judgment of someone else or by force.

Finally, Aquinas moves to consider the satisfactory value of prayer, especially the objection that it seems to lack the characteristic of painfulness necessary for authentic satisfaction. Still prayer, along with almsgiving and fasting, remains one of the three traditional means of penance which the Church enjoins on sinners in order that they might make satisfaction.[12] Thomas explains this threefold division of satisfaction, summarizing the principal elements of his definition from the Liber and Anselm. First, he cites the Anselmian element: Satisfaction should be such that it subtracts something from us for the honor of God. We have three kinds of possessions, namely, those of the soul--spiritual well-being; those of the body--corporal well-being; and our wealth--material well-being. Hence, almsgiving aims at taking something away from our fortunes. Fasting affects our bodily comfort. And prayer, while it cannot subtract or take away any good things of our soul which actually make us acceptable to God, does nevertheless help us to surrender ourselves entirely to him and in that way takes us, as it were, away from ourselves.

Next, Thomas invokes the definition of the Liber, the first part of which says that satisfaction aims at cutting out the root causes of sin. According to I John, these are three, namely, concupiscence of the flesh, concupiscence of the eyes, and the pride of life. Against the lust of flesh, Thomas suggests fasting; against the lust of the eyes, almsgiving; and, as a remedy to the pride of life, humbling oneself before God in prayer.   Satisfaction, according to this definition, aims at bolstering one's strength against sinning in the future.   Every sin constitutes a deed committed either against God (prayer warns against that) or against our neighbor (almsgiving strengthens us against that) or against ourselves (fasting serves as a preventative).   This epitomizes Thomas's method in the *Scriptum super Sententias*.   Since he is principally concerned to take account of the received traditions, he takes two established definitions of satisfaction and applies them to three conventional penitential practices of the Church, reconciling diverse strands of the tradition into unified teaching on satisfaction.

But does prayer constitute a burden?   Aquinas approaches the question from two points of view.   First, one might consider that there are two kinds of prayer.   For example, we can point to contemplative prayer which is altogether delightful, a kind of heavenly conversation that has nothing painful and therefore nothing satisfactory about it.   Or we can signify the prayer which is the cry of the sinner, a painful prayer which is indeed satisfactory.   But Aquinas teaches that all prayer has a satisfactory value because, although it does have a certain sweetness to it, it nonetheless always afflicts the body.   Here Thomas quotes the authority of Gregory the Great, who observed that, as the power of intimate love takes hold of us, the power of the flesh is proportionately weakened.   That is why when Jacob wrestled with the angel his thigh was put out of joint; he had seen God but went away limping.   In sum, Thomas concludes: "Whatever is part of bodily affliction belongs to fasting; whatever is spent on the well-being of one's neighbor belongs to almsgiving; and whatever is offered to God in praise belongs to prayer" (d. 15, q. 1, a. 4, *quaes* 3, ad 5).   Aquinas proves himself able to bring different elements of the tradition together into a synthesis.

All in all, satisfaction remains an act of justice, in particular of penitence, and forms part of that justice which deals with redressing offenses.   It restores to God an honor lost by sin (though this loss is of course on the sinner's side rather than God's), even when the offense has been directed toward one's neighbor, since an offense against one's neighbor remains an offense against God.   Satisfactory works also aim at weakening the dispositions to sin within us, and thus serve to strengthen us against a repetition of the same sin in the future.   Since the satisfaction goes beyond mere restitution, it can only be accomplished within the broader context of friendship.   More than a simple restoration of something taken or the cessation from some hurtful activity, satisfaction rather rehabilitates a relationship through the redress of personal offense.   Thus there is no question of performing a "bona fide" satisfaction apart from God's help; for, as Aquinas insists, without charity there is no satisfaction.   The presence of charity, however, does not rule out the possibility of suffering. Christian satisfaction requires that the one who performs it be separated from something he cherishes in order that the equilibrium of justice be restored. But satisfaction is a Christian act and thus the very charity which prompts it can also ease its penal character. The man who loves more suffers less. Far from decreasing the value of satisfaction, love of this kind increases it.

Satisfaction for Another

We move to another important feature of satisfaction and its general characteristics. The Christian mystery provides Thomas the occasion to ask if one person is able to satisfy for another. While the working definition of satisfaction, developed from the two definitions, does not immediately suggest that one could satisfy for another, Thomas nonetheless recalls a New Testament text, Galatians 6:2, "Bear one another's burdens, and so fulfill the law of Christ." Next, he begins his explanation of this question by recalling the familiar twofold aim of satisfactory punishment, namely, to restore an equilibrium and to cure bad habits. With regard to the latter, satisfaction's preventative purpose, it remains clear that one cannot satisfy for another since, as Thomas succinctly puts it, "by the fast of one man, another's flesh is not controlled" (d. 20, q. 1, a. 2, *quaes.*, 3). However, with regard to the former, namely, the restoration of an equilibrium, one person can satisfy for another provided he or she remains in the state of charity so that the works themselves retain a satisfactory character. Since there is greater love present in such an act, less punishment is required than otherwise would have been the norm. Furthermore, it is not necessary that one be incapable of making the satisfaction oneself, as the practice of the Church which encourages suffrages for the dead makes clear. If we can satisfy for the souls in purgatory, so also can one satisfy for another living person.

This establishment that one person can satisfy for another completes the first phase of the investigation. Thomas's soteriology unquestionably originates in the practice of the Church. There he discovers the way in which satisfaction occurs among Christian men and women. Hence the discussion of the possibility of one satisfying for another serves as a transitional step to the next important element of his early theology, *viz.*, the pivotal place of Christ in the schema of satisfaction. So, in order to pursue the question of how Christ was able to satisfy for sinners, we now turn to consider the christological questions in the Book Three of the *Scriptum super Sententias*.

Scriptum super Sententias, Book Three: New Perspectives on Traditional Materials Concerning the Satisfaction of Christ

Thomas thus announces the theme of his christological discussions: "Ad locum unde exeunt, flumina revertuntur ut iterum fluant." Thomas begins the prologue to Book Three of his *Scriptum super*

Sententias: "To the place where the streams flow, there they flow again" (Eccles 1:7). His introductory essay points to waters flowing from the mountains, because "high mountains are among the noblest of creatures" (*in loco*).[13] The streams represent the inexhaustible goodness of God, which constitutes the ultimate source of being and existence for all things. The incarnation remains a point of conjuncture at which human nature, having come forth from God, returns to him, just as the waters return whence they came. It is Christ, the incarnate Son, who alone makes it possible for us (in whom the corporeal and spiritual orders of reality unite) to return to our true Source. The waters that flow again, but now from Christ, in whom the divine and human natures remain hypostatically united, represent the gifts and virtues which God bestows on every member of his body. Aquinas invents this application of the coming forth and returning ("exitus-reditus"). The third book of the *Scriptum* treats of the incarnation as well as the virtues and gifts which we receive from Christ. Although Aquinas alters this structure in the *Summa theologiae*, the present arrangement puts a great deal of emphasis on Christ as exemplar and efficient cause of the moral life.

D. 1, q. 1, a. 2: The arguments

First of all, however, Aquinas asks whether it was fitting that God became man. In this long article, Thomas cites nine arguments which suggest that God should not have become incarnate. Since many of these arguments reoccur throughout the systematic discussions of satisfaction, we give the complete text.

1. Just as goodness and evil are opposed, so are majesty and lowliness. It would have been unwise of God to associate with lowliness since his wisdom would have dictated that he avoid whatever is opposed to his majesty.

2. Furthermore, the sin of Adam and the sin of the angels were both sins of pride, yet God did not assume an angelic nature. Why, then, should he have assumed a human one?

3. There is a relation between creation and restoration, but God assumed no human nature to create. Why, then, did he assume a human nature to restore?

4. It would have been more fitting for God to show the greatness of his mercy than the severity of his justice. Mercy dictates forgiveness of sins without satisfaction. Thus God could have saved man without assuming a

human nature and even have wrought greater praise from mankind since he manifested greater mercy.

5. A merciful God does not ask more than man can give. Yet man is able to satisfy in part for himself, and thus there was no reason for God to become man.

6. Furthermore, in this regard, man is able to make satisfaction for mortal sin. Thus he should be able to make satisfaction for original sin, since the latter is less malicious--as it is less voluntary--than the former.

7. Likewise, the first parents satisfied for the original sin insofar as it was an actual sin on their part. Why could not man, then, have satisfied for original sin?

8. Furthermore, according to the Dionysian view of the world the angelic nature is placed between human nature and divinity. If man could not have satisfied sufficiently, then surely the angels would have been able to accomplish this.

9. Lastly, since the good of the entire human race is still a created good, it would not have been impossible for God to have created a creature whose goodness exceeded the good of the entire human race and who could have made up for the corruption of the human race. Thus it would not have been necessary or fitting that God become man (III d. 1, q. 1, a. 1, obj 1-9).

These arguments obviously represent a wide diversity of approaches to the incarnation.

Next we examine the *sed contra* arguments, although in the reverse order from that of the text. The fourth *sed contra* deals with the question of the devil's role in the our fall. To be sure, the medieval tradition spoke about a ransom to Satan, but Aquinas always gives a decided nuance to the position. Pride moved Satan both to envy the human creature and to seek to enthrall him. "Thus it was entirely fitting," writes Thomas, "that the all-powerful God oppose the devil's wickedness so that man might not only be snatched from his power but indeed be made his master" (d. 1, q. 1, a. 2, sc 4). Since there is no nature above the angelic except the divine, it was entirely right for God to do this and to become incarnate. Even from his earliest works, Thomas eschews a "rights of the devil" theory, instead stressing the injustice of the devil's enslavement of mankind.

The third *sed contra* simply quotes the Wisdom of Solomon 8:30--"But against wisdom evil does not prevail"--and shows how it was right for God to do all that he could to conquer the wickedness of the devil who had thrown mankind into such an unhappy state of sin and misery. Next, the second *sed contra* presents an even simpler assertion: no single creature's good exceeds the good of human nature considered as a whole, and hence it would have been impossible for any creature to have made recompense for the whole human race. The first *sed contra*, however, presents a principal argument which guides Thomas's discussion of satisfaction at this point in its development. The first half of the argument runs as follows: (1) It was not fitting that human nature, which is among the noblest of God's creatures, suffer frustration in reaching its goal; (2) yet such was the result of original sin since by it man was deprived of beatitude; (3) therefore, to restore human nature required that the sin be dismissed--"but it is not just that a sin be dismissed without satisfaction" (*in loco*). Thus, we see how fitting it is that satisfaction be made for a sin which affected the whole human race.

The second half of the first *sed contra* continues: (1) satisfaction cannot be fittingly accomplished except by him who ought to satisfy and who is able to satisfy ("nisi ab eo qui debet satisfacere et potest"); (2) but man ought to satisfy since man sinned; (3) still, only God can satisfy. Although Thomas does not refer to Anselm by name, we recognize the argument of the *Cur Deus homo?*: Since every creature already owes his whole being to God, a mere creature could not satisfy; not even man himself, since sin has left him unworthy. Thus, in order that satisfaction be made for the sin of human nature (original sin), it is fitting that God become incarnate. Although Thomas will radically alter the meaning of the Anselmian doctrine of satisfaction, the principle enunciated in this *sed contra*, "qui debet et potest," nonetheless remains fundamental for his systematic discussion of the satisfaction of Christ.

The solution: God's mercy, justice, and wisdom

In the actual solution to d. 1, q. 1, a. 2, Thomas centers his resolution of the question around the divine attributes of mercy, justice, and wisdom. He gives Anselm a fresh and original interpretation. Anselm's argument stressed why we needed a God-man in order to be saved, but Thomas emphasizes the divine initiative to undertake our salvation as a manifestation of goodness. It is not unusual that the arguments presented in the *sed contras* are not taken up in their original form in the responses. This shift of emphasis marks only one way, however, that Thomas modifies the argument of *Cur Deus homo?* He also challenges Anselm's method. Mysteries like the incarnation depend sheerly on the divine will. Thus, Aquinas argues that the student of theology may only show that such mysteries do not constitute the impossible or appear inappropriate. Chenu writes that "the School was always haunted by Anselm's *necessariae rationes*, but the masters, like Anselm, upheld these bold conceptions and necessary relationships only within the realm of mystery wherein faith had led them."[14]   In this early work Aquinas still manifests some of this skittishness, so he stresses the arguments of convenience as expressing only the appropriateness of the incarnation.

Each of the three arguments possesses a common supposition: "Since human nature has fallen, but was still reparable, it was fitting ("decuit") that God repair ("repararet") it" (III d. 1, q. 1, a. 2).   This is true for three reasons: (1) Since God's goodness obliges him to do what he could to restore fallen human nature, which remains reparable even after the fall, a full exercise of the divine mercy points to the incarnation;   (2) the immutability of God's justice, against which no one may sin without making satisfaction, urges the incarnation so that someone from among mankind was able to make the required satisfaction;   (3) divine wisdom itself ordains that God most suitably accomplish this reparation.   But Aquinas notes that to restore human nature constitutes the most fitting way to bring about satisfaction, so that we might the more easily find what we had lost by sin.   (If an angel, for example, had been chosen to save us, such would not have been the case, since man's beatitude would then have been inferior to that of the angels.)   Not only did the divine wisdom ordain that the restoration be integral but that our task of reaching God would be made easy.   Hence God chose to save man in a visible way, since in this life man is drawn to things which he can sense externally.   Thus, as the preface for the Christmas Mass reminds us, "through him whom we can see, we are drawn to the love of the God whom we cannot see."   Goodness, justice, and wisdom in God combine to bring us Christ.

The responses: qualification of Cur Deus homo?

The responses to the arguments complete this development of the motive of the incarnation.   The notion of satisfaction and the doctrinal points which touch upon the necessity of an incarnate God to accomplish it receive adequate treatment in the responses to arguments 3,4,5,6,7, and 9.   These responses offer us the opportunity to contrast Thomas's teaching with that of Anselm, who used many of the same arguments in the course of his Cur Deus homo?   For example, the response to the third objection includes the Anselmian premise that we require an incarnate God for satisfaction because only man owed ("debet") satisfaction. Thomas replies that although the work of creation required no created instrument, satisfaction does; since without a man to perform the work, the due satisfaction could not have been rendered.   In this respect, then, the work of re-creation does not conform to the same principles as the work of creation.

Next, Thomas invokes a fundamental principle of theology, namely, that we can place no contradiction in God.   Hence, there can be no contradiction between the divine mercy and justice. In fact, Thomas observes, a mercy which would eliminate justice would be a kind of foolishness rather than a virtue. The incarnation manifests both the mercy and the justice of God. It manifests his mercy because the incarnation remains a greater demonstration of mercy, given all that it entails in the kenosis of the Word, than would have been the case had God chosen to absolve us without the satisfaction of an incarnate God. Likewise it manifests his justice since Christ does in fact satisfy justice's demands by his expiatory death. Thomas appends two observations that are important. First, God, since he judges all, had no choice but to fulfill the demands of justice and preserve its order. If he had done otherwise, it would have given the impression that judges of a lesser order could follow his example and do likewise. Second, since God is goodness itself, he alone has the right to vindicate, according to Deuteronomy 32:35, "Vengeance is mine, and recompense." All the more ought he to take vengeance on a sin committed against himself. Of course, in these replies we gain access to some of the standard theological concerns of the 13th-century, and they prove to be quite similar to those we hear about today.

The three points given in this response to the question why God's mercy would not have been more manifest by a simple deliverance from sin rather than by satisfaction are drawn from *Cur Deus homo?* I, c. 12. There we find that the Doctor of Canterbury appeals, in turn, to the disorder inherent in forgiving a sin without punishment, to the incongruity of God's acting differently from that which is the rule of justice among men, to God's sole right to take vengeance, and finally to the harmony of the divine attributes. But Thomas can clarify a detail of Anselm's theology when it appears ambiguous in *Cur Deus homo?* For instance, the fifth objection treats the relationship between the gravity of the offense and the quality of the satisfaction for it. Thomas distinguishes two ways in which the gravity of an offense might be considered: either as an insult to the divine majesty or as an injury to the one who sins. In the first point of view, sin causes an effect of relatively infinite ("infinitatem quamdam") magnitude precisely because of the infinite majesty that is offended. From the second perspective, however, sin's effect is decidedly finite, even in the case of the original sin, whose effects touch upon all the descendants of Adam. This clarification clearly shows Thomas's careful theological analysis of the reality of sin and, moreover, his willingness to correct what remains ambiguous in Anselm, who in several chapters of *Cur Deus homo?* suggests that the salvific death of a God-man is required precisely because the sins of mankind reach infinite magnitude.[15] Thomas's minor qualification, "a relatively infinite character," remains an important contribution to the argument.

Thomas continues his response by outlining the kind of satisfaction that must be made so that we can account for the effects of sin, both the finite ones and the relatively infinite one. Satisfaction must first restore to us whatever finite good we have lost by sin and secondly redress the sin as an offense against God. Thus, grace is required to make adequate satisfaction because only grace, since it merits an infinite reward, can be said to give satisfaction the somewhat infinite value required to compensate for a somewhat infinite offense. The human creature alone is unable to satisfy for his sins because he has no claim to grace. But God can give man what he needs to satisfy for his sins and the divine willingness to do so means that the demand for such grace-filled satisfaction does not constitute an injustice.

The sixth response treats the difference between the satisfaction required for original sin and that for actual sin. Thomas explains why an incarnate God is required to satisfy for original sin. In responding to this question, Aquinas confronts a second related question, namely, whether one person can satisfy for any sin apart from a definitive relationship to Christ. First, he describes two differences between original sin and actual sin, one regarding the origin of sin and the other regarding its effects, or the kind of goods which the respective sins corrupt. With respect to the origin of sin, any actual sin possesses a far greater voluntariness to it and therefore remains of greater vituperation than the original sin. The latter, says Thomas, has a less well-defined beginning (one can even speak, in the individual, of a certain necessary character with respect to original sin) and subsequently remains less a willed offense against God. With respect to the effects of the two kinds of sins, however, the contrary obtains. Original sin affects the entire human race while actual sin affects the good only of the one who commits it. According to Thomas's terminology, actual sin is a greater fault ("culpa"), but original sin a greater evil ("malum"). Still, we recognize that Aquinas accounts for the breadth of sin in order to emphasize the amplitude of Christ's satisfaction.

In line with St Anselm's principle that no individual creature could offer to God a good equal to or exceeding the good of the whole human race, no individual creature would thus be able to satisfy for the original sin which corrupted that goodness. Only one whose worth was more than that of the whole of human nature could restore the good lost by original sin. In the context of this discussion it would follow, as the next response makes clear, that Adam would have been able to satisfy for whatever there was of personal sin for him in the original sin, but not for the effect that his personal sin had on the human race. Aquinas then qualifies his remarks in two ways. First, he explains that even for the satisfaction of actual sin the aid of grace is required. This recalls the need for God's grace to render man's satisfaction relatively infinite so that it would correspond to sin's relatively infinite offense against God. The second qualification deals with Christ's role as the mediator of such grace. But here Thomas hesitates. He simply acknowledges that certain theologians (among them, Alexander of Hales)[16] hold the opinion that even the satisfaction made for personal sins is without value apart from the satisfaction made by Christ. Thomas's hesitation on this point stems less from doubt about Christ and more from his concern for the satisfaction of the holy ones who lived before Christ. The theologians to whom Thomas refers appear to have taught that the satisfactions accomplished by the holy ones of the Old Testament were efficacious because of their belief in the redemption that Christ would subsequently accomplish.

The response to the ninth objection treats the question whether God could have created a hypothetical creature who would have been able to make the kind of satisfaction required. Such a created goodness would have to be of such magnitude that the creature would be able to return to God a good at least equal to that corrupted by the original sin. Thomas offers three reasons why such an hypothesis is unworkable. The first he borrows directly from St Anselm, namely, that every creature owes whatever good it possesses to God since he is the creator. Therefore there could be nothing supplementary wherewith any created being might make satisfaction. The second reason, likewise defined by Anselm, is that satisfaction demands that at least an equal good--if not a greater good--be restored in place of what sin has destroyed. No creature could be created whose worth would exceed the good of human nature taken in its global sense. Of course, St Anselm refused to consider any creature capable of making the required satisfaction for original sin since his conception of the relationship between God and man, modeled upon that of a feudal lord and a serf, prohibited such a possibility. Indeed, both the master's right of possession and free disposition towards the serf as well as the obligation of the slave to belong entirely to the master remain undisputed principles in Anselm's theology. So he would reject satisfaction made by anyone whom God has created, no matter what his created goodness, since that goodness would itself derive entirely from God.

Although Aquinas does not favor hypothetical arguments in theology, he does recognize a final reason for not considering redemption as accomplished by a hypothetical creature of whatever amount of goodness. He points to the effect of the satisfaction accomplished by Christ, namely, that we are elevated to an order that remains above the natural order ("ad gradum superiorem"). If we are raised above the created order of things, it is impossible to think that any created instrument would alone suffice to accomplish such a work. God alone can elevate human nature. This final reference to the beatific life recalls an emphasis that Thomas earlier chose to develop, namely, the divine goodness in bringing about the incarnation in order that the human creature might reach his goal.

In the *Scriptum*, then, the fitting motive which explains why the Son of God became incarnate centers on the notion of satisfaction. And Thomas will refer to the principles established here throughout his subsequent discussions of Christ's satisfaction in the Book III. Hence a brief summary of the article will be useful. The starting point of the discussion remains the fact of original sin. The sin of the first parents finds its malice in the fact that it, unlike the personal sins of others, affects the entire progeny of Adam, namely, the entire human race. It is thus a sin of nature, which by reason of its communicability has a relatively infinite character to it. This sin, like the personal sins of any man, separates the individual from God. Man remains thwarted in reaching his ultimate goal. Sin not only affects man but also constitutes an offense against the infinite majesty of God. As such, even sin takes on a kind of infinite distinction.

The malice of the devil, however, remains no match for the wisdom of God. Moved by the incongruity of seeing the noblest of his creatures blocked from reaching the destiny God intended, he chooses a way that will both restore man to his lost dignity and make it possible for us to reach the goal of beatitude. The way that God chooses at once manifests his mercy and preserves his justice. Since it is man alone who should ("debet") redress the original sin, as we committed it, but God alone who can ("potest") redress it, because of the kind of infinite character inherent in this evil, it follows that only one who is both God and man can make the kind of satisfaction which is required. In the incarnation God's mercy is manifest in Christ's taking on our human nature and his justice is safeguarded in Christ's suffering for our sins. Because of the satisfactory act of Christ, we find restoration in union with God and can satisfy for our own sins as well, since grace now suffuses these actions with the infinite character they would otherwise lack.

The Satisfaction Accomplished by the Passion:
Redemption not Liberation

Next, Thomas discusses the relationship between the passion of Christ and the satisfaction whereby we find liberation from sin. A single question of five articles treats four major subjects: d. 20, q. 1, a. 1 treats the reparation of human nature; d. 20, q. 1, a. 2 deals with whether another besides Christ could have satisfied for human nature; d. 20, q. 1 a. 3 considers whether satisfaction was appropriately accomplished by the passion of Christ; and d. 20, q. 1, a. 4 asks whether the human race could have been liberated in any other way. An examination of these texts affords the opportunity to see how Thomas talks about the satisfaction brought about by the expiatory death of Christ.

Until now, the christological discussion between the first and twentieth distinctions draws frequently on the principles established in d. 1, q. 1, a. 2. For example, we find the suitability of Christ's having assumed human flesh frequently explained in terms of the need for someone of Adam's race to make satisfaction. Again, we require unity in the person of Christ because otherwise no single person exists who combines the ability ("potest") with the liability ("debet") required for satisfaction. Then the passion of Christ shows his willingness to suffer by bearing the greatest sorrow. Even the weakness of human nature presents no obstacle to making satisfaction since the strength whereby Christ overcame the power of the devil remains a source of power and virtue. Lastly, Aquinas sometimes speaks about the satisfaction of Christ as the price he paid for our sins.

D. 20, q. 1, a. 1, quaes 2: *Restoration through satisfaction*

Now we move to the question whether human nature actually needed to be restored. Aquinas cites two familiar Anselmian arguments to support the fittingness of restoring human nature. First, divine wisdom could not allow a creature--particularly a creature such as man--to be thwarted from achieving the goal for which he had been created. Yet original sin results in precisely that. Second, the perfection of the universe itself entails that the human creature discover happiness. The actual solution to this first section of the article shows how the restoration of human nature manifests God's wisdom, mercy, and power. Even if we grant that human nature ought to have been restored, however, we can still ask whether satisfaction provides the best way. Two standard arguments advance the inappropriateness of satisfaction First, since creation was accomplished simply by a word from God, thus re-creation should also have been accomplished by a similar fiat instead of a creature's instrumentality. Second, forgiveness embodies mercy more than redress for an offense. So far, we note familiar lines of argumentation.

A new element, however, appears in the discussion. Aquinas points to satisfaction as really a more complete way of restoring human nature since through it we become a cause of our own restoration. Next, he invokes a parallel with merit. The one who merits an eternal reward, as opposed to simply having it given to him, can be said to have a part in what he has achieved. Thomas then makes a corollary point: By satisfaction man's sin is not simply taken away, but his nature is actually restored--"ad pristinam dignitatem humanam naturam integraliter reducere." Again, God remains free to do things according to his will, and this includes restoring human nature by satisfaction. Thomas also speaks about a partial remission of debt without satisfaction. But he insists that all satisfaction in some way relate to Christ's satisfaction. Here Aquinas also underscores the point that restoration of human nature means a new creation; therefore only God who created us would be able to re-create us in such a way that we can enjoy our former state of perfection, our "pristine dignity."

In order to distinguish the work of Christ from the derivative works of the members, however, Aquinas introduces a distinction which already existed in theological idiom. Condign satisfaction happens when the satisfaction is made in accord with the demands of strict equivalence. Thomas explains that such a condign satisfaction remains necessary for two reasons: first, so that man would be truly restored and not merely forgiven; second, that there might be a foundation upon which we all could establish other derivative acts of satisfaction. This condign satisfaction demands that the redress have a kind of infinite quality to it since the offense for which it is made touches the infinite in three ways: first, the infinite character of the divine majesty which is offended; second, the infinite dimension of the good from which sinful man is separated by original sin, namely, the good of God himself; and lastly, the unlimited--even infinite--potential of the human nature which is being restored. Human nature enjoys a kind of infinite status in this regard, since it can find instantiation in an unlimited number of individual beings. Thus condign satisfaction must have something of the infinite to it, but no creature is capable of effecting that kind of satisfaction since no creature can do anything that is infinite.

D. 20, q. 1, aa. 3,4: Satisfaction accomplished by suffering

Next we consider the relationship between condign satisfaction and the passion of Christ. Did God really require that satisfaction be made in this way? Of course, we resolve the core of the difficulty by reference to the simple declaration of Hebrews 2:10: "For it was fitting that he should make the pioneer of their salvation perfect through suffering." But the key word remains "death." Sin has made us debtors, that is, subject to death; for all sin leads to death. If one is to speak about redress in strict equivalence for sin, then the satisfactory act must involve death. Christ's passion and death made his satisfaction eminent in two ways: first, it was an act of satisfaction effected by the ultimate suffering--death--and not merely by this or that suffering; second, this kind of satisfaction serves as an example of outstanding satisfaction, a true exemplar of what satisfaction should be, in which other human satisfactions can find their model and ideal.

Still the importance of death should not conceal the central action of Christ's death. Charity and death combine to make satisfaction as required. The necessity of Christ's passion and death also explains why, for example, the lesser sufferings of Christ--his hunger, his fatigue, the shedding of his blood at his circumcision--would not have made sufficient satisfaction. Nor did the killing of Christ alone effect the satisfaction; rather the love with which he underwent this passion and gave up his life also plays an important part. Yet even surpassing love was not sufficient for satisfaction. Love could take away the sin, but sorrow or suffering is required to make satisfaction for it. Likewise the simple fact of the incarnation, in which God humbles himself to become a man, does not eliminate the need for the passion and death of the incarnate God, in which he experiences bitter sorrow.

The humility of the incarnation is an antidote for the pride of Adam's sin, but the bitter sorrow of the passion is a remedy for the delight which Adam took in the sin.

Of course, other ways of restoring human nature would have been possible. Did God possess no choice but to save the world by the passion and death of his Son? Anselm apparently taught the necessity of the incarnation. "And when the Son said that the chalice could not pass from him unless he drank of it, the reason was not that he was unable to avoid death, if that had been his will, but that the world was not able to be saved otherwise."[17] Thomas, however, posits no such necessity in God, "For with God nothing will be impossible" (Lk 1:37). Indeed, God possessed ways other than satisfaction in order to accomplish the restoration of human nature. Still such a hypothetical salvation would rather constitute a liberation than a redemption since, insists Aquinas, no price would have been paid. On the other hand, for man there remains only the way God ordained since we cannot satisfy for ourselves but must accept satisfaction as a free gift. Aquinas further asks whether some more appropriate way to save man exists. But he refuses to speculate on this question. At the same time, if such a way did exist it would require an entirely different order of events, changing the practice of the Christian faith. In short, Aquinas prefers to interpret the position set forth by Anselm on the necessity of the incarnation as supposing the present order of salvation.

The actual order of salvation involves the passion and death of Christ. Satisfaction means suffering. For example, Christ's violent death expresses the satisfactory character of his sufferings more than a natural death would have done. Consequently, Christ's sufferings establish the model for the Christian way of life since we also must renounce earthly attachments and seek the joys of heaven. And we must also think of the part played by the devil in this drama. Indeed, Thomas consistently refuses to give the devil any rights over the human creature, but he does acknowledge that sin merited our enslavement to the devil's wiles. As a result, like Anselm himself, Aquinas recognizes the fittingness of salvation through painful humiliations. He even remains willing to acknowledge some metaphorical justice in the argument since we, as it were, can consider ourselves justly liberated. Thomas sees a further parallel between our sinning as a result of the devil's temptations and the human responsibility in Christ's death at the devil's instigation. Thus, for instance, Aquinas sees no reason to suppose that the devil should have been Christ's executioner. As this medieval tradition demonstrates, theology always has to battle against the tendency to accept mythological explanations.

Summary

The 20th-distinction discusses the necessity of the Cross. Why does satisfaction for original sin require the physical sufferings and death of Christ? Aquinas considers two issues: first, why does satisfaction require Christ's death, and second, does God remain free to choose some other means of satisfaction? The response to the first of these issues simply observes that new life for the human race points to the destruction of old life. The several references to our "pristine dignity" restored by the passion and death of Christ suggest the parallel Aquinas establishes between the state of original justice and redemption. Of course, only condign satisfaction (accomplished according to the demands of a strict equivalence) remains powerful enough to bring about this kind of re-creation. So the satisfaction of Christ remains preeminent in the Christian dispensation since it serves as the chief exemplar and point of unity for the satisfactions required of every Christian. These in turn dispose the believer to anticipate the true happiness of heaven.

Aquinas's response to the question of the divine freedom recognizes both the absolute transcendence of the divine liberty as well as the actuality of the historical events which constitute saving history. Thus he posits no necessity in God. Everything God does, he does freely. By the same token, Thomas refuses to speculate on this freedom. For the mere possibility that God could have acted otherwise does not supply sufficient reason to imagine other courses of action. So, given the present order of salvation as recorded in the New Testament, Thomas acknowledges that the satisfactory death of Christ remains both the most fitting way for God to have saved us and the most beneficial way for us to have been saved. In this, Aquinas demonstrates a theological modesty proper to one who serves God's word.

Aquinas emphasizes the satisfactory aspect of Christ's death in his discussion of both the motive for the incarnation and the passion and death. Of course, the theme of satisfaction does not figure prominently in the 12th-century text of Peter Lombard. There Abelard's "moral" interpretation of the passion and death of Christ influences the Lombard's work to the extent that the word "satisfaction" does not even appear in the twentieth distinction of the Sentences.[18] Thomas and his contemporaries, however, must treat the Anselmian notion of satisfaction, since by the 13th-century it had become part of every serious theological discussion of the mystery of Christ.

But Aquinas gives the theory a fresh reading. For example, at the very end of Cur Deus homo?, St Anselm asks Boso his interlocutor to consider the "great" reason why the death of Christ actually accomplished salvation of the human race. There he speaks about the recompense ("retributio") which God the Father owed to the Son because of his death on the cross--which Anselm in this context calls a

great gift ("tantum donum") to the Father. Then Anselm poses the
question:

> Anselm: If the Son wished to give to another
> what was owed to him, could the Father
> justly prohibit him or deny the one to
> whom the Son wished to cede his
> rights?

> Boso: Indeed not! I think the Father would
> have to acquit the debt of the one to
> whom the Son wished to give his
> recompense. . . .

> Anselm: To whom would the Son more fittingly
> cede the fruits and the recompense
> which his death was worth than to those
> for whose salvation he became man?[19]

For Anselm, the reason why Christ's satisfaction effects our salvation,
in the final analysis, is to be explained on a mercantile model. The
death of Christ provides a unit of exchange with which the Savior
could pay the debt owed by sinful man.

Although Thomas acknowledges that the reason why our salvation
constitutes a real redemption ("redemptio") and not merely a liberation
("liberatio") involves the price ("per solutionem pretii") paid for our sins
by Christ's satisfactory death, still the value of Christ's satisfaction
exceeds whatever his death realizes. The passion of Christ was not
satisfactory by reason of the killing of Christ, concludes Aquinas, but
because of the way in which he underwent his sufferings. He wished
to suffer with the greatest love and thus the passion was acceptable to
God. For Aquinas, satisfaction surely does not constitute a barter
between the Father and the Son over the latter's death.

Of course, Aquinas does have his preferred model for interpreting
the passion. And this interpretative model can also impede the
development of an authentic evangelical doctrine. Indeed, in the
Scriptum we recognize that Aquinas still speaks about satisfaction as if
it were a legal entity. Moreover, he remains within this juridical
framework to the extent that the demands of justice both predominate
and influence his theologizing on satisfaction and the mystery of the
incarnation.

At the same time, we also see the influence of moral
interpretations of satisfaction in Aquinas's early theology. This derives
especially from the definition of satisfaction found in the
pseudo-Augustine's Liber ecclesiorum dogmatum, which speaks about
the curative and preventative effects of satisfaction. Thus, Thomas
explains that both dolorous passion and maximal love serve to satisfy

completely for our sins. As he says: "Contrition not only finds its value in love but also in sorrow. While charity wipes away the stain of sin, it is sorrow which we consider as the satisfaction for the punishment due to sin" (d. 20, q. 1, a. 3, ad 1). Two streams of influence converge then in these early writings on the *Sentences*. First, Anselm provides Aquinas with a model for exchange between Christ and God. Second, the *Liber* furnishes him with the anthropological significance of satisfaction. As a result, Thomas's early redemption theology steers a course between the Scylla of a purely moral interpretation of Christ's passion and the Charybdis of a harshly mercantile description. In other terms, Aquinas accomplishes the task of a young theologian with success, for he develops his own line of interpretation as a result of carefully considering two dominant 12th-century models for the redemption: Abelard's theory of encouragement and Anselm's theory of exchange.

The theologian concerns himself with Christian revelation and the relationship it establishes between Christ's saving actions and the personal histories of those called to belong to his body. Like Christ, we too are required to make satisfaction for our sins. In order to introduce this subject, however, Thomas first describes the difference between the gravity of original sin and the gravity of actual sin. This difference points to the uniqueness of the incarnate Son in establishing the ground for all subsequent satisfaction within the Church. Since original sin affects the good of the whole human race, only someone whose own worth exceeds the good of the whole human race can adequately compensate for it. Actual sin, on the other hand, directly affects only the good of a single individual, with the result that each person can make due satisfaction for it.[20] Of course, Thomas consistently held that grace alone gives value to authentic satisfaction. Hence even Adam satisfied "with the help of God's grace" for the original sin (insofar as it also constitutes for him a personal sin) but could not make satisfaction for the sin as it affected the whole human race. Likewise, Thomas held the view that the holy ones of the old dispensation could satisfy for their sins, for instance, by observing the rituals of the old law, but they were not admitted to the vision of God because "the corruption of nature has not yet been healed by the satisfaction of Christ" (III, d. 1, q. 1, a. 1, ad 5).

Consequently, the ancients did perform satisfactory actions which, although valid in themselves, produced no definitive effect towards eternal life. The satisfaction of Christ had not yet opened the gates of heaven. Aquinas thus maintains the unity of the two dispensations: satisfaction belongs to both dispensations, but achieves its perfection only in Christ. The following text demonstrates this clearly.

The remission of punishment which is accomplished by all men, especially satisfactory punishments, is founded on the value of Christ's satisfaction, which more than accounted for the removal of all the punishment due to sin, considered in itself. Hence it is necessary that individual acts of satisfaction be founded on the condign satisfaction of Christ (d. 20, q. 1, a. 1, *quaes.*, 3, ad 3).

Of course, the distinction between the stain of sin ("culpa") and the debt of punishment to sin ("poena") permits Thomas to make an important separation here. He can at once demand satisfactory recompense for the punishment due to sin even after the stain of sin has been wiped away and at the same time affirm the full reality of divine forgiveness. Those who performed satisfactions before the death of Christ reversed the ordinary procedure since they first made satisfaction and then received full remission of "culpa" once the death of Christ again opened up the kingdom of heaven.

Scriptum super Sententias, Book Four: The Satisfaction of the Members

In the prologue to Book Four of his *Scriptum super Sententias*, Thomas introduces the major theme of the book with a quote from Psalm 107:20: "He sent his word, and healed them, and delivered them from destruction." Peter Lombard viewed the last book of his *Sentences* as a unique section dealing with the augustinian "signs" of the economy. Thomas, on the other hand, writes in the prologue to Book Four: "There is a continuity between the two books since in Book Three the mission of the Word made flesh was discussed and in this present [fourth] book the effects of that mission of the incarnate Word" (*in loco*). In particular, Thomas discusses three effects, namely, the sacraments, the resurrection of the dead, and the glory of those who rise.

His discussion of the sacraments and of the last things helps us further understand the relationship he posits between the satisfaction of Christ and the satisfaction of the members. Thomas first explains how we stand under the penalty of death in terms of the distinction between "culpa" and "poena"

> Because sin by its nature is something willed, punishment must be of a sort that it is contrary to our will. Sin ("culpa") reduces man to a state of weakness; punishment ("poena") subjects man to death. Sin is the road to punishment; weakness is the road to death (IV, prologue).

But the satisfactory punishments we undertake transform the punishment due to sin into an instrument of healing. Therefore, "satisfactory punishments heal sin in two ways. First, they constitute a recompense for sin, and so the expiatory satisfaction of Christ heals sin.

Second, they are a healing medicine by means of which a sick member is cured" (d. 2, q. 1, *quaes.*, 2, ad 2).

We find another clarification of this teaching in the discussion of the sacraments of baptism and penance. First, Thomas discusses the effect of this sacrament of initiation, baptism. He begins by examining whether baptism could remove all of the temporal punishment due to sin. Since faults are not rectified without some punishment, either man undertakes the satisfaction himself or else he is punished by God.[21] But Aquinas asserts that the principle does not hold for the sacrament of baptism. Why? "Christ by his death satisfied sufficiently for the sins of the whole human race, even if they would have been more than they actually are" (d. 2, q. 1, *quaes.*, 2). Consequently, since we are baptized into the death of Christ, as Romans 6 teaches, the baptized person receives the full effects of Christ's passion and death. By "full effects" Aquinas means liberation not only from sin ("culpa") but also from all satisfaction ("poena satisfactoria"). Thomas explains this special effect of baptism in terms of attributing to the believer the benefits of Christ's sufferings. So he cites I Corinthians 12:26: "If one member suffers, all suffer together," and Isaiah 53:4: "Surely he has borne our griefs and carried our sorrows." Although he lacks the philosophical capacity fully to explain this faith teaching, the singular exception to general rule for satisfaction emphasizes the strong union which Aquinas recognizes between Christ the head and his members.

We can see this same emphasis when Thomas talks about the final coming of Christ in glory. He poses the question: "Will Christ, when he comes in judgment, appear in the form of a glorified body?" Indeed, answers Aquinas. For Christ is called a mediator between God and man for two reasons: first, he satisfied for us and, secondly, he pleads for us before the Father, communicating to us divine things. Thus Christ carries our sins to God and God's gifts to us. In his first coming, then, it was appropriate that he appear in the form of our lowliness since the purpose of that coming was to satisfy for our sins. But in the second coming he will manifest the justice of God. Hence the appropriateness of his appearance in glory, since at that time he will show the glory of the divinity which was his from the beginning. But the Church of glory begins at baptism, and so the newly baptized perform no penance. Instead they participate fully in the power of the risen Christ.

The *Scriptum super Sententias* remains a work of Aquinas's youth. Still, the central features of his satisfaction theology already appear in these early theological exercises. First, Aquinas establishes the general features of Christian satisfaction in his gloss on the two definitions then current in the literature. Satisfaction embraces more than an arithmetical restitution for an injustice; it involves persons and attitudes. Next, satisfaction necessarily includes the painful since it both restores past defects and prevents subsequent failures. Finally, since one person can satisfy for another, satisfaction ordinarily occurs within the context of friendship and community. Secondly, Aquinas considers the explicitly theological implications of satisfaction as a motive for the incarnation. Here the 12th-century theology of St Anselm plays an important role since Aquinas must develop his own position in light of the arguments advanced in the *Cur Deus homo?* Although we judge that Aquinas does not fully escape the categories of law and justice in this first attempt to define the contours of his soteriology, he nevertheless succeeds in surpassing the controlling feudal imagery of Anselm's satisfaction theory. Finally, satisfaction forms part of a larger ecclesiological arrangement which establishes the Church of glory here and now. For Aquinas, the sacramental system points to a privileged bond between Christ and the members of his body. Baptism especially points to the full mystery of Christian grace and life, since at the very beginning of life it communicates a full share of the salvation which Christ accomplished for us on the cross. We now turn to consider these christological aspects of satisfaction which provide a remedy for sin and effect the salvation of man.

NOTES

1. Edition used: *Scriptum super libros Sententiarum* I-IV, reprinted Parma edition, vols. 6,7 (New York: Musurgia, 1948-50).

2. See Chenu, 273-75 for further information on the important differences between the two *summae*.

3. See his *Defensiones Theologiae Divi Thomae Aquinatis*, ed Ceslaus Paban and Thomas Pègues (Tours: A. Cartier, 1900-1907). For further information on John Capreolous (c.1380-1444), see T.M. Pègues, "La Biographie de Jean Capreolus," *Revue Thomiste* 7 (1899), 317-334. In the beginning of the 16th-century, Ignatius Loyola, for example, was among the first ones at Paris to study theology out of the *Summa*. Some years later, he accordingly made a point of including in his rule a provision stipulating that the members of the Society should also learn theology from the *Summa* instead of from the *Sentences*.

4. Here Aquinas shows the influence of the Victorine position on sacraments. Since Hugh of St.-Victor, the medieval theologians asserted that the sacraments contain grace as in a vessel, thus the preferred metaphors for the sacramental economy remain medicinal ones. For more information, see David Schaff, "The Sacramental Theory of the Medieval Church," *The Princeton Theological review* 4 (1906), 206-35. Aquinas will later nuance this position.

5. See Weisheipl, 435-6, n.31. For further information on the authorship of this work, see C.H. Turner, "The *Liber Ecclesiasticorum Dogmatum* attributed to Gennadius," *The Journal of Theoloigcal Studies* 7 (1906), 78-99. He suggests that the unknown Gennadius may represent the author who put the treatise in its present form. We refer to the author as Pseudo-Augustine.

6. In the text published by Turner, 94, chapter 23 contains the definition which reads as follows: "Paenitentia uera est paenitenda non admittere sed amissa deflere, satisfactio paenitentiae est causas peccatorum excidere nec earum suggestionibus additum indulgere."

7. See Anselm of Canterbury, *Cur Deus Homo?* I, c. 11, edited by René Roques (Paris: Les Editions du Cerf, 1963). 266: "Sic ergo debet omnis qui peccat, honorem Deo quam rapuit solvere; et haec est satisfactio, quam omnis peccator Deo debet facere." In a separate appendix, I have provided a summary of Anselm's satisfaction theory.

8. See Aristotle, *Nicomachean Ethics* Bk V, c. 3, translated by W.D. Ross, *The Basic Works of Aristotle*, ed Richard McKeon (New York: Random House, 1941), 1007. Of course, Aquinas used the Latin Aristotle, which

as L. Minio-Paluello has shown, came by direct translations from the Greek. See his *Opuscula: The Latin Aristotle* (Amsterdam, 1972).

9. For further information on the question of theological authorities in the middle ages, see Chenu, especially, 134-5. Special attention, however, should be given to the 8th-century Greek theologian, John Damascene, whose *De Fide Orthodoxa* in Latin translation provided the Middle Ages with access to the Greek fathers, especially for the doctrine of Christ.

10. See Bk II, c. 3 1104b14-17. Aristotle makes this remark in the context of his discussion on "habitus."

11. Although Aquinas actually refers to a work of Gregory the Great, the citation comes from Augustine, *De civitate Dei* I, c. 8. This happened frequently in he middle ages where collections of texts sometimes separated citations from their proper authority.

12. The practice is based on Mt 6:2-18. For a complete discussion of the historical development of satisfaction in the context of sacramental absolution, see P. Galtier, S.J., "Satisfaction," *Dictionnaire de théologique catholique*, Vol. 15 (Paris: Létouzey, 1939), 1129-1210.

13. Like Thérèse of Lisieux, Aquinas was also struck by the grandeur of the alpine scenery which he witnessed on his trips between Italy and Paris. Both saints remark that high mountains reflect the majesty of God.

14. See Chenu, 186. Of course, Anselm and the monastic school which followed him hardly expected the enthusiasms to be generated by the introduction of the *logica nova* and the misadventures that dialectics could introduce into theology. For an interesting study, see Enzo Maccagnolo, "David of Dinant and the Beginnings of Aristotelianism in Paris" in *A History of Twelfth-Century Western Philosophy*, ed by Peter Dronke (Cambridge: Cambridge University Press, 1988), 429-42.

15. For example, see *Cur Deus homo?* II c. 14 (404); c. 15 (406); c. 18 (440).

16. Although not Alexander's own work, *Summa theologica seu sic ab origine dicta 'Summa fratris Alexandri'* is the product of the Franciscan school he formed. John of La Rochelle, in fact, composed Book III which first accepted the arguments of *Cur Deus homo?* into the medieval discussion concerning the necessity of the incarnation. See the *Summa theologica* III, 1, q. 5, aa. 1,2, ed PP Collegii S. Bonaventurae (Quaracchi, 1948).

17. See *Cur Deus homo?* II, c. 19.

18. By contrast, Aquinas cites *Cur Deus homo?* 13 times in the *Scriptum*: I, c. 5 (2x); c. 10; c. 11 (6x); c. 20; II, c. 4; c. 11; c. 18. See Charles H.

Lohr, *St. Thomas Aquinas Scriptum super sententiis: An index of authorities cited* (England: Avebury Publishing Company Ltd, 1980).

19. See *Cur deus homo* II, c. 16. This text of course provides a good example of the mercantile imagery which gives Anselm's theology a commercial tone, especially when read in the light of different cultural settings. Aquinas's development of a metaphysical theology reduces this risk.

20. Aquinas recognizes that individuals can satisfy for their actual sins only on the condition that they possess grace. For example, *Scriptum* III, d. 1, q. 1, a. 2, ad 6 even speaks about "gratia humana." Here the lack of a critical edition of the *Scriptum* (presently in progress by the Leonine commission) impedes an accurate understanding of the text. M.F. Moos, O.P. observes, for instance, that several codices replace "humana" with "divina." See his edition of the *Scriptum* III (Paris: Lethielleux, 1933), 18. But Aquinas may actually have used the phrase "gratia humana" since in the same reply he remarks that "certain [other] authors hold the view that a mere man ("purus homo") cannot sufficiently satisfy even for actual sins."

21. The thesis actually comes from Augustine: "Iniquitas omnis, parva magnave sit, puniatur necesse est, aut ipso homine poenitentiae, aut Deo vindicante." See his *Enarrationes in Psalmos*, (58), n. 13.

CHAPTER IV

"A REMEDY UNTO THE SALVATION OF MAN"

Poena and Culpa in the De Malo

All in all, Aquinas has made it clear that in order to grasp fully the meaning of Christian satisfaction, the theologian must also accurately understand the meaning of sin in the Christian life. Indeed, Thomas always explains satisfaction (whether the satisfaction of Christ for original and subsequent sin or the satisfaction of the members for personal sins) in the context of the punishment ("poena") incurred by some disordered act ("culpa"). Like much he treated, Aquinas inherited this division of the evil of sin into "culpa" and "poena" from St Augustine. In the *De libero arbitrio*, Augustine wrote that there are two species of evil: that which we do ("culpa") and that which we suffer ("poena").[1]   In his early writings, Thomas distinguished between a defect of nature ("malum naturae"), any privation of a good which should form part of a determined form, and a fault ("peccatum"), any privation of some perfection in the operations of that form.   According to this stance, a defective operation at the level either of natural things or of art remains a "peccatum." But at the level of free choice, we call "peccatum" voluntary and refer to it as sin ("culpa") because of the dominion which rational creatures have over their actions. Likewise in rational creatures a defect of nature takes on an added significance, namely, that as an evil it is contrary to one's will and is referred to as punishment ("poena").[2]

However, in the disputed question *De malo* q. 1, a. 4, Aquinas develops a different philosophical analysis of this important augustinian principle.[3]   First, he eliminates the above-mentioned threefold distinction and now speaks simply of two aspects of sin, the "malum culpae" and the "malum poenae."   Then he asks whether one can consider these two qualifications an exhaustive division of evil. He replies that rational (and intellectual) creatures relate to good and evil in ways different from other creatures; the rational creature's freedom to choose accounts for this difference. He then refers to a text of Fulgentius of Ruspe (though attributed in the Middle Ages to St Augustine) which says: "Twofold is the evil of the rational creature: the one whereby he willingly turns from the highest good; the other whereby he is punished in his life."[4]   On the physical level, for example, blindness constitutes a deprivation of form, but it produces a defect, namely the inability to see, rather than originating in a defective action. For the rational creature, on the other hand, a defective act can only originate in a deliberate choice or "culpa."   Of course, we can consider deprivation of forms, both material and spiritual, in rational creatures, but these always constitute some form of punishment or "poena." To be sure, recognition that all such evil constitutes punishment for sin escapes most philosophical analysis; therefore Aquinas argues that only the teaching of the faith ("secundum fidei catholicae sententiam") makes it clear. In any event, he clearly points to the connection between disordered activity and human misery.

This leads to three considerations about "poena." First, "poena" affects rational creatures as a result of "culpa". Every disordered action, then, embodies its own punishment. Besides, the Christian tradition teaches that all "poena" results either from the sin of nature or from personal sins. Second, because the will naturally inclines to the good and shrinks from evil, "poena" always remains contrary to the creatures's will. Third, since it does not proceed from our natural inclinations but from some external cause which deals violence to nature, "poena" necessarily involves suffering. Punishment, then, emerges as a result of human abuse directed towards the structures inherent in the universe and the person.

Next, Thomas contrasts "poena" and "culpa." First, "culpa" remains an evil operation whereas "poena" amounts to an evil that inheres in the subject of the operation. On the level of physical things, an evil disposition in the subject results in a defective operation, for example, when a lame thoroughbred is unable to finish a race. On the other hand, the free creature incurs "poena" only through a disordered operation or "culpa." In this way, observes Thomas, divine providence rectifies the "malum culpae" by means of the "malum poenae." Second, "culpa," even though defective, remains something willed, but "poena" always goes against our will . Third, "culpa" is something that man does, but "poena" something he endures, as Augustine mentions in the text of the De libero arbitrio. These axioms serve as presuppositions for the issues which Aquinas treats concerning sin and sinning.

In particular, he looks at four issues. First, he turns to the text from Augustine's Confessions: "You have ordained it, Lord, and thus it is so, that every inordinate desire is its own punishment."[5] But if sin itself is punishment, then no sufficient reason exists to regard each as a different class of evil. Thomas responds that sin is never willed as something inordinate in itself, but always as an apparent good; still, the fact that it is willed at all suffices for the definition of "culpa." To be sure, in choosing to sin man unwillingly suffers sin's disorders, but this rather points to the definition of "poena." Second, if every sin concomitantly produces a punishment, how could original sin fulfill this definition since no sin existed previously to cause it? Thomas replies that punishment relates to sin more as an effect than as a cause. In this sense, even original sin has punishment associated with it, although it cannot be considered to have been actually precipitated by some previous disordered act or by the deprivation of grace which is the result of sin. Third, he considers another definition of evil given by Augustine in his *De natura boni,* cc. 35-37 which suggests that every evil forms a punishment since it constitutes a corruption of some natural mode, species, or order. Thomas responds that this serves as a generic definition of evil. However, if the corruption is something suffered by a subject, then we refer to a specific definition, i.e., "malum poenae." On the other hand, if the corruption is in an action, then we refer to the subject's "malum culpae."

Fourth, Aquinas opens a discussion pertaining to evil and satisfaction. If punishment serves satisfaction, how can punishment involve evil? Those who perform satisfaction, for example, receive praise since they willingly take on punishment for their sins. Aquinas distinguishes:

> Punishment, considered in relation to the subject, is an evil because it deprives him of something (in one way or another). However, when it is considered in relation to the one who imparts punishment, it can be considered as a good, when the punishment is a just one (*De malo* q. 1, a. 4, ad 9).

Thus, if satisfaction is willingly undertaken by a penitent, in effect the one who imparts the punishment and who suffers it constitute one and the same person. From this perspective, we can conclude that some punishments do constitute good deeds.

These two aspects of evil, the "malum culpae" (which we translate as the "stain of sin") and the "malum poenae" (the punishment due to sin) unquestionably comprise major elements in the doctrine of satisfaction. The *De malo* provides a philosophical analysis of these concepts. Elsewhere, in the *Summa theologiae,* Aquinas will elaborate a fully theological analysis of sin. In brief, we call the "malum culpae" the stain of sin because it chiefly refers to the culpable alienation from God implied in the Christian notion of sin. Sin sullies the Christian soul. In addition, the metaphor of stain also points to the permanent character of sin or the debt of punishment ("reatus poenae") which describes the abiding condition present in the sinner. Although the Christian tradition regards sin as a serious matter, both "poena" and "culpa" surrender before the power of Christ's love and obedience.

The Satisfaction of Christ the Head

De Veritate: Satisfaction and the Graced Humanity of the Word

Q. 29 a. 3: *The grace of Christ*

Several texts from the disputed question *De Veritate* offer Thomas the occasion to develop further his teaching on satisfaction.[6] First, in q. 29, he treats the topic of the grace of Christ. "Is the grace of Christ infinite?," asks Aquinas. Anselm in fact argued for the infinite merit of Christ as a condition for satisfaction. But Aquinas again distinguishes this point as a first step towards answering the question.

> Anselm in *Cur Deus homo?* proves that God had to be incarnated because satisfaction for human nature could not be made except through infinite merit, which could not be that of a mere man. From this it is evident that the merit of Christ as man was infinite. But the cause of merit is grace. The grace of Christ was therefore infinite, because an infinite effect cannot proceed from a finite cause (*De veritate* q. 29, a. 3, ad 4).

Citing a biblical text, Thomas moves to qualify this position and to introduce a distinction: "For he whom God has sent utters the words of God, for it is not by measure that he gives the Spirit" (Jn 3:34). A medieval biblical commentary, the *Glossa ordinaria*, uses this text as a basis for affirming that the grace of Christ is infinite.[7] Thomas, on the other hand, points out that the habitual grace of Christ properly refers only to the created grace which Christ possesses as a consequence of the hypostatic union. Moreover, we distinguish this grace from the "gratia unionis" precisely because it remains a created grace and therefore finite in itself.

Still, Aquinas can also consider Christ's habitual grace in some way infinite. For one can consider something infinite under one formality but finite under another. Suppose, for instance, an infinite white body. Since something even whiter can still exist, this body's whiteness does not actually amount to an infinite quality in intensity. But the whiteness does reach the infinite by extension or indirectly. Or, suppose a sentient soul which possessed every perfection of sense. While still calling such a soul essentially finite because of its limited act of existence, we could also describe its formality of sensing as having a sort of infinite character because in this case its powers of sense would not be limited to any particular mode of sensing. Likewise Thomas can explain how the habitual grace of Christ, although essentially finite, nonetheless points to an infinite mode of grace. He writes:

> In like manner, I say the habitual grace of Christ is essentially finite because its act of being is limited to a particular species of being, that of grace; yet it is infinite in the line of grace. For, although a person's perfection in point of grace can be considered to be any one of an infinite number of modes, no one of them was wanting to Christ, but he had grace in all fullness and perfection to which the formality of this species, grace, can extend (*De veritate* q. 29, a. 3).

Thomas can now respond to the question concerning the infinite character of Christ's merit.

First, Aquinas affirms that we cannot properly speak of Christ's merit as infinite since no human action can attain the infinite in intensity. The merit of Christ originates in a finite form, namely, his habitual grace. Nevertheless we can speak of a certain infinity with reference to the merit of Christ on account of the uniqueness of his divine personhood. Thomas explains: "But it had a certain infinity from the circumstance of the person who was of infinite dignity; for the greater the one who humbles himself, the more praiseworthy his humility is found to be" (*De veritate* q. 29, a. 3, ad 4). Christ's grace, then, will provide the source and cause of all subsequent grace in the Church.

Q. 29, a. 7: Satisfaction and merit

In this text, Thomas treats the distinction between merit and satisfaction. He includes under merit every positive action which disposes us for glory and under satisfaction every burdensome action or passion which removes some obstacle to our attaining glory. Then he shows how both merit and satisfaction apply to the human activity of the incarnate God. Thomas next demonstrates why the merit and satisfaction of Christ can spiritually affect ("spiritualiter influere") the members of his Church (as I John 2:2 puts it, "He is the expiation for our sins"). Christ, he explains, is the head of his body the Church; and just as the head in a physical body functions not simply for itself but for all the other parts of the body, so Christ's work also remains meritorious for his members. Moreover, Thomas continues, the headship of Christ of course implies a union between Christ and the members of his Church. In describing this foundation for the whole economy of salvation, Aquinas searches for an analogy and, in a striking phrase, even affirms that Christ and the Church constitute "quasi" one person.[8] Hence Christ was able to merit for others as if he were actually in their persons. The full implications of this intuition, however, appear only in the course of Aquinas's sacramental theology, especially his teaching on the Eucharist.

Merit and satisfaction are the principal activities to which Christ gives himself for our sakes. These actions point to the two ways in which we participate in the Church of glory. Merit addresses human unworthiness, especially in a sinner, whose sin puts an impediment between him and *visio beatifica* inasmuch as one who does not possess divine charity lacks the required dignity for attaining beatitude. Thomas writes: "As the act of sin results in a certain deformity of the soul, so meritorious acts result in restoring a certain beauty and dignity in it" (*De veritate* q. 29, a. 7). Satisfaction, on the other hand, points to the debt of temporal punishment due to sin. It removes liability to any penalty which stands in the way of attaining the reward of eternal life. Thomas explains: "And so this human work is ordered to glory much like the price paid to free a man from a penalty due; in this way the human work takes on the character of a satisfaction" (*ibid.*). Here then we have working definitions from the tradition which serve as a point de départ in the discussion.

Next, Aquinas applies these categories to the work of Christ. First, he addresses merit. Since merit positively disposes someone to participate in the reward of glory, human merit can only benefit the person who performs the meritorious deed. Hence, we cannot merit condignly for others. Christ, however, can. Why? The answer involves a basic theological axiom enunciated by the Greek fathers, namely, the humanity of Christ serves as an instrument of his divinity. So Christ through his humanity can spiritually influence other men and women ("spiritualiter influere potuit in alios homines"). Accordingly he can supply them the dignity indispensable to entering into glory. Second, Thomas treats satisfaction. He first recalls the general rule that one person can satisfy for another, provided that the former maintains a state of charity. But only Christ can satisfy for the whole human race. Aquinas explains:

> Although one man can satisfy for another, he cannot satisfy for the whole race because the act of one mere man is not equal in value to the good of the whole race. But the action of Christ, being that of God and man, possessed a dignity that made it worth as much as the good of the entire human race, and so it could satisfy for others (*De veritate* q. 29, a. 7).

Since Christ remains united to God in the person of the Logos, he can accomplish what no other individual can for our salvation. We recognize the importance Aquinas attaches to the hypostatic union, and why he affirms that unless one holds to this mystery the whole of the Christian faith unravels.[9]

We should observe carefully the terms Thomas uses to describe the effect of Christ's meritorious actions. Christ's merit gives us a worthiness ("dignitas") or a fitness ("idoneitas") for glory. Just as sin leaves the soul in a deformed state ("in quamdam animae deformitatem"), so merit effects an opposite result since it brings the soul into splendor and gives it an excelling worth ("in quamdam animae decorem et dignitatem"). On the other hand, merit does not necessarily imply satisfaction. Thomas explains this in the context of the death of Christ. "Although every one of Christ's acts was meritorious for us," he writes, "still to make satisfaction for the debt of human nature, which was made liable to death by the divine sentence, as in Genesis 2:17, he had to undergo death in the place of all" (*De veritate* q. 29, a. 7, ad 6). This way of distinguishing satisfaction from merit points to its special character in the Christian dispensation. Recall that original sin kept the Old Testament saints, even though they had personal grace to merit for themselves, from attaining glory. Sin places a weight on the world, and, therefore, a special kind of remedy is required for the salvation of man. At the same time, Aquinas adopts a clear position on the graces granted before Christ: "Personal grace was never given to anyone after the sin of the first man except through faith, either explicit or implicit, in the Mediator" (*De veritate* q. 27, a. 7, ad 7). The Church of both testaments relies on the satisfaction of Christ.

Thomas clearly moves away from the main lines of St Anselm's satisfaction theory. The juridical mentality which predominates in both Anselm and the early Thomas begins to give way to a personalist perspective grounded in the love and grace of Christ himself. "Christ and the Church remain 'quasi' one person." As a result, Christ can spiritually affect the members of his Church. What is more, Christ must undertake a work which reverses the cosmic effects of sin. But although Aquinas affirms this personal union, he does not at this point draw out the implications of the assertion for a doctrine on the mystical body and on spirituality.

Q. 29, a. 4: The headship of Christ

In the scholastic tradition, the term "head" signifies a principle of order and perfection inasmuch as the head exercises a vital influence on the body.[10] In article 4, Thomas applies this analogy to Christ. Even though the whole Christ in both natures together constitutes the head of the whole Church, Aquinas insists that Christ remains the head of the Church especially according to his human nature. He justifies this conclusion on the basis of Colossians 1:18-20, expounding a threefold signification of the term "head." First, Christ stands at the head of the Church's order as one who possesses the authority to govern: "He is the head of the body, the Church; he is the beginning, the first-born from the dead that in everything he might be preeminent." Second, Christ embodies the highest dignity in the Church as one who possesses a principle of perfection: "for in him all the fullness of God was pleased to dwell." Third, Christ can exercise a vital influence on his members: "and through him to reconcile to himself all things." Christ's headship then includes authentic spiritual authority which mediates God's work in the world.

The capital grace of Christ, as we call the grace of headship, remains ordered towards satisfaction and reconciliation. Thomas recognizes that Christ the head satisfied for the sin of nature in his visible humanity. The incarnate Son did this in order to heal the wounds of sin which left each one of us disinclined to submit to the invisible government of the Word.[11] This functional parallel between the eternal Word of creation and the incarnate Son of redemption marks Aquinas's whole christological perspective. Christ then did not serve as head of the Church prior to the incarnation, except proleptically in the faith of the Old Testament saints who awaited the day of his coming. Since the definitive act of satisfaction requires a passible body, only the incarnate Son can fulfil its requirements. As Hebrews 10:6,7 puts it, "but a body hast thou prepared for me; in burnt offerings and sin offerings thou hast taken no pleasure. Then I said, 'Lo, I have come to do thy will, O God.'"

Q. 26, aa. 6,9: The suffering of Christ

The death of Christ remains a principal stumbling stone for those drawn to the Christian confession of faith. "For Jews demand signs and Greeks seek wisdom, but we preach Christ crucified, a stumbling block to Jews and folly to Gentiles, but to those who are called, both Jews and Greeks, Christ the power of God and the wisdom of God" (ICor 1:22-24). Aquinas nonetheless realizes that the death of Christ remains linked to the punishment of death due us on account of Adam's sin. First, Thomas addresses these sufferings as they affect the person of Christ himself. Christ more fittingly merited the glorification of his body by his sufferings than he did by the meritorious acts which preceded his passion, since the "splendor of the resurrection is by a certain fittingness properly a reward of the passion, just as exaltation is the proper reward of humility" (*De veritate* q. 29, a. 4). Second, he addresses the role suffering plays with respect to his members. Here Christ's passion also merits differently from his previous merits "inasmuch as by his passion he gave satisfaction for the sin of the whole human race" (*ibid.*). Furthermore, Thomas points to the purpose human suffering serves in rectifying disordered passions so that "retribution by way of suffering remains required for satisfaction as a sort of compensation for the pleasure of sin" (*ibid.*). Aquinas favors explanations which return to the soteriological significance of the passion, thereby establishing links between the sufferings of Christ and those of the Church. In his view, the very difficulty involved in enduring great suffering contributes to our merit. To be sure, moral challenges sometimes reduce the willingness to undertake suffering and therefore place merit at risk. On the other hand, Aquinas argues, a person can also make an effort against such difficulty, with the result that merit in fact increases. Of course, quantitative evaluations of spiritual values only partially express one dimension of Aquinas's analysis of merit. He prefers to stress the relevance of the believer's union with Christ.

For example, he raises the question whether Christ experienced sorrow in his higher reason. The question represents a lingering suspicion which derives from Alexandrian christology and its hesitations in the face of a fully human Christ. Indeed, Christ's human "pathos" raises especially difficult questions for crypto-monophysitic interpretations of the hypostatic union.[12] If moreover, as Aquinas holds, Christ perfectly possessed the beatific vision at every moment of his life, including the passion, psychic suffering or sorrow in his "higher reason" would appear excluded since perfect contemplation arrests sadness or sorrow. On the other hand, satisfaction should correspond to the fault committed, and Christ satisfied for the fault of the first man which reached even the higher reason; thus the passion of Christ must also reach his higher reason. In his reply, Aquinas seeks to reconcile both values indispensable to Christ's redemptive mission.

> Christ's passion would not have satisfied except insofar as it was undertaken voluntarily and from charity. It is accordingly not necessary, just because the fault was in Adam through the operation of higher reason, that suffering be in the higher part of Christ's reason as regards its proper operation; for the sufferer's movement of charity, which is in the higher part of reason, corresponds for the purpose of satisfaction to whatever fault was to be found in higher reason (*De veritate* q. 26, a. 4, ad 2).

Here we see Aquinas's preference for theological balance. The charity of Christ again emerges as the dominant consideration in explaining the efficacy of his satisfaction for us.

Summa Contra Gentiles: Satisfaction
"ex dignitate personae patientis" and
"ex maiori caritate procedens"

Book Three: The notion of satisfaction accomplished in love

In *Summa contra gentiles* III, Thomas again discusses the human need to be liberated from sin in order to reach beatitude.[13] The discussion touches on two familiar issues, namely, the role that love plays in satisfaction and how one person can satisfy for another. First, Aquinas considers the eminence of Christ's created charity as an instrument of God's love in the world.

We can again consider several psychological factors which demonstrate the need for punitive action as a response to wrongdoing. For instance, paying a price for something helps us appreciate its worth. Again, since our sensible nature recoils from what causes suffering or pain, Thomas argues that punishment for sins of the past lessen the attractiveness of sin in the future. Likewise the delight which attracts one to subsequent wrongdoing will be less forceful in the future if one has previously undergone punishment as a result of the sinful pleasure. Although current penitential discipline does not easily persuade us of its importance, the medievals recognized that undergoing a chastisement plays a significant role in psychological liberation from sin. Moreover, when we freely undertake these corrections, they amount to godly satisfaction. When, on the other hand, God inflicts these as punishments on the sinner, they constitute purgations ("purgatoria") more than satisfaction.

While this description of the psychology behind satisfaction accords with the teaching of the *Scriptum* on the medicinal effects of satisfactory punishments, now Aquinas better recognizes the evangelical importance of theological charity. He already had affirmed that Christ's love for mankind (which exists in his higher reason) satisfies for whatever sin Adam committed in his higher reason. Granted the purpose of punishment remains both a firmer attachment to God and a lesser attraction to evil, it follows that the strength of one's love for God and the abhorrence of one's past sins measure the need for punishment. Aquinas even imagines a case where the force of personal love reaches such magnitude that it cancels entirely the need for any satisfaction. "There is no fear in love, but perfect love casts out fear. For fear has to do with punishment, and he who fears is not perfect in love" (IJn 4:18).

Thomas applies this principle to the sacrament of penance. A common opinion, held even by medieval theologians, urges sinners to confess past sins again and again. The theory is based on the supposition that in each confession, a partial remission of the temporal punishment due to sin occurs. Thus repeated confession would eventually eliminate all of the punishment due as a result of a given sin. By itself, such a position still has a metallic ring to it, but within the context of Aquinas's teaching on the sacraments, we encounter a new understanding of charity's effects. Since each celebration of the sacrament renews and strengthens the sinner's union with Christ, whatever reduction of punishment then results from repeated celebrations of the sacrament occurs not from sheer repetition but from the work of Christ's superabundant love. This love draws sinners closer to the heart of Christ, where they enjoy the full purifying effects of that union.

This recalls an earlier distinction Thomas made between restitution and satisfaction. The former entails giving something back voluntarily or under constraint, for example, property owed to another; the latter, however, constitutes compensation for the personal offense committed against another person. Satisfaction, then, prevails within an interpersonal relationship in which love figures prominently. Since to redress an offense requires love, satisfaction increases to the extent that love increases. At the same time, this emphasis on the role love plays in satisfaction moderates Aquinas's earlier position in which he stressed the repair of justice and the restoration of an established forensic order.[14]

In the *Nicomachean Ethics*, Aristotle observed that what we do through a friend we really do ourselves.[15] This in turn leads Aquinas to consider in c. 158 the relationship between friendship and satisfaction. Friendship, he writes, forms two individuals into a kind of unity ("ex duobus facit unum"), especially when love constitutes the binding force. Again, he points to Galatians 6:2, "Bear one another's burdens, and so fulfill the law of Christ." Thomas affirms that one person can satisfy for another provided both are united in the state of charity. Of course, since Christ's satisfaction remains the ground and condition for this arrangement, his death for sinners constitutes an exception to this general rule. Indeed, vicarious satisfaction actually points to an increase in love. And Aquinas gives us the reason:

> The punishment which a friend suffers on behalf of another does not escape entirely the one for whom the satisfaction is undertaken. It is as if he himself were undergoing the punishment, suffering as he does with the friend who is making the satisfaction. This is so much more the case as the guilty one realizes that it is because of himself that the friend is suffering. Furthermore, the charity which moves the friend to undertake the satisfaction makes the work more pleasing to God than if the guilty one had performed the satisfaction himself. The former is prompted by love while the latter would have been moved by necessity (*Summa contra gentiles* III, c. 158).

To be sure, we can remark in this passage the influence of the New Testament as much as that of the *Nicomachean Ethics*. In fact, three factors control the way Aquinas develops his satisfaction model: first, a philosophical paradigm, inspired largely by Aristotelian ethics; second, a christological pattern, developed mainly out of the tradition; third, an ecclesiological model, which constitutes Aquinas's original contribution to the theology of satisfaction. First, then, we examine his christology.

Book Four: The satisfaction of Christ

In cc. 50-55, Aquinas treats the motive and purpose of the incarnation. "De convenientia Incarnationis" accordingly includes two principal topics: original sin and the incarnation itself. This juxtaposition represents a unique arrangement in the *Summa contra gentiles*. The theological grounds for this particular scheme rests on the nature of communicability associated with Adam's sin. If Adam's sin reaches the whole human race, why did not his satisfaction as well? Thomas responds that Adam's nature possessed an original excellence forfeited by his sin. As a result, he communicated his sin to the whole race but not the satisfaction which he performed after sin, which consequently remains a purely personal act. This explanation clearly points to the role and person of Jesus Christ.

C. 53: Arguments against

In all likelihood, Aquinas wrote the *Summa contra gentiles* to help missionaries. Hence we find here a larger number of arguments than ordinarily happens when a text represents the record of an classroom instruction; in fact, Aquinas never taught the *Summa contra gentiles*. Of course, the Christian mystery of the incarnation appears to challenge philosophical arguments which support the transcendence of the divine nature, especially as developed in certain schools of Arab and Greek philosophy. Thus, Thomas devotes considerable attention to explaining why in fact the incarnation does not infringe upon the divine transcendence. At the same time, he takes account of at least seven different arguments which inquire about the fittingness of Christ's satisfaction. First, it seems unfair to say that Christ had to become a man in order to die for our sins since justice demands that the one who sinned should be the one who satisfies; second, if there was a need for satisfaction by someone greater than a mere man, certainly an angel would have sufficed; third, one sin cannot satisfy for another, hence Christ's death should have been a natural one and not a violent act as it was. A second group of arguments considers whether Christ's death alone can satisfy for sin: First, Christ could not have satisfied for our personal sins, since then it would seem that Christ should die frequently inasmuch as we sin frequently; second, since it would be foolish to assert that the death of a single man accomplished what the combined efforts of all mankind could not, the death of Christ could not erase Adam's sin; third, if Christ did satisfy for the sin of Adam, why then are we still urged by the Christian scriptures to accept suffering as a punishment for sin; fourth, if the death of Christ remains adequate to take away the sins of mankind, why are Christians still told to seek absolution from a priest? These arguments supply the topics for Aquinas's discussion of the incarnation and satisfaction. We should observe that the first set raises questions about the purpose of the incarnation and the second concerning the motive for Christ's redemptive mission.[16]

C. 54: Arguments in favor

Following the list of arguments which represent objections which either Moslem or Jew might employ to challenge the Christian faith, Thomas provides a series of positive arguments which point to the incarnation as entirely befitting the divine goodness. Each of these arguments of fittingness rests upon the natural desire in every man and women to achieve perfect happiness. First, the incarnation remains a most efficacious help for us to attain beatitude because it closes the breach between humanity and divinity. Next, it reminds us of the universal call to holiness and helps us to know certain truths about God in a way that conforms to human psychology. Then, Christ incarnates the love God has for each one of us, thereby giving us hope for a share in divine friendship since we now experience the required equality which must exist between friends. Again, the incarnate Word also gives us a concrete example of the virtues which otherwise would have remained just abstract ideals. Finally, Christ assures us that our sins are forgiven lest the experiential knowledge of our sinfulness keep us from trusting in the power of God's love. Altogether these arguments for the fittingness of the incarnation cohere harmoniously towards showing the plan of God's love. "For he has made known to us in all wisdom and insight the mystery of his will, according to his purpose which he set forth in Christ as a plan for the fullness of time, to unite all things in heaven and things on earth" (Eph 1:9,10).

Still, we need to consider the role that satisfaction plays in this recapitulation of all things in Christ. Aquinas again refers to the tradition of the Church concerning original sin. Since this involves the good of the whole human race, an individual or indeed the whole human race itself remains inadequate to the task of satisfaction. A sort of justice nonetheless requires that whoever sinned should themselves satisfy. Therefore satisfaction requires someone who both could perform it ("potest") as well as one who ought to perform it ("debet"). Since the angels, although naturally higher than humans, nonetheless remain our equals with respect to the call to beatitude, only an incarnate God fulfills the required conditions for making satisfaction. This argument substantially follows that given in *Cur Deus homo?*. Perhaps the distinctive purposes of the *Summa contra gentiles* persuaded Thomas to consider Anselm's "rectus ordo" argument for satisfaction a compelling one for his audience.

C. 55: Responses to objections

Thomas's responses to the seven original arguments further develop his position in this text. First, he treats the objection that vicarious satisfaction appears to contradict the principle that the one who sinned should also make satisfaction. On the other hand, he observes, one friend can satisfy for another; such satisfaction, moreover, pleases God because he prefers love to sacrifice as Hebrews 10:5ff explains. But-- next--an angel could not serve as this kind of friend to us. Indeed, argues Aquinas, there is something repugnant about such a suggestion since the human race should not have to look to the angels for salvation. Third, the actual worth of Christ's death does not chiefly lie in physical death, especially when considered as an act perpetrated by violent and sinful executioners, but in the charity with which Christ freely bore such a wicked death ("ex caritate ipsius, qua voluntarie mortem sustinuit"). Fourth, Christ need not undergo such a death each time that we sin. The worth of his one satisfaction derives from a love so intense that it is sufficient to satisfy for whatever punishments subsequent sin might require. Also, the dignity of his person itself makes his death once and for all more than sufficient for a full satisfaction. Aquinas summarizes this important argument: "tum propter eximiam caritatem qua mortem sustinuit; tum propter dignitatem personae satisfacientis." Then he responds to the objection that since Christ died in his human nature, his death amounts to nothing more than the death of any other individual. But Christ's death instantiates a value which results from both his greater personal dignity and his superabundant love, demonstrated especially in the fact that he willingly undertook punishment for others who remain separated from him in both dignity and love. Aquinas's actual phrase, "ex dignitate personae patientis" and "ex maiori caritate procedens," recalls the expression of Romans 6:10, "The death [Christ] died he died to sin, once for all, but the life he lives he lives to God."

In the subsequent replies, Aquinas addresses the satisfaction performed by Christ's members. Although Christ's satisfaction remains "once for all," each member of Christ still remains bound to fill out the sufferings in the body. First, the fact that certain penalties ("poenalitates") associated with sinful disorder still exist in the world does not point to an inadequacy in the satisfactory work of Christ. On the contrary, these penalties actually provide the Christian believer the opportunity to accept a share in the effects of Christ's passion and death through the sacramentalization of human suffering. Finally, argues Aquinas, the sacraments themselves do not duplicate the satisfaction of Christ in the Christian economy of salvation. Rather, since they mediate Christ's benefits to each member, the seven sacraments, especially baptism and penance, extend Christ's satisfaction throughout time and space. They do not, however, constitute duplications of what remains "once and for all" a perfect offering.

Book Four: Sacraments and the satisfaction of the members

In the *De veritate*, Thomas employed a striking Pauline phrase, "Christ and the Church are 'quasi' one person," in order to establish the ground for Christ's merit. Similarly, in the *Summa contra gentiles*, Aquinas places a consistent emphasis on the dignity of the person of the incarnate God; and this continues his personalist perspective on the satisfaction of Christ. For example, when he refers to the death of Christ as a kind of universal cause of salvation ("quasi quaedam universalis causa salutis"), he compares the effects of Christ's death to those effected by Adam's sin. But the Church must apply a universal cause to many individual cases. According to one tradition in the Church, carnal intercourse accounts for the application of Adam's sin to his progeny.[17] On the contrary, Aquinas explains the application of the effects Christ's death to the members through a sort of spiritual regeneration ("per spiritualem regenerationem"), which both joins us to ("conjungitur") and incorporates us into ("incorporatur") Christ himself.[18] In this, we recognize his efforts to appropriate the Pauline and Johannine teaching on the body of Christ.

The sacraments also figure in this ecclesiological vision. In fact, Aquinas considers the sacraments as so many "effects of the incarnation." Thus he recognizes their principal importance in the

Christian life. For example, although baptism inaugurates new life in Christ for the believer, sinners should still seek union with Christ by the dedication of a rectified will ("studium bonae voluntatis"). This reference obviously refers to the life of virtues, gifts of the Holy Spirit, and Beatitudes which develop as a result of sacramental incorporation into Christ. Furthermore, although Christ has cleansed the world of original sin and its definitive results, still those born into the world bear the effects of original sin in their psyches and bodies. Thus God's plan includes the sacraments of salvation, especially penance, as means for growth in faith. The Christian believer then adheres to the person of Christ, thereby freely choosing to follow his direction. In other terms, to use Aquinas's own phrase, Christ becomes for each of his members an authentic personal good ("personale bonum").[19]

Thomas further explains this dynamic in the context of the sacrament of baptism, where he clearly indicates the divine initiative operative in the personal salvation histories of believers.

> Our union ("conjunctio") with Christ in baptism is not a result of our operation, as if originating from within us (since nothing generates itself as such), but a result of Christ's operation, in whom we have been born anew to a living hope. The remission of sins in baptism is accomplished, then, by the power of Christ himself perfectly and fully joining us to himself. Thus not only the stain of sin is removed, but the debt of punishment is also absolved (IV, c. 72).

By the same token, Thomas also indicates a difference between baptism and penance with respect to their diverse effects on the temporal punishment due to sin. Baptism removes all the temporal punishment due to sin. This represents the power of Christ, which predominates in every sacramental action. Penance, on the other hand, leaves certain penalties incumbent on the penitent. This points to the need for a progressive reformation of the image of God, which Christ also achieves in the penitent.[20] But even in this case, the absolute priority of the divine action in each believer's life can work according to its own design. Thus, Thomas again refers to the case of one whose psychological turning toward God and to the merits of Christ ("conversio mentis in Deum et ad meritum Christi") coupled with his detestation for sin itself suffices to cancel entirely the debt of sin.

Finally, Thomas discusses holy anointing. In this sacrament, the priest can validate past sufferings as well as virtuous actions into proper satisfaction for the sins confessed at the end of one's life. Still, he does not counsel us to delay satisfaction nor persuade us that satisfaction remains optional. On the contrary, he urges that we ponder the rewards or punishments that await us immediately after death and therefore emphasizes the importance of penitential satisfaction as a means of preparing oneself for eternal glory. Since the vision of God totally exceeds our natural faculties, no one can be admitted to glory without such purification. Thus, we choose either satisfaction now or purgation later.[21] Spiritual torpor offers no advantages in Aquinas's convictions about the spiritual life.

Summary

The emphasis of the *Summa contra gentiles* on Christ's great love and on the high dignity of his person controls Thomas's theology of satisfaction. To be sure, satisfaction for the temporal punishment due to sin remains both fitting and required, but the power of Christ's love for the sinner prevails over the medicinal purposes of Christian satisfaction. When the sinner turns to Christ as a "personal good," this action transforms satisfaction from an expression of penitence into an authentic act of reconciliation. Such a conversion on the part of a repentant sinner establishes an attachment to God that remains the goal of Christ's salvific work and the consummation of spiritual regeneration.

This development clearly marks an advance from the juridical model which controls Aquinas's use of satisfaction materials in the *Scriptum*. In the *Summa contra gentiles*, Thomas remains focused upon the dignity of the person of the incarnate God and the intensity of his love. Can we explain this development? Two factors suggest possible avenues of investigation. First, we know that during the composition of the *Summa* Aquinas became exposed to several fresh theological influences. During his stay at the papal court, for example, he had the chance to develop a renewed interest in Eastern theology.[22] We owe the composition of *Contra errores Graecorum*, begun at the request of Urban IV to help with ecumenical discussion, to this exposure. Scholars agree moreover that the composition of the *Contra errores Graecorum* precedes that of the fourth book of the *Summa contra gentiles*.[23] Byzantine thought and its characteristic emphasis on divinization and spiritual theology more than compensate for the juridical attitude of satisfaction and morals bequeathed to Aquinas by the western tradition. In the *Summa contra gentiles* we see results of this theological alembic.

Other new sources of theology also figure in the development of his thought. For at the same time that Thomas began the composition of the *Contra errores Graecorum*, he also began a "glossa continua" on the four gospels. The *Catena aurea* still remains a valuable commentary on the Scriptures. Before he begins the gloss on Mark, Luke, and John (completed sometime after the death of Urban IV in 1264), Thomas explains his method: "That this commentary may be more complete and have more continuity, I have had many works of the Greek doctors translated into Latin, and I have added extracts of them to the commentaries of the Latins, being careful to place the names of the authors before their testimonies (*Catena aurea, Expositio in Marcum,* introduction).[24] To be sure, the date of composition for the *Catena aurea* (1262/63-1267) does not allow us to assume that Thomas was actually working on it at exactly the same time as the *Summa contra gentiles* (1259-1264). On the other hand, he was at least actively engaged in collecting and examining patristic sources, especially commentaries on the New Testament. This fresh look at the Word of God also undoubtedly influenced his theology in the *Summa contra gentiles.*

In addition, we recognize a different perspective on theological method evident in the opening pages of the *Contra gentiles*. For there Aquinas urges prayerful meditation on the revealed mysteries of the Christian faith as an indispensable starting point for understanding them. Thus, Chenu describes *Summa contra gentiles* as a "work of contemplation of truth" inspired, for example, by Hilary of Poitiers' *De Trinitate.*[25]

> Undertake in faith, move ahead, be persistent. You will not reach the end, I know, but I shall congratulate myself on your progress. For he who pursues the infinite in piety of mind will always become more proficient as he goes onwards, even if, as will happen, his efforts do not always succeed. But do not betake yourself into that mystery, do not plunge yourself into the arcanum of that unending nativity, presuming to comprehend the sum total of intelligence; understand, rather, that those things are incomprehensible (*Summa contra gentiles* I, c. 8).

Above all, Thomas's mature and meditative reflection upon the sources of theology led him to emphasize charity's role in both christological satisfaction and in satisfaction by the members. In addition to the scriptures, these sources include the patristic authors of both east and west. By this time, Aquinas had reached theological maturity.

De Rationibus Fidei: Satisfaction and the Humility of the Suffering Servant

In contrast to the emphasis on the dignity of the incarnate Word and the charity of Christ, the *De rationibus fidei* takes another approach to the issue of satisfaction.[26] Aquinas wrote this work in response to a request from an anonymous cantor in Antioch for theological help. The cantor's questions direct Aquinas to specific issues relative to satisfaction, especially the humility of the Suffering Servant and the institute of justice. In this text, Thomas explains the folly of the cross and the wisdom of God in a way reminiscent of St Paul's discussion in I Corinthians 1:18. He especially wants to show that for the Word of God to suffer and die for our salvation involves no affront to common sense. In short, he must explain the fittingness of the kenosis.[27]

Thomas first explains how a poor, humble, and obedient Christ eminently suits the accomplishment of man's salvation. Indeed, the earthly life of the incarnate God embodies a judgment on our inordinate attachment to material riches, which only obstruct the attainment of our final goal. Christ's poverty and sufferings, moreover, set an example for us. They instruct us and confirm the divine character of Christ's message. Then Thomas accounts for the poor circumstances of Christ's life and the bodily weaknesses which he endured. These help us measure temporal fortunes and misfortunes, since by his willing acceptance of death Christ taught us not to allow any difficulty, not even the fear of death itself, to keep us from following a life of virtue.

The incarnate Word teaches us concretely by his human words. Christ confirmed his teaching by miracles to insure that we would accept it not as just another human teaching but as a divine truth from God. The poverty of Christ, of course, meant that he had no human resources, and thus the miracles he performed could only be the result of divine power. As a result, those who actually witnessed the miracles could hardly conclude that they were the products of human power. So they would be more disposed to listen and accept the teaching of the poor Christ as an authentic revelation. All in all, the example set by the poor life of Christ and the credibility which his poverty gave to his teaching provides reason enough to establish the fittingness of the "kenosis." Anyone who refuses to accept the wisdom manifest in the incarnation, concludes Thomas (in an exceptional remark), must have a head harder than rock, because at the death of Christ even the rocks were split asunder.

Thomas pursues this discussion by establishing a connection between the "kenosis" of the Word and the motive for the incarnation. Since Christ redeems us by sharing our infirmities and uniting those infirmities to divine life, the power of God can shine through human weakness. Thus, Christ at once liberates us from the sin of pride and disobedience whereby Adam preferred himself to God and also teaches us humility, namely, that we must not prefer ourselves to God's glory. Humility also leads us to trust in God for the blessings which the incarnate Word achieves by his death. In this way, concludes Thomas, an authentic order of human justice emerges since we realize that the creature remains entirely subject to God.

But there remains another aspect of the order of justice that Aquinas considers. For he links the discussion of the poverty of Christ to the satisfaction of Christ. First, he explains that the order of justice demands a certain balance, "as when a judge takes from him who, having received the goods of another, has more than he ought to have, and gives what has been taken to someone who has less" (*De rationibus fidei* 7 [160-64]). Likewise sin indulges a created will at the expense of right reason and the eternal law. To right the balance requires some form of punishment either by suffering an evil or giving up some good. Aquinas accordingly establishes the anthropological grounds for satisfaction. And from there he moves to the christological argument.

First, given that the entire human race was under the guilt of sin, only some penalty could right the balance of justice. Then Aquinas repeats the Anselmian formula pointing to the need for a God-man to perform the required satisfaction. Thomas concludes by asserting that the Saracens' contention that God should have saved us without human satisfaction or should have preserved us from sin altogether fails for two reasons. First, the order of justice requires that one make satisfaction for an offense. Second, human nature, which endows man with freedom of choice, obliges us to approve punishment for the blameworthy just as it requires reward for the praiseworthy. Thus a marvelous wisdom manifests itself in the way God's providence orders the course of salvation history. Thomas writes:

> In all of this does the wisdom of God especially make itself manifest since through the incarnation and death of his Son God both preserved the order of justice as well as the dignity of human nature and at the same time mercifully provided a remedy for the salvation of man (*De rationibus fidei* 7 [224-8]).

The humbling of the Word of God, concretely manifested in the poverty of the Savior's earthly life, discloses the reparation of Adam's unjust pride and disobedience. God's wisdom triumphs in the unexpected and diminutive features of Jesus of Nazareth's human history. To this model, satisfaction draws us.

Compendium Theologiae: Summary of Basic Teaching

The *Compendium theologiae* constitutes an abbreviated course in Christian doctrine.[28] Although we discover recapitulations of Thomas's teaching on christological satisfaction, the work does not mark a decided advance in his theology. Still, Chenu insists on the importance, for example, of the ordering of questions in the *Compendium* as a means towards a fuller understanding of Thomas's doctrine.[29] So, for instance, although Chapter 200 repeats what already has been said concerning the question: "That only an incarnate God ought to have restored human nature", still the context makes a difference. For in the previous chapter, Thomas gives two reasons: First, we would not be able to arrive at perfect beatitude unless the infection of sin were removed. Second, we need help consistently to seek good and avoid evil. Neither Adam nor any "homo purus" could restore human nature since no individual's worth compensates for a sin which affects the whole of the human race. Likewise, no "homo purus" can cause grace. Even the angels, by reason of their gratuitous call to beatitude, could not repair human nature. God alone can save man ("potest"). God, however, could not ignore or bypass the demands of the "ordo justitiae." Thus Christ alone fulfills the conditions required for satisfaction.

In Chapter 226, Aquinas treats the physical and psychic limitations accepted by Christ in light of his salvific mission. Thomas repeats the Aristotelian principle that one friend can suffer a penalty for another friend since love is a kind of unitive force which makes two individuals a kind of whole. Granted that no single individual can make condign satisfaction, still Christ, the incarnate Son, can satisfy. An angel could not serve as such a friend for us since angels lack the infinite dignity required to repair an offense that involves something of the infinite inasmuch as it offends God. Again, because sins merit punishment, the human nature assumed by Christ must be able to suffer whatever punishments we owe. But two kinds of punishment result from sin: Satisfactory punishments which can draw us closer to God and chastisements which serve to separate us from God. Clearly Christ did not take on the latter category of punishment, which includes sins such as ignorance, disordered passions, and the like. But Christ did assume those defects which make the endurance of satisfactory punishment possible. These include whatever ordinary human sufferings form part of our human nature or what the saints call the non-embarrassing defects. In any event, Christ's defects remain ordered to his salvific purposes.

In Chapter 227, Thomas continues the discussion of Christ's death on the cross. Besides assuming the defects that allow a God-man to suffer, Christ actually had to undergo his passion and death. Aquinas summarizes Christ's intentions in dying. First, to make satisfaction for our sins ("remedium satisfactionis"); second, to be a sacrament of salvation ("salutis sacramentum"); and third, to give an exceptional example of virtue, especially charity, patience, fortitude, and obedience ("exemplum perfectae virtutis").

In Chapter 228, Thomas underscores the importance attached to the mystery of the cross by repeating three purposes. But he also includes two allegorical interpretations to emphasize his points: (1) that Christ our friend really satisfied for all our sins; (2) at the same time he paid a debt which he himself did not owe. Thus, quoting the Wisdom of Solomon 11:17: "One is punished by the very things by which he sins", he refers to the death of Christ on the wood of the cross as satisfaction for the sin which Adam accomplished through the instrumentality of the wood of the tree of the knowledge of good and evil. Next Aquinas puts the words of Psalm 69:4, "What I did not steal must I pay back?", on the lips of Christ. In addition, Chapter 231 describes other bodily sufferings of Christ which he endured in satisfying for the sin of Adam. These include those punishments which derive from our wounded nature, such as hunger, thirst, and weariness, as well as those which befall us, such as wounds and beatings.

Motivated by the text of I Corinthians 13:13, Aquinas intended to organize the *Compendium theologiae* into three parts, each dealing with one of the theological virtues-- faith, hope, and charity. For he judged that every perfection of the present life consists in the exercise of these virtues. Although he finished the first section of his project, he did not complete the work as planned. In section one, however, he treats the elements of systematic theology where the discussion of Christ's satisfaction appears in the context of original sin, the incarnation, and the passion and death of Christ. This work still serves as a compact summary of the principal arguments found in the *Summa theologiae*.

Satisfactory Acts of the Members

Satisfaction plays an essential role in the Christian life. For this reason, Aquinas recognizes that satisfactory works also form an integral part of religious life. For example, *De perfectione spiritualis vitae, Quaestio de quodlibet* III, and the disputed question *De caritate* each discusses Christian satisfaction within the context of the evangelical counsels, i.e., poverty, chastity, and obedience. Furthermore, since satisfaction also pertains to the rite of penance and the granting of indulgences, Aquinas raises these issues in *Quaestio de quodlibet* III and II. The quodlibetal questions, since they deal with practical theology, especially provide new perspectives on the purposes and goals of satisfaction in the Church. In these theological essays one also finds emerging the distinctive personalist perspective characteristic of Aquinas's mature work.

Satisfaction and the Perfection of Charity

The *De perfectione spiritualis vitae*, a treatise on spiritual theology and religious life, undertakes to explain why we can consider religious life itself as an eminently satisfactory work.[30] Thomas first cites the authority of both St Augustine and Cicero, who explain the meaning of the word "religion" as pertaining to the worship of God. Then, drawing from Gregory the Great's commentary on Ezekiel, Aquinas explains that sacrifice gives worship to God in one of two forms.

There is a difference between sacrifices and holocaust. While every holocaust is a sacrifice, not every sacrifice is a holocaust: in a simple sacrifice it is the custom to use only a part of the animal; when it is a question of a holocaust the entire heifer is offered up. When, therefore, someone vows one thing to God, but holds something else back, that is a sacrifice; when, on the contrary, he vows to God everything that he has, all that with which he lives, all that he knows, that is a holocaust (*De perfectione spiritualis vitae* 12 [36-49].

Thomas concludes that since those who pronounce the vows of poverty, chastity, and obedience dedicate themselves to God in a total way, we fittingly refer to them as religious. Why? Because such religious men and women make of themselves living holocausts, thereby performing a supreme act of the virtue of religion.

But in the Old Testament we also discover other kinds of sacrifices, including the sin-offering. Religious life also fulfills the command to satisfy for sin, imposed even on the saints of the old dispensation. Since holocaust forms a perfect sacrifice, the vows of religion remain means whereby those who pronounce them can make perfect satisfaction to God ("perfecte homo Deo satisfacit"). Accordingly, religious life forms both a state of perfect charity and a state of perfect penitence. Hence the Church does not impose religious life as a satisfaction on even the most serious sinner, even if, as Aquinas insists, the vowed life transcends all other satisfactions. On the other hand, we can imagine a case where one might be counseled to enter religious life rather than bear an even heavier burden of satisfaction such as would be imposed if the sinner remained in secular life. At one time, in fact, this was actually part of the practice of the Church.[31]

Quaestio de quodlibet III, q. 5, a. 3 again considers whether sinners should enter religious life.[32] But now Aquinas advances reasons which explain the advantages of religious life for those who have sinned. Among the principal reasons which he adduces is satisfaction's twofold medicinal function, namely, healing sin's wounds and strengthening us against sin in the future. Granted the perfect state of penitence which religious life embodies, no other satisfaction is comparable to the penances performed by those in religion. Furthermore, no better protection can be found against committing sin in the future than religious life. Aquinas holds firmly to this position. "It is stupid," he writes (in a rare mood of exasperation), "to say that someone who is weaker because of sins committed in the past should not seek out a securer life style" (*Quaestio de quodlibet* III, q. 5, a. 3, ad 1). Of course, religious life points beyond the penitential aspect of satisfaction to a life of steady union with God. Aquinas explains this important point as follows:

> It is difficult for those in the world not to be enticed by the world's riches. Chrysostom, commenting on Matthew 19:23-24, says that the Lord is teaching that a rich man who clings to his possessions with inordinate attachment ("per amorem") will not enter the kingdom of heaven, and that a rich man who has many possessions will do so only with difficulty (*Quaestio de quodlibet* III, q. 5, a. 3).

Thus satisfactory acts (in this case religious poverty) both atone for sin and dispose us for that charity which merits eternal life.

De caritate q. 1, a. 11, also raises the question of the relationship between charity and the vows of religion.[33] Are we all obliged to possess perfect charity? Aquinas replies that the perfection of Christian life chiefly consists in charity which remains a virtue of the will ("ad interiorem mentis dispositionem, et praecipue in actu caritatis"). From a different perspective, however, the perfection of Christian life also consists in certain external things, such as virginity and poverty. Thomas goes on to offer three reasons why even external goods belong to the perfection of charity. First, they remove whatever impediments exist to loving God freely. Thus, for example, "poverty belongs to perfection only inasmuch as it disposes one to follow Christ" (*De caritate* q. 1, a. 11, ad 5). Second, they manifest the effects of charity in the soul, such as we observe in one who loves God perfectly and therefore diligently avoids those things that can separate him from God. Third, for reasons already established elsewhere, religious life constitutes perfect satisfaction for sin.

Aquinas enunciates an important distinction here, one which applies, moreover, to all kinds of satisfactory actions. External actions as such, for instance, fasting, almsgiving, social welfare involvement, and so forth, embody the perfection of Christian living only in a derived sense. In fact, we measure their value according to the ways in which such actions relate to the principal perfection of eternal life, namely, the soul's adhering to God in charity. For this reason, Aquinas explains:

> Whence it does not follow that the poorer a man is the more perfect he is. Perfection in such things should be measured by reference to that in which perfection principally consists. Accordingly, a man would be said to be more perfect whose poverty drew him further away from earthly occupations and made it easier for him to serve God (*De caritate* q, 1, a. 11, ad 5).

To be sure, the hardships of religious life, such as poverty and celibacy, do promote the medicinal benefits of satisfaction and atone as well for past sins. Even so, these satisfactory actions only dispose us to maintain a personal union with God. The perfection of the Christian life prevails in the theological virtues, especially charity. In other terms, religious life demonstrates that satisfaction and charity combine to complete the Christian mystery.

Sacramental Satisfaction

A Prayer for Penitents

Aquinas also considers satisfaction in the context of penance. In *Quaestio de quodlibet* III, q. 13, a. 1, he asks whether a certain prayer added by the priest after the formula of sacramental absolution in fact constitutes an extension of the sacramental satisfaction. In this, Thomas is addressing a question of practical importance, since the medieval rite of penance included a prayer asking that "whatever good you do be the cause for the remission of your sins."[34]   Although the wording of the petition seems to imply a sacramental satisfaction, it nonetheless leaves the specification of the penance vague.   Since the discipline of penance requires that the priest impose a specific penance, the practice appears to pose a difficulty.   Still, Aquinas maintains that even satisfaction of an undetermined kind qualifies as sacramental if, through an exercise of the power of the keys ("ex vi clavium"), the priest places it under the power of the sacrament.

Based on Matthew 16:19, the "power of the keys" represents the sacramental efficacy of penance. In the *Summa contra gentiles* IV, c. 72, Thomas explains this theological idiom by reference to the grace of Christ.   The power of the keys (exercised in penance) derives its full efficacy from the passion of Christ.   Since Thomas allows for the removal of punishment either by the power of the keys or, as we have seen, through the penitent's superabundant sorrow, he can interpret the prayer after the absolution as a means of extending the benefits of Christ's cross even to every good act subsequently performed by the penitent.   Accordingly, the importance he assigns to the mediation of Christ's passion in the sacraments, especially through the power of the keys, provides the reason behind his welcome flexibility with regard to imposing a determined penance. It also explains his frequent counsel that a priest impose a light penance in order to sustain the penitent's desire to draw more closely into the mystery of Christ's forgiveness. In short, Thomas prefers to emphasize the healing effects of penance, accomplished by the repentant sinner's personal union with Christ and commitment to the power of his death realized in the sacrament.   He holds the juridical requirement that a priest match a given sin with a determined penance as secondary in the theological explanation of the sacrament.   Thus he urges priests to add the prayer "Whatever good you do" when imposing a penance in the confessional because "even though such undetermined satisfaction might not be of great efficacy for guarding against future sin, nonetheless, as a sacramental satisfaction, it will expiate for past sins because of the power of the keys" (*Quaestio de quodlibet* III q. 13, a. 1).

The Dead Crusader

In another quodlibetal debate, Aquinas considers the case of satisfaction and the dead crusader. *Quaestio de quodlibet* II q. 8, a. 2 asks whether grounds exist to allow the benefits of an indulgence for one who accepts the crusader's cross, receives the papal indulgence granting full remission of sins, but dies before he reaches the Holy Land and therefore prior to sustaining the hardships of the crusade.

The crusader has fulfilled the legal requirements expressed in the papal bull, namely, that one be truly sorry for and confess past sins, but he has not completed the penitential work for which the Church grants the indulgence.[35] The question undoubtedly reflects a pastoral situation current in the 13th-century, which may include the fate of the French king Louis XIII who died while setting out for his second crusade.

The opening arguments persuade us that the crusader should receive the full benefits of the indulgence since he had fulfilled the requirements of the papal bull which promises remission of all punishment due to sin. But Thomas first quotes St Augustine's adage, "it is one thing to take out the arrow, another to heal the wound." He interprets "taking out the arrow" to mean the remission of sin and "healing the wound" as a reference to the image-restoration ("reformationem imaginis"). Of course, image-restoration requires satisfaction. Thus, Aquinas provisionally argues that a crusader who dies before suffering the burdens of the crusade avoids satisfaction and, therefore, cannot enter immediately into glory.

On the other hand, we know that one friend can satisfy for another. But now Aquinas introduces a new concept into the theology of satisfaction, namely, the collective merits of Christ and of the saints. Theologians earlier referred to the satisfaction of Christ and the saints as a kind of treasury ("thesaurus") for the Church.[36] This allows Thomas to suggest a better fate for the unfortunate crusader.

> Christ shed his blood for the Church and did and underwent many other things whose worth is of infinite value because of the dignity of his person. Likewise all the other saints had the intention that those things which they did and suffered for God would be useful not only for themselves but for the whole Church (*Quaestio de quodlibet* III q. 13, a. 1).

The one who presides in the Church, principally the Pope, can dispense benefits from this "thesaurus" to anyone united through charity with the Church. Thus, the crusader can benefit from what the indulgence promises even if he himself does not suffer the hardships of the crusade. But what power effects the required reformation in the crusader who had not yet "learned obedience through what he suffered" (Hebrews 5:8)? Aquinas replies that "the passion of Christ and of the other saints is imputed to such a one as if he had suffered sufficiently for the remission of his sins."[37] In other words, the indulgence itself eliminates the need for satisfaction ("cedit in locum satisfactionis").

In order to clarify this line of argumentation, Aquinas recalls the distinction between the medicinal and vindicative purposes of satisfaction. Satisfactory deeds remain ordered to the restoration of the image of God in the believer, which principally requires the healing or preventative functions of satisfactory deeds. Although the indulgence satisfies for the vindicative aspect of satisfaction, namely, the remission of all punishment due to sin, it cannot substitute for satisfaction's medicinal effects. To put it differently, the indulgence does not uproot the causes and enticements which lead to sin in the first place since only the actual working out of satisfaction ("labor satisfactionis") can accomplish this. Accordingly, Thomas encourages crusaders who survive the battle freely to take on satisfactory acts for the sake of their own work of image-restoration. In any case, such medicinal effects of satisfaction are unnecessary for one who is dying; it is the liberation from the debt of punishment that is important for him.

However, there is an ambiguity in the text at this point. Although Aquinas refers to the healing role of satisfaction as a "labor satisfactionis," he also seems to diminish the importance of actually undergoing such labors. For example, after stating that crusaders should undertake such satisfactory acts as precaution against sin in the future, he adds, "Nor is any burdensome labor required for this" ("nec ad hoc requiritur aliquis labor"). The reason given for this apparently contradictory assertion is that the "labor" of Christ's passion suffices. It might be that, by appealing to the burden of Christ's own sufferings, imputed by jurisdiction to the crusader, Aquinas exempts the latter from the normal medieval external forms of satisfaction which are directed towards the always-necessary self-reformation. This could be seen in terms of public penitential pilgrimages, etc. which a man on a boat, armed with a papal bull, need not undertake. Or it could be that Thomas is simply referring to that lightening of his burden which a man united to the passion of Christ by the sacrament of penance would experience as he undertook the task of self-reformation. All in all, as Aquinas's developed doctrine of satisfaction clearly shows, Christ remains the source of all spiritual integrity in the Church.

NOTES

1. Augustine writes: "Duobus enim modis appellare malum solemus: uno, cum male quemque fecisse dicimus, alio, cum mali aliquid esse perpessum." See his *De libero arbitrio* I c. 1, 1 (*Corpus Christianorum, Series Latina*, Vol. 29, 212). We also find the distinction employed by Peter Lombard, see *Sententiae* II, d. 35, c. 6 (536): "Aliud est enim culpa, alius poena. Alterum est Dei, id est poena; alterum diaboli vel hominis, id est culpa." Aquinas, however, will interpret punishment from God in terms of the intrinsic moral meaning which the Eternal Law establishes in the universe.

2. See *Scriptum* II d. 34, q. 1 for this first attempt to put Augustine's distinction to work in a theological context.

3. Edition used: *Quaestio disputata de malo* (Turin: Marietti, 1953).

4. The text appears in *De malo* q. 1, a. 4, *sed contra*. But the patristic source, *De fide ad Petrum*, c. 21, was written by the North African bishop Fulgentius of Ruspe (c.462-527)

5. Augustine writes in *Confessionum* I, c. 13 (*PL* 32: 670): "Jussisti enim, et sic est, ut poena sua sibi sit omnis inordinatus animus."

6. Edition used: *Quaestiones disputatae de veritate*, Leonine edition, vol 22 (Rome, in three parts, 1972-76).

7. *Glossa ordinaria* at Jn 3:34 (*PL* 114:370): "Hominibus dat ad mensuram, filio non dat ad mensuram, sed sicut totum ex seipso toto genuit Filium suum, ita incarnato Filio suo totum spiritum suum dedit, non particulatim, non per subdivisiones, sed generaliter et universaliter." Although once attributed to Walafrid Strabo (808-849), the *Glossa ordinaria* represents a compilation of the 12th-century, drawing in part from earlier authors. It was adopted by the Parisian masters as their standard guide or commentary on the Bible. For further information, see Smalley, 31-45.

8. Since this text enunciates a basic principle of Thomas's ecclesiology, we give it in full: "Christus et Ecclesia sunt quasi una persona; sed ratione unitatis praedictae ex persona Ecclesiae loquitur, ut patet in glossa super Psal. 'Deus, Deus meus, respice in me;' ergo et similiter ratione unitatis praedictae Christum quasi ex persona aliorum mereri potuit." *De veritate* q. 29, a. 3, ad 4). Augustine and Irenaeus also emphasized the unity of the Church in similar ways.

9. See IIIa q. 2, a. 1. There Aquinas emphasizes the need for a personal interpretation of the union that escapes both the several theories of accidental union favored by divisive christologies and, on

the other hand, the view that the union occurs in the natures, with its reverberations of confusion and distortion in either the divine or human nature.

10. For more information on this theme, see Thomas Potvin, *The Theology of the Primacy of Christ according to Saint Thomas and its Scriptural Foundations* (Fribourg: Editions Universitaires, 1973). Also, John Boyle, "The Structural Setting of Thomas Aquinas's Theology of the Grace of Christ as he is Head of the Church in the *Summa theologiae*" (University of Toronto: Unpublished doctoral dissertation, 1989).

11. Aquinas points indirectly to the natural law, the participation by the rational creature in the Eternal Law. God's wisdom, which Trinitarian theology appropriates to the Logos/Son, establishes the moral order as a matter of native finality and appetite in the human person. Human freedom remains, for Aquinas, a characteristic, but not an absolute goal, of each one's personal appropriation of the theological life.

12. The early Alexandrian christologists, for example, refused to acknowledge any kind of change in Christ. Thus, Clement of Alexandria, *Miscellanies*, n. 9 (*PG* 9:921): "For he ate, not for the sake of the body, which was kept together by a holy energy, but in order that it might not enter into the minds of those who were with him to entertain a different opinion of him. . . . But he was entirely impassible, inaccessible to any movement of feeling either pleasure or pain."

13. Edition used: *Summa contra gentiles*, Leonine edition, vols. 13 - 15 (Rome, 1918-1930) as published in *Liber de veritate catholicae fidei contra errores infidelium*, vols. 2,3 (Turin: Marietti, 1961).

14. In general, Aquinas emphasized the importance of justice and equivalence in his treatment of satisfaction in the *Scriptum*. Even when he speaks about one friend satisfying for another, he remains conscious of the remedial benefits of satisfaction which risk being lost for the guilty party. For more information on this point, see Joseph Lécuyer, C.S.Sp., "Prolégomènes thomistes à la théologie de la satisfaction," *Studi Tomistici* (Rome: Cittá Nuova Ed., 1974), 82-103.

15. Aristotle actually makes this point in his discussion of the virtuous action: "What is possible is what we could achieve through our agency [including what our friends could achieve for us]; for what our friends achieve is in a way, achieved through our agency, since the origin is in us." *Nicomachean Ethics* III, c. 3 (1112b27-29).

16. A comparative analysis of the arguments found in the *Scriptum* with those in the *Summa contra gentiles* discloses that Aquinas now

treats entirely new material. Only the question of the hypothetical angel as redeemer remains from the earlier discussion.

17. For a thorough presentation of this topic, see T.C. O'Brien, *Original Sin* (1a2ae. 81-85), Vol. 26 (New York: McGraw-Hill, 1965), especially appendices 1,3,7.

18. See *Summa contra gentiles* IV, c. 55, ad 6. In this, he follows the lead of St Augustine who recognized the fulfillment of this total Church in heaven: "Adiungitur ista Ecclesia, quae nunc peregrina est, illi coelesti Ecclesiae, ubi Angelos cives habemus . . . et fit una Ecclesia, civitas Regni mundi" (*Sermo* 341.9.11 [*PL* 39:1500]).

19. See *Summa contra gentiles* IV, c. 55, ad 7. In fact, personal union with Christ forms the heart of Aquinas's spirituality. Since he recognized the importance of the human psychology for theology and life, Aquinas develops a spiritual doctrine which encourages use of both heart and mind as instruments of divine union.

20. The same doctrine appears in the *De articulis fidei*, 2 [# 616]: "Effectus autem Baptismi est remissio culpae originalis et actualis, et etiam totius culpae et poenae, ita quod baptizatis non est aliqua satisfactio iniungenda pro peccatis praeteritis, sed statim morientes post baptismum introducuntur ad gloriam Dei. Unde effectus Baptismi ponitur apertio ianuae paradisi." Edition used: *De articulis fidei et sacramentis ecclesiae ad archepiscopum Panormitanum* (Turin: Marietti, 1954). For further information on this work, see Weisheipl, 392-3.

21. See *Summa contra gentiles* IV, c. 73. This religious intuition animated the life and doctrine of Thérèse of Lisieux who wished to offer herself as a holocaust to God's merciful love. At the same time, the Little Flower emphasized the triumph of love in this sacrifice. See Philippe de la Trinité, "Le thomise de Sainte Thérèse de l'Enfant-Jésus en matière de Rédemption," *Vie Theresienne* 8 (Oct., 1962), 1-8.

22. For further information, see I. Backes, *Die Christologie des hl. Thomas von Aquin und die grieschen Kirchenväter* (Paderborn, 1931). Also, Gottfried Geenen, O.P., "The Council of Chalcedon in the Theology of Saint Thomas," *From an Abundant Spring* (New York: P.J. Kenedy & Sons, 1952), 172-217. Finally, I.T. Eschmann explains: "It seems that in the first part of [Aquinas's] Italian sojourn, in the years of Urban IV, Thomas, in a way, discovered Greek theology, the part it played in theology, and the consequences which would ensue, if it were neglected, as indeed it was neglected, in a theology that was nourished by Latin thought." Cited in Weisheipl, 173.

23. For further information, see H. Dondaine, O.P., "Le *Contra Errores Grecorum* de S. Thomas et le IVe livre du *Contra Gentiles*," *Revue des Sciences Philosophique et Théoloqiques* 30 (1941-1942), 156-58.

24. "Beginning with the *Glossa in Marcum*, Saint Thomas's research in Greek Patristic sources becomes more and more intense. For the purpose of broadening the range of his information, he procured new translations of certain Greek Fathers. Because of this research into Greek theological sources, the *Catena* marks a turning point in the development of Aquinas's theology as well as in the history of Catholic dogma." See, I.T. Eschmann, "A Catalogue of St. Thomas's Works," in Etienne Gilson, *The Christian Philosophy of St. Thomas Aquinas*, trans L.K. Shook (New York: Random House, 1956), 397.

25. Chenu, 295. Hilary of Poitiers (c. 315-67), whose *De Trinitate* in 12 books earned him the title, Athanasius of the West, was a 4th-century bishop in France and adversary of the Arian heresy there.

26. Edition used: *De rationibus fidei contra Saracenos, Graecos et Armenos ad Cantorem Antiochiae*, Leonine edition, vol. 40 (Rome, 1968).

27. The *kenosis* refers to the fact that Christ abandoned his heavenly riches (the usual metaphor for divine glory and possessions, the state of Christ in his divine existence) and has made himself poor (as a member of the human race) in order to gain heavenly rewards and blessings for mankind. See, Lucien Cerfaux, *Christ in the Theology of St. paul*, trans G. Webb and A. Walker (New York: Herder & Herder, 1966).

28. Edition used: *Compendium theologiae ad Reginaldum socium suum* (Turin: Marietti, 1954). [ET: *Compendium of Theology*, trans C. Vollert (St. Louis: B. Herder, 1947)]

29. Chenu, 332.

30. Edition used: *De perfectione spiritualis vitae*, Leonine edition, vol. 41 (Rome, 1970), B69-B111. [ET: *The Religious State, the Episcopate, and the Priestly Office*, trans J. Procter (Westminster, MD: Newman, 1950)]

31. Aquinas records a case in *Quaestiones quodlibetales* III, q. 5, a. 3: "Stephenus Papa quemdam uxorem interfecerat, inducit ut ingrediatur monasterium, et humiliatus sub manu Abbatis cunta observet quae tibi fuerint imperata, alioquin iniungit ei gravissimam poentitentiam, si eligit in saeculo remanere."

32. Edition used: *Quaestiones de quodlibet I-XII*, ed. R. M. Spiazzi (Turin: Marietti, 1956). [ET: *Quodlibetal Questions 1 and 2*, trans Sandra Edwards (Toronto: Pontifical Institute of Mediaeval Studies, 1983).

33. Edition used: *De caritate* in *Quaestiones disputatae*, ed P.A. Odetto (Turin: Marietti, 1949), 2:754-91 [ET: *On Charity*, trans L.H. Kendzierski (Milwaukee: Marquette, 1960)]

34. We still find this prayer in the revised *Rite of Penance*, n. 93.

35. For further information on the question of indulgences and the crusades, see Maureen Purcell, O.P., *Papal Crusading Policy. The Chief Instruments of Papal Crusading Policy and Crusade to the Holy Land from the final loss of Jerusalem to the fall of Acre, 1244-1291*, Studies in the History of Christian Thought, ed. Heiko A. Oberman (Leiden: E.J. Brill, 1975).

36. For further information, see Carl J. Peter, "The Church's Treasure ("Thesauri Ecclesiae") Then and Now," *Theological Studies* 47 (1986), 251-72.

37. This employment of satisfaction actually refers back to the original context within which the term gained currency for theology. For more information, see Jean Rivière, "Sur les premières applications du terme 'satisfactio' à l'oeuvre du Christ," *Bulletin de Littérature Ecclésiastique* 25 (1924), 285-97; 353-69. The *Sacramentum Veronese*, 8, 35, ed. L.C. Mohlberg (Rome: Herder, 1966), 17 contains a reference to the merits of the saints as grounds for granting the petitions of the Christian community: "Uere dignum: prostrato corde poscentes, ut quamuis tanta sint nostra facinora, quibus etiam cum innumeribus sanctorum suffragiis laboremus, tu tamen inmensa pietate concedas, ne scelera magis nostra praeualeant quam satisfactio pro nobis copiosa justorum."

CHAPTER V

"FOR THE WORSHIP OF HIS GLORY"

Summa theologiae Ia-IIae: Punishment as Restorative

Sin and Punishment

In his catechetical work *Jacob and the Happy Life*, St Ambrose exclaims: "My guilt became for me the cause of redemption, through which Christ came to me."[1] The paradox of the fortunate fault, as Milton's *Paradise Lost* reminds us, controls a Christian view of history.[2] In addition, the debt of punishment, incurred as a result of personal and original sin, remains at the center of the theology of a redemptive incarnation. In the *Summa theologiae*, then, Aquinas sets forth a theology of atonement which recognizes this essentially 'cruciform' character of our Christian life.[3] For reasons which touch on the structure of the *Summa* itself, however, Aquinas nevertheless treats sin in the *secunda pars* as part of his general theory of morals.

In fact, Thomas discusses the reality of sin in the *prima secundae*, as part of his analysis of the Christian moral life. There, in q. 72, a. 1, ad 2, we discover what might be considered his preferred definition of sin: "actus debito ordine privatus." That is, sin lies in an action which lacks due order with respect to human flourishing. In Aquinas's view, this due order embraces all those actualities which human life requires for proper development and perfection. At the same time, it extends to an interpersonal order which ultimately points to the reality of the Church:

> Each man's actions have the quality of merit or demerit through
> being directed to another person (considered either as an
> individual or as a member of the community). In both respects
> our acts, good or bad, are meritorious or otherwise in the sight
> of God (Ia-IIae, q. 21, a. 4).

For a moral realist, then, human actions embody moral meaning chiefly in their very structure, that is, as concretely related to a world of real persons, thoughts, sentiments, or things. Sin, therefore, never points to some merely extrinsic reality, such as a human law or moral obligation, but always involves intrinsic objects of human concern and meaning.[4] These moral objects and the relationship which exists between them, in turn, find their ground in the eternal law, *viz.*, how God knows the world as actually existing.

Aquinas's theory on what constitutes a proper human action thus identifies a stream of internal finality which directs human activity from its origin to its end. And this primarily interpersonal order marks out the arena in which the rational creature, always through free activity, advances toward God. Sin, on the other hand, disrupts that finality, breaking out of the "ordo rerum" which Aquinas calls natural law. For Aquinas, natural law signifies nothing more than the rational creature's participation in the eternal law.[5] Interpreted in an interpersonal context, moreover, natural law can establish the norms which govern an individual and society.

Although natural law admittedly plays a preliminary role in Aquinas's method for moral theology, it nevertheless does point to the normative relationships which God's creative agency establishes for the rational creature. In the same way, the punishment which sin deserves also remains intrinsically correlated to this created relationship. Furthermore, as the scriptural notion of covenant reminds us, natural law achieves a high form of interpersonal expression in Christ. Thus, it is the incarnate Logos who, since he remains the natural Son of the Father, can also instruct us about the requirements for adoptive sonship and daughterhood. But even if the sinner (for whatever reasons) ignores the personal implications of sin and its effect on his relation with Christ, punishment nonetheless issues as a necessary consequence of each bad human action. In other terms, the sinner willy-nilly incurs "poena," which eventually reveals itself in the sinner's personal life.

Since due order derives from the eternal law which governs the whole of creation, it applies to any creature. But it takes on added significance in the rational creature where the "ordo debitus" actually becomes an "ordo justitiae." In fact, Aquinas speaks about justice only in connection with intelligent beings. He explains the basis for this decision in various places throughout the *prima secundae*.

> Things possessing intelligence set themselves in motion towards an end, for they are masters of their act through their own free decision, of which they are capable by reason and will (Ia-IIae q. 1, a. 2).

> Intelligent creatures are ranked under divine providence the more nobly because they take part in providence by their own providing for themselves and others. Thus they join in and make their own the eternal reason through which they have the natural aptitudes for their due activity and purpose ["ad debitum actum et finem"] (Ia-IIae q. 91, a. 2).

All in all, these texts express the central feature of Aquinas's teleological ethics. Although Christ expressly appears only in the *tertia pars*, Thomistic moral theology considers the human person as set between God and God, and, at the same time, as capable of freely recapitulating the salvation history originally lived by Jesus of Nazareth.

Since each disordered human action necessarily encompasses both fault ("culpa") and punishment ("poena"), Aquinas integrates these aspects of sin into his moral teleology. First, our capacities for accurately apprehending the meaning of human flourishing and for freely making the ultimate end of human existence the object of our choices both reflect the divine reason or order intrinsic in creation. "We are left with the conclusion," Thomas continues, "that only in voluntary activity do good and bad constitute the reason for praise and blame and that in these, evil ("malum"), sin ("peccatum"), and culpable fault ("culpa") are identical" (Ia-IIae q. 21, a. 2).[6] Aquinas, then, inserts reason and order into his interpretation of sin. These elements of his explanation, however, do not substitute external obligation for inner finality, but rather point to the proper and formal way in which man is subject to his own inner finalization.[7] In a moral teleology, human independence always remains ordered to human perfection, with the result that goal-centered morality coincides with the evangelical notion of freedom.

Of course, the attitude toward sin and punishment which such a conception develops differs profoundly from the perspectives of casuist moral theology. Much like today's revisionists, the casuist moral theologians developed their systems emphasizing the right and wrong choice, individual commandments and negative precepts, and especially the prerogatives of mature conscience and human autonomy. The Christian tradition, on the other hand, stresses good and bad decisions, virtues and vices, and especially the gifts of the Holy Spirit and the evangelical beatitudes. Thus, Aquinas understands eternal punishment as the unavoidable result of a failure to pursue a virtuous life. For God is not an afflictive avenger. Punishment for mortal sin simply remains the violent state of separation and estrangement which the rational creature suffers only after being finally deprived of reaching his or her supernatural destiny.[8] To put it differently, "God does not turn further away from anyone than the person has turned away from him" (IIa-IIae q. 24, a. 10). In short, Aquinas invariably points to charity as the proper goal of Christian life.

Q. 87, a. 6: Re-ordering of Sin's Effects

Charity also controls Aquinas's interpretation of sin's effects in the human person. First of all, Thomas poses the question whether a debt of punishment follows upon sin. Three initial arguments suggest reasons why those whose sins have been forgiven should therefore also escape punishment. At the same time, II Samuel 12:13-14 recounts that, although God forgave David's sin of adultery, the child of that union nevertheless died. From this point, Aquinas proceeds on two levels. First, he argues that divine vindicative justice requires recompense for sin. In the following passage he explains the reasons for this.

A sinful act makes a person punishable in that he violates the order of divine justice. He returns to that order only by some punitive restitution that restores the balance of justice, in this way, namely that one who by acting against a divine commandment has indulged his own will beyond what was right, should, according to the order of divine justice, either voluntarily or by constraint be subjected to something not to his liking (Ia-IIae q. 87, a. 6).

Accordingly, even after sin has been forgiven, there still exists a penal debt. Aquinas, however, shifts the emphasis from righting an impersonal balance of justice in an "ordo universalis" to restoring justification in the sinner whose appetites remain skewed by the remnants of sinful behavior.

Second, Aquinas distinguishes simple "poena" from "poena satisfactoria." The restoration of the soul's splendor in fact results from the sinner's willing acceptance of the divine justice and the satisfactory punishments which it requires for a complete psychological restoration, that is, one which permeates the whole person. Thomas explains this as follows:

As to the taking away of the stain of sin, clearly this cannot be wiped out except by the soul being rejoined to God; it was by drawing away from him that it incurred the impairment of its own splendor which constitutes the stain of sin. Now the soul is joined to God through an act of the will which embraces the order of divine justice (Ia-IIae q. 87, a. 6).

In this text, Aquinas points to an act of charity. This act of conversion and of repentance turns the repentant sinner back to God from whom he has previously turned away by sin. An act of love informs the satisfactory punishment which the sinner undertakes.

The introduction of love into the discussion also permits Thomas to enlarge on what it means for the sinner to "embrace the order of divine justice." In brief, the sinner must either undertake satisfactory punishment or at least patiently bear whatever punishments are imposed. In either case, an act of the will makes the punishments satisfactory. From this perspective, at least, satisfactory punishments do not inflict the demands of an abstract order of justice but rather constitute something willingly suffered as a condition for realizing divine reconciliation. In other terms, the sinner now embraces God's saving justice as an expression of the divine goodness. On the other hand, punishment precisely implies something that goes against one's will. Satisfactory punishment accordingly embodies real punishment only in a diminished sense of the term. As the language of the scholastics puts it, satisfaction "simpliciter est voluntaria, secundum quid autem involuntaria". Simply speaking, satisfaction is voluntary, but in another and more literal sense of punishment, it remains involuntary. All in all, we should appraise the debt of punishment which exists after sin more as an opportunity for satisfaction than as an outright punishment. In any case, Aquinas recognizes the analogical character of satisfaction.

Indeed, as he developed a more personalist explanation of our relationship with God, he gradually altered his conception of "poena" and "macula." In fact, he began to fathom the "ordo justitiae" as something more than simply a juridical structure. In other words, he personalized Anselm's "ordo universitatis." As a result, he discovers that the juridical concept of "poena" is itself purely personal, something which is already clear for "macula." Even when the stain of sin is wiped out, "poena" still constrains the capacities of a soul deformed by sin. It remains then a question of looking at the same reality--the disruption of the whole person caused by sin--from two sides and thereby indicating a substantial link between concepts previously understood only as juridically related. As St Augustine imprinted on the western moral consciousness, every disordered deed constitutes its own punishment.

Since he knew that the believer's union with Christ can turn simple "poena" into satisfaction, a truth of revelation helped Aquinas frame this conception of "poena." Again, he realizes that "poena" can lead the individual through submission of the whole person to human nature's own supernatural finality. Still, it remains a gradual submission because sin is not simply a "macula" to be wiped clean even by charity but also a "poena" to be healed by the exercises of the Christian life. "Through him we have obtained access to this grace in which we stand, and we rejoice in our hope of sharing the glory of God. More than that, we rejoice in our sufferings, knowing that suffering produces endurance, and endurance produces character, and character produces hope" (Rom 5:2-5). Thomas can even look at "poena" from the side of divine vindicative justice according to a fresh perspective. Although punishment is called for in order to right the balance of justice, personal and human values also result when one fulfills this demand of justice. Punishment, he argues, remains necessary for justice's sake "and to undo scandal, namely that those who have been scandalized by the sin may be edified by the repentance; this is clear from the example given about David" (Ia-IIae q. 87, a. 6, ad 3). Satisfaction then institutes a new moral value in the human community.

Q. 87, aa. 7,8: Remedial Punishments

Satisfactory punishments, however, do not always occur as a result of an individual's own sin. For example, we can choose to take on the punishment actually due another, as when an innocent person willingly undertakes satisfaction in someone else's place. Love makes this possible. Thomas explains the ground for the exchange: "In some cases those who are different in their purely penal obligations remain one in will, through their union in love" (Ia-IIae q. 87, a. 7). This recalls his teaching developed in the *Summa contra gentiles*: a friend can satisfy for another to whom punishment is due. Again, Aquinas points out that something may appear punitive when in fact it does not possess the full weight of punishment. For example, we can suffer providentially ("secundum divinam providentiam") the loss of certain lesser human goods, such as bodily health or financial security, in the interests of our own salvation, of the salvation of others who are warned by such punishments, or even for the glory of God. We need such "bitter potions" in order to progress in virtue through adversity and to realize that in this life the supreme values remain those of the spirit. In any event, Aquinas recognizes that we can convincingly employ the notion of satisfaction in many different areas of theology.

He altogether differentiates three aspects of punishment: satisfaction, penalty, and healing. Although one person can satisfy for another by reason of a caritative bond between them ("inquantum sunt quoddammodo unum" in the phrase of Aquinas), purely penal punishments on the other hand necessarily afflict only the individual who sins. Thomas recognizes, however, that in some circumstances someone can suffer even penal punishment on account of another's sins. This usually happens when a relationship, such as parent-child or master-servant, already exists. Hence an entire family, for example, can suffer on account of a profligate father. But such punishments borne by innocent persons always involves temporal goods and, as Aquinas understands God's providence, will necessarily redound to their spiritual benefit. Of course, no innocent party can suffer spiritual punishment as a result of another's sin. To sum up, remedial sufferings show the errant sinner where happiness and human fulfillment lie, but satisfactory punishments actually bring the whole person progressively into conformity with that beatitude. We call this state an affective experience of personal union with the triune God through love and knowledge. In another treatise, Aquinas modifies this distinction to include the role which positive actions can play in image-restoration. "The act of mercy, however, is directed against sin," he writes, "either by way of satisfaction when it follows justification, or by way of preparation, for 'the merciful obtain mercy,' when it can precede justification" (Ia-IIae, q. 113, a. 4, ad 1). In any event, because of the incarnation, the Christian gospel can only proclaim fortunate faults.

Summa theologiae IIIa q.1: Satisfaction
Subordinate Theme of a Redemptive Incarnation

The God-Centered Dynamism of the Human Person

Especially in its treatment of the virtues and vices, the whole of Aquinas's *secunda pars* examines the return of the created image to God.   Here Aquinas spells out his view of the central factor in salvation history: God, insofar as he is the goal of our life in life everlasting.   God is the point to which all creation is tending, whether unconsciously and in obedience to a law of development written into its being, or consciously and in freedom, and therefore hazardously, with the possibility of eternal frustration.[9]   God, however, is not to be thought of simply as final cause of the rational creature separated from creation as the finish-line is separated from a runner at the start of a race.   Rather, as transcendent cause of all that exists, God is really present to creation as an active cause, even as creation tends toward him as final cause of its perfection.   Furthermore, we can account for God's presence to creation in at least two ways.   First, he is present to all that exists as an active cause of its being.   Second, he is present to those called to communication in charity as a direct object of knowledge and love.[10]   For Aquinas, theology always remains a "sermo de Deo," a word about God.

Christian faith alone can competently proclaim the special presence of God to those who live according to the design of his love.   Since grace establishes a real union between the believer and the persons of the blessed Trinity, such a union, although rooted in our human psychologies, nonetheless requires a radical adjustment of our natural capacities.   "No man has ever seen God; if we love one another, God abides in us and his love is perfected in us" (IJn 4:12).   But God himself can never form part of a creature, created grace, as it is called, effects the required adaptation.   Grace, then, provides this necessary proportion between the human knower and the divine persons known, between the human lover and the divine persons loved.   This mediation, moreover, originates in the grace of the incarnate Word and draws the believer into fellowship with the community of all those who claim that Jesus is the Son of God.   "Whoever confesses that Jesus is the Son of God, God abides in him, and he in God" (I Jn 4:15).

The *Summa theologiae* values satisfaction as an instrument which conditions us for this personal relationship with Father, Son, and Holy Spirit.   Through these penitential activities, we actively embrace an order of divine justice which instantiates the order of divine final causality inherent in the God-centered dynamism of the human person. Created in the image of God, the human person bears the "imago Dei" as a sign of both its origin and final destiny.   The notion of image, however, is not a static concept, for it suggests a dynamic movement towards a goal. Thomas remarks that "man is not only said to be an image, but to the image ("ad imaginem") of God, by which is signified a certain movement toward perfection" (Ia q. 35, a. 2, ad 3). Sin, an act directed away from God, renders the image sterile and paralyzed, marring its splendor and beauty.

Satisfactory punishments make the image once again fruitful and operative. Although human effort is involved, we cannot complete this work of restoration by ourselves. Thomas writes: "Even before sin, man needed grace for achieving eternal life, and that is what grace is principally for. But after sin man also needs grace over and above this for the remission of sin and the support of his weaknesses" (Ia q. 95, a. 4, ad 1). According to Aquinas, whatever difficulty we encounter in appropriating this grace accounts for its satisfactory character. "But when Christ had offered for all time a single sacrifice for sins, he sat down at the right hand of God, then to wait until his enemies should be made a stool for his feet. For by a single offering he has perfected for all time those who are sanctified" (Heb 10:13-14). The perfect and consubstantial image of the divine nature becomes incarnate and through his human service to the Father accomplishes the perfect work of restoration. As Colossians teaches, Christ remains "the image of the invisible God, the first-born of all creation" whom God sends into a sinful world of sterile, vestigial images.[11] Since all other satisfactions find their value in Christ, he bears the inner dynamism which carries creation toward its fulfillment, "making peace by the blood of his cross" (Col 1:20).

The texts of the *tertia pars* which treat of satisfaction form part of Aquinas's christology. Aquinas divides the treatise into two parts. First, he considers the mystery of the incarnation in itself, "Christus in se" (qq. 1-26); then he treats what was done and suffered by our Saviour, "Christus pro nobis" (qq. 27-59). These questions allow us to examine the satisfaction of the head of the body. Of course, Thomas only completed part of his treatise on the sacraments. He considers the sacraments of the new law "conformed in a certain way to the incarnate Word as in the mystery of the incarnation the Word of God is united to sensible flesh" (IIIa q. 60, a. 6, ad 3). So we can also examine satisfaction performed by the members of the body which is the Church.

Programmatic Essay: The Incarnation and Our Attainment of Beatitude

The first question of the *tertia pars* contains what we might describe as a programmatic essay for Aquinas's whole treatise on the economy of salvation. He treats the fittingness of the incarnation under two headings: "Whether it was fitting ("conveniens") for God to become incarnate" (IIIa q. 1, a. 1) and "Whether the incarnation of the Word of God was necessary for the restoration of the human race" (IIIa q. 1, a. 2). We consider each of these articles in turn.

Q. 1, a. 1:   *Arguments for fittingness*

In the *Scriptum*, Aquinas subordinates the incarnation to the requirements placed on the human race by original sin, namely, the need that God himself to repair its effect. Thus, his earlier systematic work stresses both God's justice and mercy. In the *Summa theologiae*, however, Thomas addresses the purpose of the incarnation from a fresh perspective. For example, he cites Romans 1:20 which speaks of our need to be drawn to the invisible things of God by those things which we can see. Again, he refers to John Damascene's *De Fide Orthodoxa* which alternatively describes the incarnation as an expression of God's goodness, wisdom, justice, and power. In a special way, then, the divine goodness controls Aquinas's discussion of the incarnation in the *Summa theologiae*: "good things are said to pour forth their being ("diffusivum sui") in the same way that ends are said to move one" (Ia q. 5, a. 4, ad 2). While goodness for Aquinas certainly implies final causality, it also presupposes efficient and formal causality This puts the incarnation at the center of both the "sacra doctrina" and of salvation history.

In the *Summa theologiae*, Aquinas consciously develops a theology of satisfaction. Since the incarnation embodies a self-communication of the divine goodness, it restores the splendor of our God-like image through the "super-abundant" satisfaction of the incarnate Word. The divine goodness, it restores the splendor of our God-like image through the "super-abundant" satisfaction of the incarnate Word. The divine goodness, however, does not compare simply with the divine generosity. On the contrary, God's goodness both implies our free activity and constitutes the condition for its possibility. To put it differently, the term, "bonitas divina," amounts to Thomas's shorthand for the whole system of God-man relations as he conceived it. "For God so loved the world that he gave his only Son, that whoever believes in him should not perish but have eternal life" (Jn 3:16). Luther called this verse "the Gospel in miniature." Only when this basic teaching about the incarnation serves as the primary hermeneutical principle, can we correctly interpret those texts of Aquinas which treat of satisfaction. For example, we find references to satisfaction among a wide range of topics treated in the *tertia pars*, namely, in relation to the physical and spiritual disabilities undertaken by Christ in his human nature (qq. 14, 15), in relation to his priesthood and mediation (qq. 22,26), in relation to his passion (qq. 46-48) and the effects of his expiatory death (qq. 49, 50, 52), and finally in relation to the sacraments and the satisfaction of the members (qq. 68-90)

First, we ought to consider the incarnation as the self-communication of the divine goodness.

Whatever is truly suited to a thing is so by reason of its distinctive nature; for example, discursive reasoning befits man who is by nature rational. But the very nature of God is goodness, as Dionysius makes clear. Therefore whatever forms part of the meaning of the good befits God.

But goodness implies self-communication, as Dionysius shows. Therefore it is appropriate for the highest good to communicate itself to the creature in the highest way possible. But, as Augustine teaches, this takes place above all when "he so perfectly joins human nature to himself that one person is constituted from these three: Word, soul, flesh." Clearly then, it was right for God to be incarnate (IIIa q. 1, a. 1).

At the very beginning of the treatise, then, Aquinas establishes the incarnation as the eminent and principal expression of God's love in the world.

The union of the Word of God to a human soul and flesh constitutes at once the wonder and scandal of the incarnation. Indeed, the earliest christological heresies retreated from affirming the full reality of Christ's humanity. They judged it unfitting that God, the supreme uncreated spirit, should find compatibility with a material body which remains as distant from him as wickedness from supreme goodness. But Aquinas recognizes a suitability which serves the purposes of satisfaction. He writes:

Since God, who is uncreated, unchanging and incorporeal, brought changing and bodily creatures into being out of his goodness, all those characteristics whereby they differ from the creator are established by his wisdom and ordained towards his goodness. Likewise the evil of penalty ("malum poenae") is brought in by his justice because of his glory (IIIa q. 1, a. 1, ad 3).

Whatever incompatibility might seem to be present in the Word's assuming a human nature (along with its imperfections) in fact points to God's wisdom. Thomas even refers to the "malum poenae" as something which God allows "because of his glory." In short, everything which God does in the world remains ordered to the "bonitas divina" as an end. Christ brings justification to a sinful human race for the worship of the Father's glory.

By the same token, Christ does not assume the "malum culpae" along with human nature, since his redemptive mission would not be served by sin itself.

> But the evil of fault is committed by a turning aside from the plan of God's wisdom and the order set by his goodness. Accordingly God could rightly take to himself a nature created, changeable, bodily and liable to penalty, but not one subject to moral ("malum culpae") fault (IIIa q. 1, a. 1, ad 3).

Here then we find two basic principles for Aquinas's satisfaction theory. First, he cites the providential character of the "malum poenae" which explains why the Word assumed a human nature capable of suffering. Second, he notes the absence of "malum culpae" in the assumed nature which illuminates the sinlessness of Christ, or, to put it differently, the perfection of created charity possessed by the soul of Christ.

Q. 1, a. 2: Necessity of the Incarnation

Next Aquinas examines the necessity of God's choice to save us by the incarnation. "For God sent the Son into the world, not to condemn the world, but that the world might be saved through him" (Jn 3:17). First, he distinguishes between two kinds of necessity. One, absolute necessity, never obliges the divine freedom in anything outside of its own nature. But there is a necessity which operates in something required for a better and more expeditious attainment of a certain goal, such as our furtherance in good and deliverance from evil. In the second sense, the incarnation is necessary for us.

Since we can only expect to discover indications of the latter--which one might call the usefulness for the incarnation--the following arguments represent Aquinas's balanced conception of what constitutes the Christian life, the "sequela Christi." Aquinas divides his list between those ends which refer to our furtherance in good ("ad promotionem hominis in bono") and those which refer to our deliverance from evil ("ad remotionem mali"). Each explains why "there was no other course more fitting [than the incarnation] for healing our wretchedness."

The first five arguments consider how the incarnation contributes to our furtherance in good.

> First, with regard to faith, greater assurance is guaranteed when the belief rests on God himself speaking. Thus Augustine writes: "Truth itself, the Son of God made man, established and confirmed faith that men more confidently might journey to it."

> Second, as to hope, which is lifted to the heights, for, to quote Augustine, "nothing is so needful to build up our hope than for us to be shown how much God loves us. And what is a better sign of this than the Son of God deigning to share our nature?"

Third, as to charity, which is most greatly enkindled by the incarnation for, as Saint Augustine asks, "What greater cause is there for the coming of the Lord than to show God's love for us?" He goes on: "If we have been slow to love, let us not be slow to love in return."

Fourth, as to right living, we are set an example. Augustine says, in a Christmas sermon: "Not man, who can be seen, should be followed, but God, who cannot be seen. So then, that we might be shown one who would be both seen and followed, God became man."

Fifth, as to the full sharing in divinity, which is true happiness and the purpose of human life. This comes to us through the humanity of Christ, for, in Augustine's phrase, "God was made man that man might become God" (IIIa q. 1, a. 2).

The second set of five arguments describe how the incarnation remains useful in delivering us from evil.

First, for our instruction, lest we put the devil above ourselves and go in awe of him who is the author of sin. And so Augustine writes: "When human nature is so joined to God as to become one with him in person, these proud and evil spirits no longer dare to vaunt themselves over man because they are without flesh."

Second, we are taught how great is the dignity of human nature, lest we sully it by sin. To the point Augustine writes: "God showed us the exalted place that human nature holds in creation by appearing to men as a true man." So also Pope Leo: "O Christian, acknowledge your dignity! Having been made a sharer of the divine nature, refuse to fall back into your previous worthlessness by evil conduct."

Third, to do away with human presumption "the grace of God, with no preceding merits on our part, is shown to us as in the man Christ." So writes Augustine.

Fourth, as he adds: "The pride of man, which is the greatest obstacles to our union with God, can be rebutted and cured by such great humility on the part of God."

Fifth, it rescues man from thralldom. This, as Augustine writes, "should be done in such a way that the devil is overcome by the justice of a man, Jesus Christ," which was accomplished by Christ making satisfaction for us. One who was merely a man could not make satisfaction for the entire human race, and how could God? It was fitting, then, for Jesus Christ to be both God and man. On this Pope Leo says: "Weakness is received by power, humility by majesty, that one and the same mediator between God and man might die from the one and rise from the other, and thus we were fitly restored. Unless he were truly God, he could not provide a cure; unless he were man, he could not offer an example" (IIIa q. 1, a. 2)

The fifth argument, the last in the series of ten, points directly to Anselm's *Cur Deus homo?* and satisfaction, the so-called "necessary reason" for the incarnation. On the other hand, we observe an important feature of Aquinas's own theological method in these texts. He situates the tradition, especially represented by St Augustine, within a context Thomas draws from his experience, that is, from a deliberate judgment made concerning the nature of the Christian life.

To sum up, the first series of texts considers our image-perfection: first, because the incarnate Word speaks the truth which we accept in faith; second, because Christ moves us to hope that the promise of eternal life remains attainable; third, because the charity of the wayfarer is greatly enkindled by the evidence of God's love; fourth, because all of these virtues are more effectively communicated by concrete example than by abstract instruction; and fifth, because it is through the humanity of Christ that we receive a full sharing in divinity which alone constitutes "true happiness and the purpose of human life." The second series considers aspects of image-restoration: first, because Christ liberates us from the devil's blackmail; second, because we no longer indulge in despising our own nature; third, because Christ removes the evil of presumption in our own abilities; fourth, because Christ shows us the evil of pride; fifth, because Christ's satisfaction for sin delivers the human race from servitude to sin.

The patristic authorities dominate this major text of Aquinas. St Augustine, for example, joins Damascene in portraying the incarnation as an expression of the divine goodness. At the same time, although *Cur Deus homo?* already had eliminated the notion from theological currency in the West, the "ransom from the devil" theory obliquely appears in connection with Christ's satisfaction.[12] But Aquinas also includes a reference to Leo the Great, whose *Tomus ad Flavianum* plays an important role in the early development of christology. As a direct link with the Council of Chalcedon (451) and its dogmatic definition, Leo speaks of Christ as the "mediator" between God and man ("unus atque idem Dei et hominum mediator"). The mediator acts in a way that befits our restoration for he died to weakness and was raised up from humility. This same pattern of activity marks the member of Christ who embraces satisfactory punishments. In other words, Leo interprets Christ's "ransom" as a form of mediation.[13] In any event, the authentic tradition in large measure provides Aquinas with the essential features of his doctrine.

For the satisfactory works of the members

Resistance to the utter gratuity of the redemption marks every major period of the Christian dispensation. History assigns the name of the Celtic monk Pelagius to the perennial tendency, latent in each of us, to serve as our own savior.[14] In the *Summa*, Aquinas again faces objections which suppose that the incarnation is superfluous since the creature should be able to effect his or her own reconciliation with God.[15]

> Moreover, the only thing necessary for the restoration of human nature fallen through sin is that man should satisfy for his sin. For God ought not to require more than man is capable of. Now God is more inclined to show mercy than to punish; and thus, as the act of sin is charged to man, so too, it seems, the contrary act cancelling it should be credited to him. Therefore the incarnation of the Word of God was not necessary for the restoration of the human race (IIIa q. 1, a. 2, ad 2).

Although this view of the divine clemency seems to enhance God's stature, Aquinas recognizes that any alternative to Christ's unique mediation distances itself from the revealed sources of the "sacra doctrina."

The objection, however, allows Thomas to explain the relationship between the satisfaction of Christ and the satisfactory actions of the members. In the first place, he speculates whether the satisfaction of the members might find validation from some other source than the grace of Christ. Cajetan, in an extended commentary, observes that on this point Aquinas failed to express himself clearly in the *Scriptum*.[16] But in the *Summa* Aquinas expressly teaches otherwise:

> Satisfaction can be termed sufficient in two ways, completely or incompletely. In the first way satisfaction is condign, i.e., it is a recompense equalling the fault committed.   So understood, sufficient satisfaction is beyond the power of anyone merely human, since all human nature is corrupted by sin, with the result that the goodness of any one individual or even of many would not make adequate recompense for a disability affecting the whole nature. Further, a sin against God has a kind of infinity about it, because of God's infinite majesty; the seriousness of an offence is in proportion to the dignity of the one offended. Thus for condign satisfaction the act of the one atoning should be infinite in worth--an act, that is, of one who is both God and man.

In a second way satisfaction is termed sufficient, but incompletely so, i.e., sufficient because of the willingness of the one accepting it even though it does not equal the offence. So understood the satisfaction of one who is purely human is sufficient. Yet since whatever is incomplete presupposes something complete which supports it, every expiatory work of one who is merely human derives its value from the atoning work of Christ (IIIa q. 1, a. 2, ad 2).

The distinction between condign and congruous merit still obtains in contemporary discussions of grace and reconciliation.

Aquinas subsequently proposes two approaches to the question of autonomous satisfaction. First, since the sin of nature extends to every member of the human race, satisfaction requires one whose personal goodness can compensate for such extensive corruption. In like manner, Anselm argued that one can not satisfy "unless he returns a thing of greater value than that for which one ought not have sinned."[17] But original sin affects the good of the whole human race. Hence, even the whole human race lacks the necessary resources to make a condign satisfaction. Second, since it offends the divine dignity, any sin constitutes a sort of infinite transgression. But we define condign satisfaction as paying back in full measure for an offense. Thus, only the one who is both God and man ("Dei et hominis existens") can effect such satisfaction. Simply put, God alone can effect our image-restoration.

By the same token, Aquinas also indicates that created satisfactions possess their own proper value. It is true, of course, that God's willingness to accept our satisfaction as sufficient constitutes the principal cause of their efficacy. On the other hand, divine acceptance alone does not enact the present economy of salvation, as Aquinas's immediate reference to the condign satisfaction of Christ indicates. Every satisfactory action of a member of Christ derives its power to atone for sin only from the perfect satisfaction of Christ. But this condition points to something more than a forensic requirement imposed by an offended God. On the contrary, it rather attests to our "full sharing in divinity" which only the incarnate Word makes possible. Since only the incarnation secures image-perfection for a sinful race, we could not expect to find similar results if the creature alone satisfied for human sin.

Q.1., a. 3: Motive of the Incarnation

Since Rupert of Deutz first raised the question in the early 12th-century, theologians have carried on a debate concerning the universal primacy of Christ.[18] Unfortunately, the formulation of the question, "If man had not sinned, would God nevertheless have become incarnate?"

tends to conceal rather than to disclose the theological issue actually at stake. Thus, some hold that the controversy, carried on for nearly eight and a half centuries, remains largely academic.[19] But Aquinas understands that an important truth for Christian living is involved. For the only Christ we know is the crucified and risen Lord whose death and resurrection he himself interprets as salvific. Aquinas, moreover, points to revelation as the basis for his conviction: "everywhere in the sacred Scripture the sin of the first man is given as the reason for the incarnation" (IIIa q. 1, a. 3).

Of course, Aquinas does not mean that human sin in effect causes the incarnation. Although some accuse him of holding this position, he expressly rejects such an implication. "Since God wills nothing apart from himself, unless it be for an end which is his goodness, it follows that nothing else moves his will except his goodness" (Ia q. 19, a. 2, ad 2). Self-communication of the divine goodness, then, remains the only purpose of the incarnation. Still, in the actual economy of salvation we can discover a motive to explain the particular form in which this goodness manifests itself. "For the grace of God has appeared for the salvation of all men, training us to renounce irreligion and worldly passions, and to live sober, upright, and godly lives in this world, awaiting our blessed hope, the appearing of the glory of our great God and Savior Jesus Christ" (Titus 1: 11-13). In the present order, then, the recapitulation of all things in Christ cannot proceed without the satisfaction of Christ.

In short, Aquinas distinguishes between the motive and the end of the incarnation. The end ("finis") remains the very glory of Christ himself. "The glory which thou has given me I have given to them, that they may be one even as we are one (Jn 17: 22). And this glory he shares with the Father. Thus, God's purpose in communicating himself in the incarnation remains unaffected by any created activity, especially sin. Next, granted that this free decision on God's part expresses his absolute will, it still remains a contingent willing. As a result, we can legitimately uncover in revelation indications concerning God's motive in choosing these means to save us instead of others. In this context, the motive of the incarnation remains liberation from sin. By the same token, the satisfactory work of Christ remains a subordinate element of the explanation. Since human sin could never alter divine purposes, Thomas's resolution of the question does not imply that sinful abuse of human freedom places some necessity on God. Rather, he understands that our "promotio in bono" and "remotio mali" require Christ just as the New Testament presents him.

Qq. 2-26: Presuppositions for Understanding the Satisfaction of Christ: The Perfections and Disabilities of the Incarnate God

It is because Christ is both divine Word and a man that what he does, says, and still suffers in his members, has the power to bring salvation to those whom God calls to everlasting life. In like manner, the Christian believer cannot understand what God has accomplished in Jesus Christ without careful attention to the New Testament's account of what Christ did, said, and suffered, and of his exaltation and sending the Holy Spirit on the Church. The II Vatican Council especially reminds systematic theologians to make sacred scripture the soul of theology.[20] On the other hand, some interpreters insist that we can discover only a functional christology within the pages of the New Testament.[21] As a result, these theologians and exegetes frequently question whether the dogmatic formulations, for instance, of the Council of Chalcedon, adequately represent the evangelical kerygma.[22] But Aquinas's theological method recognizes no distinction between the *Christus pro nobis* and the *Christus in se*. For example, in considering the Chalcedonian formula, Aquinas accepts the orthodox tradition, especially represented by Leo the Great, that everything which Christ did according to his humanity and his divinity both promotes and effects our salvation. In other words, Christ's functions derive their salvific import from his being the incarnate Son.

Qq. 2-15: The Ontological Structure of the Incarnate God

After the initial question of the *tertia pars*, Aquinas devotes fourteen questions to the ontological structure of the incarnate God (qq. 2-6) and the characteristic endowments of his assumed humanity (qq. 7-15). He does not aim to draw a metaphysical blueprint of Christ. Rather. as a systematic theologian, he correlates the data derived from the New Testament and the interpretive tradition of the Church with a philosophical anthropology which can support the diverse images of Christ. Although the concept of human nature and the human person which emerges from his theology demonstrates his preference for Aristotle, the chief influences on his thought nevertheless remain Christian authors and sources.

First, however, we should present a general outline of Aquinas's christology in order to become acquainted with the general topics which he treats. The specific questions in which he considers the satisfaction of Christ require this backdrop. To proceed any other way would be as if an analytic geometrician studied only algebra but completely ignored the principles of plane geometry. In qq. 2-15, then, we find the following material treated:

How are we to understand the revealed truth that the Word is incarnate?

Understanding the actual union of God and man in the light of the Church's teaching and with the aid of philosophical principles (q. 2).

Considering the mystery from the point of view of the divine person who assumes a human nature (q. 3).

Considering the mystery from the point of view of what was assumed (qq. 4-15):

The human nature and its parts assumed by the Word (qq. 4-6).

The qualities characterizing this assumed nature:

its perfections: grace (considered as personal and as capital) (qq. 7,8); knowledge (qq. 9-12); power (q. 13),

its weaknesses, accepted in view of the redemptive mission (qq. 14, 15).

In the following sections, however, we consider only those questions which bear directly on the capacity of Christ to make satisfaction.

The human nature of Jesus Christ

United to the person of the Word

The hypostatic union remains the "point d'appui" of Christian faith. The fathers of Chalcedon insisted that the two natures of Christ, undivided and unconfused in the union, come together in the one person or hypostasis of the Logos. For this reason, the Church uses "hypostatic union" as a cryptograph to express the complex of issues involved in the assumption of a human nature by the eternal Son. Aquinas first considers the hypostatic union ("de modo unionis Verbi incarnati quantum ad ipsam unionem") in q. 2, a. 2. Aided by his knowledge of texts from the great christological councils of the 5th and 6th centuries, he produces an innovative treatment in christology. The Christian philosopher Boethius, who supplied the Middle Ages with a working definition of person, also contributes to Aquinas's doctrine of the incarnation.[23] The treatise thus respects the general principles established for the "sacra doctrina," namely, to put human intelligence at the service of the faith.

At the same time, metaphysics can only supply preliminary elements for a doctrine of redemption. "Sacra doctrina" discloses the "eternal purpose which [God] has realized in Christ Jesus our Lord" (Eph 3:11). To be sure, Christ necessarily accomplishes satisfaction in his humanity since it involves change and decay. Yet the value of Christ's satisfaction derives chiefly from the dignity of his divine person. Since Anselm first introduced the notion into western theology, we find no adequate explanation for the outcome of Christ's life and death other than the fact that "truly he was the Son of God" (Mk 15:39). In short, the hypostatic union, the "gratia unionis," validates the satisfaction of one man for sins committed against the infinite dignity of God.

The eternal person of the Word assumes a human nature like ours in all things but sin. This represents the material content of the Christian tradition as developed from the New Testament until the middle of the 5th century. In 451, Chalcedon rejected two heterodox positions concerning the unity of the Lord Jesus: first, the model of natural union as proposed by the radical monophysites; second, the model of accidental union as proposed (apparently) by the hardened Nestorians. The former group taught a mythological Christ, for whom ethereal flesh which only looked like ours covered up a divine Logos. The latter group contented themselves with a rational view of Christ, in whom two complete natures functionally co-existed in an elusive and undefined unity.[24] We grasp something of the importance which Aquinas assigns to this article of faith from his concluding remarks in q. 2, a. 2:

> Consequently, all that is present in any person, whether belonging to his nature or not, is united to him in person. If, then, the human nature is not united to the Word in person, it would not be united at all. To hold that would be to abolish belief in the incarnation and to undermine the entire Christian faith. Since, therefore, the Word has a human nature united to himself, even though it does not form part of his divine nature, it follows that this union was effected in the person of the Word, not in the nature (IIIa q. 1, a. 2).

To be sure, Aquinas emphasizes the importance of personal union. Still, because he distinguishes between a possessive subject and an effective one, he can sort out the different functions of both nature and person in the mystery of the incarnation. As a personal unity, Christ enjoys only one effective subject, the eternal Logos. But besides the effective principle of unity which Christ receives through his uncreated personhood, he also enjoys two possessive subjects, since each nature does what remains proper to it.

Three points in this text require further commentary. First, since the person of the Word pre-exists, Christ's created human nature does not constitute his person but rather joins it. Second, this same infinite person also possesses the divine nature, "one in being with the Father." Third, the human nature, once hypostatically united to the person of the Word, remains an individual nature, enjoying all of the operations proper to human nature, though not in itself personalized. In the same way, since the second person of the blessed Trinity alone assumed our human nature, we can discover reasons of fittingness why the Son became incarnate instead of the Father and the Holy Spirit. Such reasons reveal more and more of the trinitarian mystery behind the redemptive incarnation.[25]

Indeed, Aquinas finds in his trinitarian theology a source for establishing the person of the Word as the one who most fittingly becomes incarnate. He resolves the personal signification of the names "Son" and "Word" when applied to the second divine person, and he explains how we can understand "Word" as the proper name of that divine person whose intra-trinitarian procession comes about after the fashion of an intellectual emanation. He writes:

In the divinity "Word" as a literal term refers to a person and is a name proper to the Son. The reason is that a word denotes a kind of coming forth from the mind; but in the Godhead the person proceeding on the basis of such an emanation of mind is called the Son, and such a procession is a begetting. Therefore it must be that in the divinity the Son alone properly has "Word" as his name (Ia q. 34, a. 2).

Trinitarian doctrine distinguishes, then, between appropriations and personal names for the persons of the Trinity. This allows Aquinas next to develop his theological intuition concerning the incarnation.

First, he identifies the Word of God as the exemplar of all creation and the means for creation's final perfection. Since rational creatures alone possess the capacity to participate in the incarnate Word, whom by appropriation we also call the Wisdom of God, they alone are ordained for the benefits of the incarnation. Next, the second divine person bears the name, Son. Aquinas relates this to our achieving beatitude.

A further reason can be taken from the purpose of the union, the accomplishment of the predestination of those who are preordained for a heavenly inheritance. To this sons alone have a right: "If sons heirs also." Appropriately, then, through him who is Son by nature men share by adoption in a likeness to his sonship: "Those whom he foreknew he predestined to share the image of his Son (IIIa q. 3, a. 8).

We can perceive a striking parallel between these texts and those found at the beginning of the *tertia pars*. There two series of arguments described the practical usefulness of the incarnation as "promotio in bonum" and "remotio mali." The incarnate Son of God returns to men and women their predestined share in God's glory through conformity to his own filial image. "We however remain sons by adoption to the extent that we remain conformed to God's son, thereby obtaining a certain participation in divine love" (*Super ad Ephesos*, c. 1, l. 2). As the word of God's true wisdom, Christ remedies the evil of fault committed when we turned away from the plan of God's original wisdom and love.

God's providential care for his creation includes special regard for the human creature made after the divine image. The disarray of sin does not definitively frustrate the self-communication of divine goodness because God transforms those disordered results into satisfactory punishments for the worship of his glory. Satisfaction both heals the disorder of sin and restores our tarnished image to its ordained splendor. But such a divine work remains unimaginable apart from a divine worker. The satisfaction of Christ, in which every human satisfaction finds its efficacy, opens up the way to man's salvation. "Our Saviour, the Lord Jesus Christ," Thomas writes in the *tertia pars*, "showed in his own person that way of truth which, in rising again, we can follow to the blessedness of eternal life" (IIIa, prologue).

Taken from Adam's stock

Since Christ remains "homöouisios hēmin," that is, one in nature with us just as he remains one in being with the Father, christology must also contemplate the human nature which he assumed. In accord with Chalcedon, Aquinas holds that Christ's body belongs to the stock of Adam. We can easily recognize the latent soteriology involved in this insistence inasmuch as it recapitulates the Pauline typological antithesis between Adam and Christ. Aquinas points out the irony of the fact that Christ conquers the devil in the same flesh which the devil had conquered when Adam sinned. Citing St Augustine in the *De trinitate*, he writes:

> As Augustine teaches, "God could have taken on human nature from another source and not from the race of that Adam who by sin enthralled the human race. Yet he judged it better to take up a man of that conquered race and through him to conquer its enemy" (IIIa q. 4, a. 6).

In *De Trinitate*, Augustine rejects the notion that Christ assumed a human nature created expressly for the incarnation and gives a reason why God "judged it better" to assume a human nature stemming from

Adam.   As we have already seen, Augustine emphasizes the poetic justice displayed in Christ's rout of the devil in Adam's flesh.

> (Satan), conqueror of the first Adam and holding in his power the human race, has been conquered by the second Adam, thus losing his grasp on the Christian race, which has been set free out of the human race and from human fault, through him who was not in the fault, although he was of the race (*De trinitate* XIII, c. 18, 23).

All in all, the tradition emphasized the authenticity of Christ's human nature as a condition for the universality of redemption.   "For if many died through one man's trespass, much more have the grace of God and the free gift in the grace of that one man Jesus Christ abounded for many" (Rom 5:15).

Aquinas adopts this line of argumentation in his own treatment, but at the same time clearly modifies the mythological conclusions concerning the devil.   So we find him speaking about the new dignity to which the divine power raises us in the incarnation.

> Three reasons can be adduced.   First of all, it seems to be a matter of justice that he who committed the sin should pay the price. Thus, that whereby satisfaction was to be paid for the entire human race was rightly assumed from that nature corrupted by sin. Secondly, it forms part of the enhanced dignity of man that the conqueror of the devil should be born of the race the devil had vanquished.   Thirdly, it more clearly manifests the power of God that from a nature abased and weakened he raised one exalted to such virtue and dignity (IIIa q. 4, a. 6).

Although other approaches to the incarnation compete for his attention, Aquinas centers his account of the incarnation in the divine goodness and glory.   This insight characterizes his mature treatment of Christ's atonement.

In 362, almost a half century after the condemnation of Arius, St Athanasius composed his "Letter to the Antiochenes" as part of an effort to reconcile the then-major schools of christological deliberation. In this document, the Alexandrian party acknowledged that Christ possesses a human soul.[26]   The "Logos-sarx" model favored by the Alexandrians had inclined towards depreciating Christ's full human status, and gnostic heresies had earlier advanced the same position.[27] The explicit recognition that Christ possesses a human soul with a full range of psychological capacities thus involved a long process of dialectic and debate, and this synodal declaration marks one of the great milestones in the early christological controversies.   Yet the character of the physical and psychological disabilities undertaken by

Christ in his human nature remained a strong point of contention even after the period of patristic theology.

Aquinas recapitulates the orthodox argument for maintaining the completeness and authenticity of Christ's human nature. Philosophical anthropology, it should be noted, does not supply an "a priori" category in the debate. Rather, the credibility of the Gospels rests on whether the Son of God assumed a true body. Thus Aquinas can argue for a real humanity.

> A second reason can be taken from what the mystery of the incarnation accomplished. If Christ's body had not been real but imaginary he would not have undergone real death; the events narrated by the Evangelists would not be factual but a kind of pretense. From that it follows that no real human salvation resulted, since the effect must correspond to its cause (IIIa q. 5, a. 1).

In sum, we find Aquinas making the same soteriological point that impressed Athanasius at the synod of 362. Our salvation "embraces the whole man body and soul" inasmuch as "the Savior really and in very truth became man."[28]

The bodily weaknesses assumed in view of Christ's redemptive mission

Although modern christology has grown comfortable with a weak and suffering Christ, the tradition of the Church recognizes that whatever impediments Christ suffers must in some way conform to the dignity of his divine person. We cannot accept the radical conclusions of kenoticists who transform Christ into a romantic, ideal figure and thereby describe his human condition and sufferings in terms perfectly identical to our own. On the other hand, Christian theology must take full account of the physical weaknesses Christ suffered as part of his redemptive mission. Aquinas first inquires whether the Son of God ought to have taken on a human nature that carried with it bodily disabilities. Difficulties about accepting Christ's bodily disabilities arise because they seem to betray the principle of perfection. This insures that whatever theologians say about the human nature of Christ, in fact, conforms to the unique mode of subsistence enjoyed by a human nature united to the Logos. Thomas consequently explains how the principle of perfection itself must cohere with other principles of interpretation, especially in those matters where the Gospels leave no room to question the authenticity of Christ's human conduct, for example, his nescience, his weeping, his distress, and so forth.

Aquinas includes actions such as these under the principles of credibility and economy. The first insures that any theological description of Christ's human conduct does not strain the human imagination beyond what the mystery of the incarnation itself requires.

Thus, we exclude the gnostic Christ. The second principle, however, insures that our conception of Christ's humanity allows him to experience the sufferings which make up our salvation. Thus, we exclude the Christ of liberal Protestantism. For example, Aquinas employs the principle of economy in the following text.

> The Son of God took flesh and came into the world to make reparation for the sin of the human race. Now one person atones for the sin of another by taking on himself the punishment due to the sin of the other. These bodily disabilities--death, hunger and thirst and the like--are punishments for the sin that was brought into the world by Adam, according to Romans: "Therefore as sin came into the world through one man and death through sin." Hence it was fitting, given the purpose of the incarnation, that he should take these penalties on in the flesh, in place of us. As Isaiah says: "Surely he hath borne our infirmities" (IIIa q. 14, a. 1).

In particular, the principle of the economy points to the satisfaction of Christ, since it allows him at once to express the highest love and to endure the greatest sufferings. Aquinas looks at this question in the context of an objection which overstates the principle of perfection, arguing that Christ's perfect moral life seems incompatible with a passible body.

> The punishments which one person suffers for the sins of another are, as it were, the material of reparation. But the principle of it is the attitude of soul which makes someone want to atone for another. It is from this that reparation gets its effectiveness; it would have no effect if it did not spring from charity. Therefore the soul of Christ had to be perfectly endowed with knowledge and virtue so that he would have the power to make reparation; and his body had to be liable to suffering so that he would not lack the material for reparation (IIIa q. 14, a. 1, ad 1).

Aquinas nevertheless distinguishes those disabilities which Christ assumes for our sins and those other forms of disability which would only have detracted from Christ's salvific purpose and which therefore, according to the same principle of the economy, he could not have fittingly embraced.

Following the principle of perfection, Thomas explains, for example, that Christ was exempt from the human disabilities which are irreconcilable with perfect knowledge and grace, such as ignorance, proneness to evil, and difficulty in doing good. Similarly he was spared those kinds of disabilities that befall individuals who have some genetic defect or which result from damage caused by some form of unhealthy activity. Drawing on a patristic tradition, Aquinas summarizes the question of Christ's disabilities as follows.

> There is a third set of disabilities that are shared by all men as a result of the sin of the first parent: death, hunger, thirst and the like. These are the disabilities that Christ assumed. They are what Damascene calls "the natural and unembarrassing afflictions:" natural because they are common to all humanity, unembarrassing because they do not imply any lack of knowledge and grace (IIIa q, 14, a. 4).

So Christ undertook the physical disabilities that satisfactory punishment requires, but only those which positively contribute to the salvific purpose of the incarnation. We should not interpret the principle of economy as a facile move on Aquinas's part or a theological sleight-of-hand. The New Testament itself demands that we look at things this way.

In the *De rationibus fidei*, Thomas faced the problem of explaining to Saracens the reason for Christian belief in a "suffering God." In that analysis of the bodily disabilities of Christ, he seeks to account for the interpretation Christian theology and liturgical practice give to Isaiah 53: 2-5, 7. This scriptural reference stands behind Thomas's theological approach to Christ's weaknesses:

> Surely he has borne our griefs and carried our sorrows;
>   yet we esteemed him stricken, smitten by God, and afflicted.
> But he was wounded for our transgressions, he was
>   bruised for our iniquities;
> upon him was the chastisement that made us whole,
>   and with his stripes we are healed.

To sum up: Aquinas remains a "magister in sacra pagina," a biblical theologian because his christology emerges from the pages of the sacred scriptures. In these texts, we behold Christ, the servant born in the likeness of men (Phil 2.7), who becomes the merciful and faithful high priest (Heb 2:17-18); he suffers the hostility of sinners (Heb 12:3) and yet shares their sinful flesh (Rom 8:3). These themes sustain Aquinas's discussion of the disabilities of Christ's body.

The disabilities and perfections of Christ's soul

Christ's sinlessness

The recognition that Christ possesses a human soul as a constitutive element of his human nature implies that Christian theology must also account for its operations. But psychological disabilities provide a greater challenge to the principle of perfection than do merely physical ones. The rational activities of knowledge and love represent the highest human capacities, and so we correctly expect to find Christ perfect in those actions which entail knowing and loving. Still, the theologian must take full account of those places in the canonical Gospels where we read that Christ suffered temptation and even lacked a clear grasp of those things we would expect one perfect in knowledge to know. Since satisfaction mainly involves the perfection of charity, the substantial holiness of the incarnate God requires special clarification.[29]

The question of whether one personally united to the Word can experience vulnerability to sin and undergo temptations has vexed Christian theologians for centuries. It would seem that the one who perfectly fulfills the law and the prophets cannot at the same time violate the law and renounce the prophets. In addition, we acknowledge that the perfection of charity in the soul of Christ radically enables him to perform a complete satisfaction for sin. But sin neither contributes to godly reparation nor constitutes a human perfection. On the contrary, sin negatively affects the same human capacities as charity, namely, those affects and thoughts whereby we live out our relationship with God.

When Thomas asks whether there was any sin in Christ, he applies principles already established earlier in the *tertia pars* to illumine the existential actualization of Christ's sinlessness and explain its relation to satisfaction. It is significant, moreover, in light of the purposes of systematic theology, that Thomas responds to no fewer than five objections from the scripture in the course of explicating Christ's sinlessness. For example, we find three scriptural citations in the following text which points out the reasons why moral weakness contributes nothing to satisfaction.

> It has been remarked already that Christ undertook our disabilities to make reparation for us, to prove the truth of his human nature and to become for us an example of virtue. On each of these counts it is clear that he ought not to have taken on sin.

> Firstly, sin contributes nothing toward satisfaction. In fact it rather obstructs the ability to make satisfaction because, as Ecclesiasticus puts it, "the Most High does not approve the gifts of the wicked." Likewise sin does nothing to authenticate human nature. For sin forms no part of human nature, a nature which has God for its cause; rather it is contrary to nature, having been introduced, as Damascene puts it, "from a seed sown by the devil." Thirdly, by sinning Christ could not give an example of virtue because sin is the opposite of virtue. Therefore in no sense did he take on the disability of sin, either

original or actual. This is what is in I Peter: "He committed no sin; no guile was found on his lips" (IIIa q. 15, a. 1).

Thomas nevertheless does take into consideration the sinful condition into which God sent his Son. "While we were still weak, at the right time Christ died for the ungodly" (Rom 5:6). Thus he can present Christ as a "victim" for sin and accordingly apply to the satisfaction of Christ the text, "He made him to be sin" (II Cor 5:21).

> God "made Christ to be sin" not by making him a sinner but by making him a victim for sin. There is a parallel in Hosea, where the priests are said to "feed on the sin of my people," because according to the Law they would eat the victims offered for sin. In the same sense we have in Isaiah: "The Lord has laid on him the iniquity of us all," meaning that he gave him up to be a victim for the sins of all men. Or "made him to be sin," could mean "in the likeness of sinful flesh," as in Romans. And this would be because of the vulnerable and mortal body which he took on. (IIIa q. 15, a. 1, ad 4).

In other terms, Aquinas insists on reading the scriptures within an interpretative framework. This method, moreover, respects not only the larger theological tradition but also the dogmatic definitions of the Church.

Christ's capital grace and his members

Although the hypostatic union remains the principle of all grace both for Christ and in the Church, theologians distinguish two further graces which belong to Christ. The first embodies his substantial holiness and accounts for his perfect charity and obedience to the will of the Father. The second points to a function of Christ which depends on both the "gratia unionis" and the created grace for its source and strength. The capital grace belongs to Christ as head of the Church inasmuch as he "has the power to infuse grace into every member of the Church" (IIIa q. 8, a. 1). In the following text, Aquinas distinguishes the capital grace of Christ from the ordinary work of sanctification which trinitarian theology ordinarily appropriates to the Holy Spirit.

> Christ as God can give grace (or the Holy Spirit) in his own right. As man he can also give it, but instrumentally. For his humanity was "the instrument of his divinity." And so his actions brought salvation to us through the power of the divinity. They caused grace in us both by meriting it and by some kind of efficient causality. What Augustine denies is that Christ as man gives the Holy Spirit in his own right. But in the

role of instrument, or minister, even other saints are said to give the Holy Spirit, as in Galatians--"Does he who supplies the Spirit to you" (IIIa q. 8, a. 1, ad 1).

The mention of instrumental causality recalls the patristic adage that Christ's humanity serves as an instrument of his divinity.[30] In this context, however, Aquinas extends the principle to include the relationship of grace which obtains between Christ and the members.

Aquinas also emphasizes the Pauline metaphor of body to express unity in the Church. In one text, we read, "Christ and his body are taken as one person."[31] And in *De veritate* q. 29, a. 7, arg. 3, he reiterates the same striking affirmation: "Christ and the Church are one body" ("Christus et Ecclesia sunt quasi una persona"). This personal relationships between Christ and his members explains how the perfection of grace, which remains chiefly and principally a personal quality of Christ, can spiritually affect the other members. In order to clarify this important theological truth Aquinas borrows and adapts a classical philosophical argument. The theological rule draws from principles of Aristotelian and Platonic philosophy, namely, that the most perfect representative of any kind exercises a causal influence on all the participants in that kind. But the text, "And from his fullness have we all received, grace upon grace" (Jn 1:16), provides an original insight into its application to the unique participation we enjoy through Christ.

> Christ received the fullness of grace so that it could be passed on ("transfunderetur"), as it were, from him to others. Hence he required the maximum grace; just as fire, which is what makes things hot, is itself the hottest thing of all (IIIa q. 7, a. 9).

Thomas can now explain the capital grace of Christ as something capable of establishing a real order in the world. This "communio" forms the Church.

The doctrine that the blessed Trinity, as "first cause" of our redemption, makes instrumental use of the humanity of Christ enjoys a long history in theology. It also furnishes a strong connection between Christ and his members. Indeed, the Church transcends the level of accidental community and approaches a direct, physical relationship with Christ himself.[32] Theology can defend a direct relationship since no other self-sufficient mediator of God and man exists other than Christ. It is physical, however, because Christ as intermediary must perform the function of a mediator, namely, to bring together, and Christ performs this function as a man, that is, in his physical body. Since he cannot easily analyze the nature of the physical causality (the actual phrase is not found in the text) exercised by the humanity of Christ, Thomas has frequent recourse to metaphor when describing how this causality works. For example, he uses some form of the verb "to pour", either "to pour onto" ("transfundere"), "to pour into" ("infundere"), or "to overflow" ("redundare"), to express the transmission of grace from Christ to the members.[33]

Aquinas's preference for figures of speech to explain instrumental causality signals a caution about how we should approach interpreting the idea. "Reality need not correspond to figure in every detail," Thomas writes, "but only in some regard, since reality surpasses figure" (IIIa q. 48, a. 3, ad 1). Thus, the figurative use of some form of the verb "to pour" points to, but does not exhaust, the meaning of the affirmation that Christ spiritually affects his members. The members, nonetheless, do remain truly affected by the grace of Christ since it becomes a principle of merit and of satisfaction for them. And since this effect remains a real one in those who receive it, we can suitably refer to the union which the capital grace of Christ effects as an ontological union, although we should not thereupon conclude that the inclusion of all men and women in Christ constitutes a physical union in the sense that final recapitulation destroys personal identity. Aquinas's phrase, "The head and the members form as it were a single mystical person," argues against such an interpretation, since the use of the modifier "quasi" always indicates that Aquinas intends an analogy. To speak without qualification in this matter would mean to speak loosely and therefore incorrectly about divine things.

The "quasi" also points out the analogical elasticity contained in the notion of person. Indeed, contemporary ecclesiology explores ways to grasp how the Church remains as one person in Christ. On the other hand, Aquinas never envisages the mystical body of Christ in purely juridical terms. In fact, he rejects outright the theory of "transfer of merit" suggested by *Cur Deus homo?* as an adequate explanation of God's plan for our salvation. The imputation of rights, even to those who firmly believe in Christ, necessarily results in a merely moral union between Christ and his members. Such an explanation remains unsatisfactory because it interprets merit and satisfaction according to a restricted point of view, as if Christ made a deposit in a bank. To be sure, the human creature can have no claim to beatitude, but the merit and satisfaction of Christ accomplish more than simply establishing such a claim for us with God. Among other reasons, the parable of the vine and the branches does not permit such a narrow interpretation of Christ's work. "Abide in me, and I in you. As the branch cannot bear fruit by itself, unless it abides in the vine, neither can you, unless you abide in me" (Jn 15:4).

Thomas's theological analysis of merit and satisfaction does not cohere with later doctrines of imputed grace. The positive perfecting of the image of God in man and the gradual restoration of our soul to dignity and glory require more than a simple imputation of Christ's satisfaction or merit. The Church experiences the benefits of Christ's passion here and now. We are the Church of glory. This happens because God ordains for us a participation in the merit of Christ.

Since we are "quasi" one person with Christ, this union bestows on us the worth ("dignitas") and the fitness ("idoneitas") required for glory. In like manner, satisfaction removes the penalty of sin that keeps us from entering into that glory. All in all, Aquinas develops a realist theology which respects the temper of Aristotelian philosophy, but even more the Christian revelation which discloses the God of Abraham, Isaac, and Jacob. It also finds a center of gravity in Augustine: "In Christ you were tempted, for Christ received his flesh from your nature, but by his own power gained salvation from you; he suffered death in your nature, but by his own power gained glory for you."[34]

Qq. 16-26: Some implications of the Hypostatic Union

Questions 16-26 complete Thomas's discussion of the mystery of the Incarnation in itself. He introduces them under the heading "De his quae consequuntur unionem." However, these implications or consequences do not directly refer to properties or functions of Christ objectively deriving from what has been said of his ontological structure in questions 2-15. Rather they concern logical deductions which may be drawn from what has already been established. The outline indicates the subjects treated in these questions:

"De his quae consequuntur unionem," on the implications of the union. Those that affect--
--Christ himself:
-statements relating to him as existing and coming into existence; (q. 16).
-as regards his unity;
(dealt with elsewhere--questions regarding unity or plurality as to knowledge and nativity; cf Question 17, Introduction).
of existence (q. 17),
in volition (q. 18),
in activity (q. 19),
--his relations with his Father:
-Christ as related to the Father;
subjection (q. 20),
prayer (q. 21),
priesthood (q. 22),
-the Father considered as related to Christ;
problem of adoption (q.23),
predestination (q. 24),
--in relation to us;
-our adoration of him (q. 25),
-his mediation (q. 26).

Christ as related to the Father: his priesthood

The priesthood of Christ, treated in q. 22, aa. 1-6, remains a central feature of Thomas's theology of satisfaction. Since the principal office of the priest entails the worship of God, Aquinas associates the priesthood with the virtue of religion. Christ the priest properly embodies the eminently religious man. Likewise, the priesthood entails communicating God's goodness to man through "gifts and sacrifices for sins" (Heb 5:1), with the result that the priest satisfies to God on our behalf. In q. 22, a. 1, Thomas establishes that Christ significantly fulfills these tasks:

> Now these functions are carried out by Christ in an eminent degree. For through him divine gifts are brought to men--"by whom [Christ] he hath given us most great and precious promises: that by these you may be made partakers of the divine nature." It was he also who reconciled the human race to God --"In him Christ it hath well pleased the Father that all fullness should dwell, and through him to reconcile all things unto himself." Consequently Christ was a priest in the fullest sense of the word (IIIa q. 22, a. 1).

The twofold purpose of the incarnation clearly emerges in this interpretation of the work of Christ: first, image-restoration through sin offerings; second, image-perfection through divine gifts. At the same time, Thomas qualifies the satisfaction effected by the sacrifices of the old dispensation, since they effected only a preliminary stage of reparation: "[F]or if perfection had been attainable through the Levitical priesthood, what further need would there have been for another priest to arise?" (Heb 7:11).

For us, Christ's salvific sacrifice alone accomplishes the fullness of the reconciliation and "perfect union with God" for ever. Thomas appropriately relates Christ's work to the purposes of sacrifice.

> Man must make use of sacrifice for three reasons. Firstly, to obtain remission of sin, by which he is turned away from God. It is, accordingly, the office of a priest "to offer up gifts and sacrifices for sins." Secondly, in order that man may be preserved in the state of grace, united at all times with God in whom are found his peace and salvation. It was for this reason that, under the Old Law, the peace victim was immolated for the salvation of the offerers. Thirdly, to win for man's spirit perfect union with God, something which will be realized fully only in heaven. This was why, under the Old Law, the holocaust was offered, that is, a sacrifice wholly consumed by fire.

Not all of these benefits have been made over to us by Christ's own humanity. For, in the first place, our sins have been blotted out--"He was delivered up for our sins." In addition we have received through him that grace which saves us--"He became to all that obey him the cause of eternal salvation." Finally, through him we have laid hold on the consummation of glory--"We have confidence in the entering into the Holies [that is, into heavenly glory] by the blood of Christ." We may conclude therefore that Christ as man was not only priest but likewise victim and, indeed, the supreme victim, for he was at once a victim for sin, a peace victim and a holocaust (IIIa q. 22, a. 2).

Three elements, then, comprise the benefits which derive from Christ's sacrifice. The first has a negative aspect, namely, the remission of sins. This, of course, Aquinas attributes to satisfaction. The second element has a positive aspect, namely, sacrifice. This Aquinas identifies with preservation in grace. The third element points to the eschatological dimension of Christ's sacrifice. This Aquinas refers to that perfect union with God characteristic of everlasting life.

Although the priestly work of Christ belongs to his humanity, the efficacy of his sacrifice remains inseparable from the divine nature of the incarnate God "whose human actions draw their efficacy from his divinity" (IIIa q. 22, a. 3, ad 1). Thomas explains the fullness of Christ's satisfaction by reference to the "macula culpae" and the "reatus poenae." Christ removes the stain of guilt by grace which turns the sinner's heart back to God. But Christ satisfies in his flesh for the liability to punishment; as Isaiah 53:4 puts it, surely he "has borne our griefs and carried our sorrows." As previous teaching made clear, however, Christ's satisfaction always finds its principal value not in suffering but in love. The priesthood of Christ observes this same norm. For "in virtue of that act of worship of his by which, under the influence of his love, he submitted with humility to his passion" the sacrifice of Christ constitutes a true satisfaction of sin. It remains this personal devotion of Christ that makes his real sufferings efficacious and wins for him the glory of resurrection. (Surely his executioners did not consider themselves as doing something pleasing for God.) Only Christ's love, then, makes his sacrifice both true worship and authentic satisfaction. Although Thomas never loses sight of the intimate connection between the sufferings of Christ and the satisfactory aspect of his sacrifice, he nonetheless stresses the priestly sacrifice of Christ, motivated by love and undertaken with humility, as the effective instrument which brings about justice in a restored creation. "Therefore he is the mediator of a new covenant, so that those who are called may receive the promised inheritance, since a death has occurred which redeems them from the transgressions under the first covenant" (Heb 9:15).

Thomas's comprehension of Christ's priesthood achieves a degree of insight unmatched by his contemporaries. Perhaps the fact that he wrote the first medieval commentary (though not gloss) on Hebrews accounts for this theological development. In any event, the pages of the New Testament leave no doubt as to the central importance of the passion in the life of Christ. Thomas reflects this concern, as the frequent references to Scripture testify, by clearly making satisfaction for sin a primary task imposed on Christ the priest. We have already remarked that Thomas frequently casts new light on the traditional ways of speaking about the incarnation as satisfying God's justice. Augustine's speaks about the justice involved in the fact that the incarnate Word destroyed, in the flesh of Adam's stock, the power of the devil over fallen man. Anselm's presents Christ's satisfaction as restoring the broken order of divine justice in the world. Thomas's discussion of the priesthood and passion of Christ incorporates the main thrusts of the these traditional approaches to Christ's satisfaction, with the result that he transforms justice into reverence and worship. The perfect worship of God's glory remains a priestly act, accomplished in the context of the virtue of religion.

Aquinas frequently refers to the fact that God's justice introduces satisfactory punishments aimed at the restoration of his glory. Although this raises a question about the propriety of vindicative justice as an instrument of the divine will, Aquinas allows the traditional understanding to remain. But his interpretation of what vindicative justice entails casts an altogether different light on Christian life than what we might expect to find in the writings of those who miss the point of Christ's priesthood and sacrifice. Thus, Aquinas's treatment of the priesthood of Christ remains of pivotal importance. Since God expects the debt of true priestly worship, he provides for this in the priestly character of the incarnate Son. Christ embodies the perfect just man, the one who alone properly offers to God the sacrifice that fits a divine "debitum." The tradition correctly grasped that an act of justice alone could not satisfy for the offense of sin. Aquinas, however, makes it clear that Christ does not simply satisfy a retributive justice. In offering a sacrifice of worship, Christ fully propitiates the divine justice and once again inaugurates the divine glory in the world.

Christ's priesthood, then, must logically be spoken about in terms of his relation to his Father. "Every high priest chosen from among men is appointed to act on behalf of men in relation to God, to offer gifts and sacrifices for sins" (Heb 5:1). Nevertheless Thomas ascribes its effects to the members of Christ. Thus "a priest is constituted an intermediary between God and man, but the only person who stands in need of an intermediary with God is one who is unable to approach God for himself" (IIIa q. 22, a. 3). By his satisfaction, Christ restores the order of justice in our relations with God, for he has entered "into heaven itself, now to appear in the presence of God on our behalf" (Heb 9:24). In brief, Christ's love restores that order of personal relationships into which our native finality draws us. Christ's worship, the religious expression of justice, opens the way to love. The satisfaction of Christ the priest does not principally appease a divine vindicative justice; rather, according to this profound understanding of the redemptive work of Christ, it makes possible the very communication of divine goodness itself.

Christ as related to the members: his mediation

Since it effects our reconciliation with God, the work of satisfaction properly belongs under the heading of those duties Christ performs as our mediator with God. But Christ's function as mediator chiefly points to his created human nature--to the fact that he is man--and on this basis we can distinguish his mediation from his priesthood. The question devoted to the mediatorship of Christ, which ranks among the smallest in the *Summa theologiae*, nevertheless explains Christ's satisfaction as mediator in terms practically identical with those used to describe his work as priest. For example, Thomas writes:

> It is quite true that the power of taking away sins with personal authority belongs to Christ as God. But it is as man that he satisfies for the sin of the human race; and it is on this ground that he is called the mediator of God and men (IIIa q. 26, a. 2, ad 3).

Aquinas now turns our attention to the anthropological aspect of Christ's satisfaction. Christ's human history unfolds before us. Everything which transpires in his life forms part of his mediation.

Question 26 thus serves as a sort of preface to the rest of the *Summa theologiae*, since it introduces the discussion of Christ's mediation contained in the mysteries of his life, death, and resurrection. The sacraments of the Church extend that mediation in space and time. Although Christ remains the one sufficient mediator for all time, he nonetheless allows others to participate in his mediation in diverse ways. In particular, the priests of the new dispensation receive the charge to carry out the office of sacrifice and worship through the continual celebration of the Eucharist, the sacrament of unity and love in the Church.

Qq. 46-59: Satisfaction:
"To Win for Our Spirit Perfect Union with God"
as the Key-Notion of Christ's Redemptive Death

Even though everything Christ said or did is part of his priestly mediation, the Gospels make it clear that the events surrounding his passion and death constitute the principal moments of God's salvation. Thomas divides his examination of the mystery of Christ's life, death, and exaltation under four separate headings.

Having gone through the matters relating to the union of God and man and the corollaries that follow from that union, we turn now to the things which the incarnate Son of God actually did and suffered in the human nature united to him. We shall examine under four headings the things involved:

first, in his coming into the world;
second, in the regular course of his life;
third, in his departing from the world;
fourth, in his exaltation after his life on earth.

We find the subjects directly related to satisfaction treated according to the following outline:

How are we to understand Christ's passion and death, whereby "he departed from this world"?

Christian reflection on the mystery of the passion, from the perspective of what Christ suffered (q. 46), as well as the causes (q. 47), modes of efficacy (q. 48) and effects (q. 49) of the passion. Christian reflection on the death of Christ (q. 50); his burial (q. 51); and his descent into hell (q. 52).

How are we to understand the exaltation of Christ?

The resurrection, considered from the point of view of its relation to the passion (q. 53); as it affected Christ himself (q. 54) and how the resurrection of Christ was manifested (q. 55); the causality of the resurrection (q. 56). The mystery of Christ's ascension (q. 57), and his sitting at the right hand of God in majesty (q. 58) and in power (q. 59).

This marks out the boundaries of the theological terrain Aquinas covers in the final section of his christology.[35]

The Method of Investigation Employed by Aquinas

The methodology which Thomas employs in his investigation of Christ's passion and death reveals something about his conception of theology's task. The uninformed student could read these questions in the *Summa* and easily arrive at the same conclusion which impressed Harnack, who, after considering the *tertia pars*, wrote: "multa sed non multum."[36]   But a more sympathetic analysis reveals that Aquinas does accomplish much, for he relates every detail in the mystery of Christ's life and death to an even more central theological truth about God's relationship to the world.   Thus for Aquinas, even christology remains principally a theo-logia, a "word about God."   He never speculates, therefore, whether historical christology can cover up for a refined theological agnosticism.   In fact, without the basic perspectives of the "sacra doctrina," christology remains as unintelligible as any mystery would seem apart from faith.   This is true, even if the search for the historical Jesus makes it appear that an alternative, independent approach to Christ really does exist.   Christology from within the "sacra doctrina," moreover, avoids the critical error of letting the study of Christ slip into the center of theological investigation, with all the dangers of thereby speaking a word principally about creatures instead of about God.

Three methodological principles control Thomas's use of his sources. His method makes it plain that, although he supplies ample references to the patristic tradition, his concept of theology as a sacred science marks a decisive departure from the methods employed by the glossators.   First, we can point to the way Aquinas applies the principles established in qq. 2-26 concerning the ontological structure of the incarnate God to the various aspects of Christ's life, death, and exaltation.   For example, Aquinas takes pains to sort out the several levels of divine causality involved in the death of Christ.   Second, he steadfastly refuses to account for the benefits of salvation by any other means than God's choice to save us through the visible humanity of Christ.   For example, we observe in these questions Thomas's practice of citing the instructive value of the mysteries of Christ's life, which, in addition to what Christ taught, also communicate divine truth.   Third, Aquinas relates the individual events of Christ's life to the central purpose of his ministry, namely, the inauguration of the new law of grace and the restoration of covenantal love between God and man.[37]

To sum up: Aquinas does not expound the details of Christ's life simply for the purpose of presenting a complete narration of his earthly mission. The scriptures themselves accomplish that commission. Aquinas, on the other hand, performs the task of a theologian. So he interprets each detail and event of Christ's life, admittedly under the light of faith, but also with that "most fruitful help," as Vatican I puts it, which the judgment of reason can supply.[38] As happens in good theology, Aquinas consequently avoids useless multiplication of data, and instead draws interpretive meaning from the revealed sources of God's word, what Schillebeeckx calls faith's "inner demand for theology."[39] Exegetes and idealists may juggle concepts and symbols, but existential judgments in theology are to be left to the Holy Spirit and those theologians who respect the integrity of the discipline.

Qq. 46, aa. 1-6: Programmatic Essay:
Redemption with all the Human Values of Satisfaction

The first question of this section of the *tertia pars* serves a twofold purpose. In the same way the first question of the *tertia pars* served as a general introduction to Thomas's christology, the initial three articles of q. 46 provide a programmatic essay for the discussion that follows (qq. 47-52). The remaining articles recall the realty of Christ's suffering from many different aspects, *viz.*, the mental and physical pain, the time and place of the passion, and so forth. In the programmatic essay, moreover, Thomas relates the passion of Christ to our salvation in much the same way that he earlier related the incarnation to the self-communication of the divine goodness. He affirms that while no absolute necessity obliged Christ to suffer, Christ's sufferings were necessary if a number of specific goals were to be accomplished easily.

Among these, Aquinas points to Christ's own bodily exaltation, to the fulfillment of certain Old Testament prophecies, but especially to our liberation. As he explains, the requirement that Christ suffer and die finds its deepest explanation in the effect it achieves within the human order.

> The liberation of man through the passion of Christ was consonant with both his mercy and his justice. It is consonant with his justice because by his passion Christ made satisfaction for the sin of the human race, and man was freed through the justice of Christ. It is consonant with his mercy because, since man was by himself unable to satisfy for the sin of all human nature, God gave him his Son to do so. According to Paul: "They are justified freely by his grace through the redemption which is in Christ Jesus, whom God has set forth as a propitiation by his blood, through faith." In so acting God manifested greater mercy than if he had forgiven sins without requiring satisfaction. Paul therefore writes: "God, who is rich in mercy, by reason of his great love with which he loved us, even when we were dead by reason of our sins, brought us to life together with Christ" (IIIa q. 46, a. 1, ad 3).

Absolutely speaking, then, other means were open to God, but given the hypothesis ("ex suppositione") that the present order of salvation history was foreknown, no other divine choice would have led to a healing of sin's wounds. In order to emphasize the positive value in Christ's suffering, Aquinas will next distinguish satisfaction from salvation as a mere liberation from sin.

If God's justice requires satisfaction, then Christ's passion must have been the only way of saving the human race. Aquinas's response distinguishes between justice taken in the legal sense and the evangelical justification of the sinner.

> Even this justice depends upon the divine will which requires satisfaction for sin from the human race. For if God had wanted to free man from sin without any satisfaction at all, he would not have been acting against justice. Justice cannot be safeguarded by the judge whose duty it is to punish crimes committed against others, e.g., against a fellow man, or the government, or the head of the government, should he dismiss a crime without punishment. But God has no one above him, for he is himself the supreme and common good of the entire universe. If then he forgives sin, which is a crime in that it is committed against him, he violates no one's rights. The one who waives satisfaction and forgives an offense done to himself acts mercifully, not unjustly (IIIa q. 46, a. 2, ad 3).

We can observe in this response a shift of emphasis from Anselm's response to the same objection and, for that matter, the response of Thomas himself in his earlier works. For Anselm and the early Thomas, the thought of God forgiving sin without punishment implied a disorder. This held true even when they took account of the divine mercy. The explanation was that, while God's justice demanded satisfaction, his mercy provided it in Christ. Besides, it was suggested, for God to forgive sin without punishment would give bad example to human judges, who are required to punish offenses justly.

Now, however, Aquinas, points to the preeminence of the divine goodness as a reason for God not to liberate us without satisfaction accomplished through the very sufferings of Christ. Perhaps the implications drawn from other kinds of human experience, e.g., the case of an individual who waives satisfaction and simply forgives an offense, contribute to modifying Thomas's previous hesitancy in this matter. Admittedly, though, a better explanation (if demonstrable) would lie in the fact that Thomas had achieved a deeper understanding of the divine transcendence and, therefore, had become considerably less hesitant to speak about God in terms other than those suggested by the norms for human conduct. In any event, bad example to human judges no longer seems a serious matter for him. He has moved from thinking of justice as a moral virtue which observes a rational mean to envisioning the satisfaction of Christ as the principal expression of evangelical justice.

The use of the term "liberate" (e.g., "pro liberatione," "modus liberationis," "ad liberationem") throughout these initial articles represents an important choice for Aquinas. He wants to preserve the absolute freedom of divine love as it communicates itself in the world and at the same time to give full meaning to the way in which God actually manifests his love in Christ. This leads him to conclude that, although God could have freed man from his sins in some other way than by the sufferings of Christ, such a decision would not have constituted a redemption with all the human values of satisfaction, but simply a liberation.

Thomas gives five reasons which specify the benefits that accrue to man by reason of a redemption by satisfaction rather than a simple liberation from sin:

> First, man could thus see how much God loved him, and so would be aroused to love him. The perfection of his salvation consists in this. Paul therefore writes: "God shows his love for us, in that while we were yet
> sinners, Christ died for us."

> Second, he gave us an example of obedience, humility, constancy, justice and other virtues which his passion revealed and which are necessary for man's salvation. Peter notes that "Christ has suffered for us, leaving you an example that you may follow in his footsteps."

> Third, by his passion Christ not only freed man from sin but merited for him the grace of justification and the glory of beatitude.

> Fourth, man thus feels a greater obligation to refrain from sin, as Paul says: "You were bought with a great price, so glorify and bear God in your body."

> Fifth, in this way a greater dignity accrues to man. Man has been overcome and deceived by the devil. But it is a man also who overcomes the devil. Man has merited death; a man by dying would conquer death. "Thanks be to God," Paul writes, "who has given us the victory through our Lord Jesus Christ." It was therefore better for us to have been delivered by Christ's passion than by God's will alone (IIIa q. 46, a. 3).

These five reasons of fittingness allow Aquinas the occasion to delineate some of the human values satisfaction entails. The centrality of satisfaction in Christ's salvific death chiefly arises from "the greater dignity which accrues to man" from it. Like St Paul, Aquinas seeks reasons to boast about the cross of Christ.

The primary symbol of the passion, of course, remains the cross, the instrument of Christ's passion and the insignia of the Christian faith. Aquinas draws together certain allegories to explain the significance of this means of execution.

Death by crucifixion was suited in every way to atone for the sin of our first parent, who in violation of God's command sinned by taking the fruit of a forbidden tree. It was fitting, in order to satisfy for that sin, that Christ should allow himself to be fixed to the tree of the cross, thus restoring as it were what Adam had stolen. "Then did I pay," the psalmist says, "what I did not take away." Augustine says that "Adam scorned the precept and plucked the fruit from the tree; but what Adam lost, Christ found again on the cross (IIIa q. 46, a. 4).

Granted the medieval curiosity about the devil's role in the first parents' fall, Aquinas still practices a decided reserve when it comes to speaking about how Christ vanquishes the devil.[40]

The question of Christ's actual physical and mental sufferings, which he experienced in the course of his passion, also forms part of Aquinas's meditation. Thomas evaluates these sufferings of Christ in accord with the principles established for discovering the disabilities of body and soul which Christ assumes in his humanity. In general, he portrays the consummate character of Christ's physical and spiritual sufferings, the sensitivity of the one suffering, and the magnitude of the sufferings themselves. Christ's psychological suffering, for example, is increased to the extent that he satisfied for the sins of the world as well as by the knowledge of his own innocence. In an especially nuanced remark, Thomas describes how Christ even suffered sadness during the course of his satisfaction.

The Stoics saw no utility in sadness and, looking upon it as completely contrary to reason, taught that a wise man should avoid it completely. Actually, however, some sadness is praiseworthy, when, for example, it proceeds from a holy love; this occurs when a man is saddened over his own or another's sin. Sadness can also be useful when it is aimed at satisfying for sin, for "the sorrow that is according to God produces repentance that tends to salvation." Christ, then, in order to satisfy for the sins of all men, suffered the most profound sadness, absolutely speaking, but not so great that it exceeded the rule of reason (IIIa q. 46, a.6, ad 2).

On the cross, Christ provides an example of right sorrow for sin. "For it was fitting that he, for whom and by whom all things exist, in bringing many sons to glory, should make the pioneer of their salvation perfect through suffering" (Heb 2:10).

Q. 47, aa. 1-3: Christ's Loving Obedience to his Father's Will

Thomas has already supplied reasons why any means other than the passion of Christ would not accomplish salvation with the human values involved in satisfaction. "Given a certain hypothesis ("ex suppositione facta"), there was no other way. It is impossible that God's foreknowledge should be erroneous and that his will or plan be frustrated" (IIIa q. 46, a. 2). He now clarifies the exact nature of this hypothesis in order to illuminate the omnipotence of God and the freedom of Christ. How can we maintain the absolutely free and transcendent will of God to save us through suffering and, at the same time, account for the fully human and, therefore, free response of Christ? Again, can we make God the cause Christ's sufferings? Or, does Christ's obedience involve him causally in his own death? The clarification of the interplay between the divine will and Christ's human will also serves as a first step in order to determine the responsibility of those who actually executed Christ. Of course, Aquinas maintains that the killing of Christ constitutes "a most grievous sin" in itself ("ex genere peccati").

Thomas's explanation of Christ's killing concentrates on three major points. Each expresses the reciprocal meshing of Christ's will with the Father's plan for our salvation. First, God delivers a command and Christ responds in obedience. Second, Christ demonstrates love for the Father and the Father welcomes the created love of Christ's heart, purified by the "gratia unionis." Third, both Christ and the Father enjoyed the absolute power to restrain those who slew Christ, but did not do so. The following texts enlarge on these points. First, we consider the Father's role in the passion of his Son.

God the Father delivered Christ to his passion in three ways.

First, by his eternal will, he ordained our Lord's sufferings in advance for the liberation of the human race. "The Lord laid upon him the guilt of us all," and, "The Lord was pleased to crush him in his infirmity."

Second, by filling him with charity he inspired in him the will to suffer for us. "He was offered because it was his own will."

Third, he did not shield him from suffering but abandoned him to his persecutors. Hence as he hung on the cross Jesus said: "My God, my God, why have you abandoned me," that is, God delivered him into the power of those who persecuted him (IIIa q. 47, a. 3).

The second series of texts (taken from q. 47, aa. 2,3 *passim*) describes Christ's response to his Father's will. First, Christ received a command from his Father to suffer.

Although obedience conveys the idea of having to do what has been commanded, it also implies the will to carry out that command. Such was Christ's obedience.

[Second], the same response prompted Christ's sufferings out of charity and out of obedience. He fulfilled the precepts of charity out of obedience and was obedient because of his love for the Father who had given him the command.

[Third], Christ suffered the violence that caused his death and at the same time died by his own will, for he had the power to prevent it.

Christ's submission to the will of the Father establishes the exemplar for all human loving. "Although he was a Son, he learned obedience through what he suffered; and being made perfect he became the source of eternal salvation to all who obey him" (Heb 5:8,9).

Several features of Aquinas's theology of satisfaction merit careful attention at this point. First, Aquinas locates the essence of Christ's sacrifice in the perfect meshing of his human will with that which the Father from all eternity wills for the salvation of the world. From this point of view, Aquinas leaves little room for a developed theory of penal substitution.[41] Second, the inauguration of the new dispensation occurs because of the love and obedience of the incarnate Son. Indeed, we recognize in Christ the perfection of the beatitude he himself taught as expressive of the new law, "Blessed are those who are persecuted for righteousness sake, for theirs is the kingdom of heaven" (Mt 5:10). Third, Christ fulfills the role of Suffering Servant as described in Isaiah and the Pauline writings. Although the biblical theme of the Suffering Servant can easily inspire an unbalanced presentation of Christ's suffering, Aquinas still manages to present Christ's obedience to God's plan of salvation without suggesting a vengeful God who exacts a terrible punishment from an innocent victim.[42] Instead, he points to the example of virtue which Christ exhibits for our edification.

All in all, the principal themes of Hebrews mark Aquinas's treatment of the passion in the *Summa theologiae*. "Sacrifices and offerings thou hast not desired. . . . 'Lo, I have come to do thy will, O God'" (Heb 10:5,7). Christ the priest of the new alliance offers to God the perfect worship of praise. Even so, it is not the sacrifice of his body on the altar of the cross in which this perfect worship mainly consists, but his personal offering of obedience and love. Since the divine will to which Christ is obedient remains identical with the salvific will of God for man's salvation, Christ's satisfactory offering opens the way up to salvation. The charity of Christ, "obedient because of his love for the Father," inaugurates the new covenant of love. "We have this as a sure and steadfast anchor of the soul, a hope that enters into the inner shrine behind the curtain, where Jesus has gone as a forerunner on our behalf, having become a high priest for ever after the order of Melchizedek" (Heb 6:19,20). In one place, Thomas illustrates why Christ, in imitation of the Old Testament holocausts, should not have been put to death by fire. The wood of the cross, he explains, is prefigured in the wooden altar used for such sacrifices, but "in the holocaust of Christ the material fire was replaced by the fire of charity" (IIIa q. 46, a. 4, ad 1).

Q. 48, aa. 1-6: Satisfaction: Key-Notion for Interpreting Christ's Redemptive Death

Aquinas now turns to the essential question of the efficacy of Christ's passion. How does Christ's death accomplish our salvation? The five modes which Thomas discusses in these articles continue to draw the attention of theologians.[43] For they provide different interpretations of the passion, by which he organizes a large amount of material in a relatively compact manner. He speaks of the passion of Christ working by way ("per modum") of merit (q. 48, a. 1); of satisfaction (q. 48, a. 2); of sacrifice (q. 48, a. 3); of redemption (q. 48, a. 4); and, finally, by way of divine (q. 48, a. 5) instrumental causality (q. 48, a. 6). In short, question 48 makes a causal assertion about the death of Christ. But like any question in the *Summa*, it must be read in context.

Although each of the modes forms part of a comprehensive explanation of the efficacy of the passion, we can nevertheless speculate about which one serves as the principal or key-notion in Thomas's theology. The reasons for undertaking such a discussion include the conviction that satisfaction is a dominant feature of the Christian life. Of course, any of the other modes account for actions and passions no less indispensable to our salvation, but the actual economy of salvation, marked as it is by human sin and frustration, requires the satisfaction of Christ as the archimedean point of the new dispensation. Aquinas, however, does not make the task of defending this position easy. Several texts, for example, seem to support the view that satisfaction remains just one of several good analogies, which accounts for the suffering Christ endured. Again, if a key-notion does exist, there is likewise a strong case to be made for the capital merit of Christ. On the other hand, since the gravitational center of Aquinas's soteriology remains the actual economy of salvation as revealed in the scriptures, the motive of Christ's mission must include a direct reference to the presence of sin in the world. Merit, however, points to reward, not failure. Hence the general perspectives of Aquinas's theology require that the notion of satisfaction constitute the initial prerequisite for image-restoration. "But as it is, he has appeared once for all at the end of the age to put away sin by the sacrifice of himself" (Heb 9:26).

Alternative interpretations of Q. 48

Some authors nevertheless reject any attempt to systematize the thought of Aquinas in this matter. In a study devoted to this question, for example, Bernard Catão definitively excludes Christ's satisfaction as the key-notion ("notion maîtresse") of Aquinas's soteriology. Rather, writes Catão, it provides "a good analogy which, among others, aids in understanding why the human act of the Saviour was one of humiliation, suffering, and death on the cross."[44] Admittedly, Aquinas does at times describe each of the modes in a similar fashion. For example, he frequently compares the headship of Christ with merit and at other times he proposes the parallel it has with satisfaction.

> We have pointed out that Christ was given grace not only as an individual but insofar as he is head of the Church, so that grace might pour out from him upon his members. Thus there is the same relation between what another man does in the state of grace and himself (IIIa q. 48, a. 1).

> The head and members form as it were a single mystical person. Christ's satisfaction therefore extends to all the faithful as to his members. When two men are united in charity one can satisfy for the other (IIIa q. 48, a. 2, ad 1).

These texts, however, exhibit only a partial view of the position Aquinas establishes in q. 48.

As is incumbent upon any theologian, Aquinas manages several strands of biblical tradition concerning the passion of Christ. So, for example, in an effort to untangle the relationship between the satisfaction accomplished by Christ and the "superabundant" satisfaction which the tradition since Anselm concluded could alone expiate our offenses, Aquinas compares the different modes. This allows him to emphasize the place satisfaction holds in the larger picture. In any event, he sets forth a synthesis of themes already discussed in other contexts.

> A man effectively satisfies for an offense when he offers to the one who has been offended something which he accepts as matching or outweighing the former offense. Christ, suffering in a loving and obedient spirit, offered more to God than was demanded in recompense for all the sins of mankind because, first, the love which led him to suffer was a great love; second, the life he laid down in satisfaction was of great dignity, since it was the life of God and of man; and third, his suffering was all-embracing and his pain so great. Christ's passion, then, was not only sufficient but superabundant satisfaction for the sins of mankind (IIIa q. 48, a. 2).

Similarly, Thomas makes the same point with respect to sacrifice: "This gesture, this voluntary enduring of the passion, motivated as it was by the greatest love, pleased God. It is clear then that Christ's passion was a true sacrifice" (IIIa q. 48, a. 3). Again, Aquinas puts the mode of redemption in terms similar to those used for those of satisfaction and of sacrifice: "Christ offered satisfaction by giving the greatest of all things, namely himself, for us. For that reason the passion of Christ is said to be our redemption" (IIIa q. 48, a. 4). Finally, he resolves merit: "It is clear that if anyone in the state of grace suffers for justice's sake, by that very fact he merits salvation for himself, for it is written: 'Blessed are they who suffer persecution for justice's sake.'" (IIIa q. 48, a. 1).

If we look only at the textual evidence, then, it seems that Aquinas places no special emphasis on any particular mode. Instead the passion of Christ suffered according to his human nature expresses different aspects of the single divine action operating in the world. The following important text contributes to this impression.

> When Christ's passion is viewed in relation to his divinity it can be seen to act in an efficient way; in relation to the will which is rooted in Christ's soul, by way of merit; in relation to the very flesh of Christ, by way of satisfaction, since we are freed by it from the guilt of punishment; by way of redemption, inasmuch as we are thereby freed from the slavery of sin; and finally, by way of sacrifice, thanks to which we are reconciled by God (IIIa q. 48, a. 6, ad 3).

This conclusion appears even more reasonable when we consider that this text appears by way of summary at the very end of Aquinas's treatment of the matter.

On the other hand, since it expresses the divine agency in a human mode of communication, we might conclude that the capital merit of Christ actually is the principal focus of Aquinas's soteriology. "All this is from God, who through Christ reconciled us to himself and gave us the ministry of reconciliation; that is, in Christ God was reconciling the world to himself" (IICor 5:18,19). To be sure, Aquinas uses instrumental efficient causality in order to explain how the meritorious and satisfactory deeds of Christ can "spiritually affect" his members. So it would seem reasonable, especially in terms of a functional christology, for Christ's mediation in the Church to supply the key-notion for interpreting his redemptive sufferings.

Instrumental causality, in fact, is not the peripheral element in the Thomist system which it is sometimes represented as being. It is rather an essential element of the synthesis. It signifies the means by which Aquinas introduced into western theology the richly suggestive intuition of the Greek Fathers that the very union of God with human nature brought redemption to all that is human. The sacred humanity of Christ, because it is united to the person of the divine Son, is the source from which salvation merited by Christ is physically communicated (that is, by efficient causality) to all who are united in the one mystical person of Christ. All in all, Aquinas seems to put great emphasis on this element of his explanatory scheme.

Morever, Aquinas had immediate recourse to this principle in order to explain the universality of Christ's merit and satisfaction in *De veritate* q. 29, a. 7. His careful analysis of Christ's human and divine activity in the *Summa*, moreover, altered somewhat his interpretation of the effects of that activity.[45] For there he prefers to assign Christ's merit to his human activity, although communication of that merit is explained in terms of the headship of Christ and the ability of a head to influence its members. Later, in the articles of q. 48, Aquinas reunites merit, headship, and instrumental causality to explain the full meaning of Christ's salvific actions. Thus, the capital meritorious grace of Christ, transmitted to the members of his body, explains why Christ's passion accomplished the salvific plan of God. G. Lafont consequently favors this conclusion when he writes that the capital merit of Christ gives the works of Christ their efficacy for us.[46] Moreover, he cites this text from Aquinas in support of the thesis.

> Christ's passion causes the forgiveness of sins by way of ransom. He is our head and has, by his passion (endured out of love and obedience) freed us, his members, from our sins, the passion being as it were the ransom. It is as if, by performing some meritorious work with his hands, a man might redeem himself from a sin he had committed with his feet. For the natural body, though made up of different members, is one, and the whole Church which is Christ's mystical body is deemed to be one person with its head, Christ (IIIa q. 49, a. 1).

By the same token, Lafont also acknowledges that Aquinas adds certain "aspects complèmentaires," *viz.*, the modes of satisfaction, sacrifice, and redemption, to bring out the full intelligibility of Christ's merit in its historical expression. Although this makes a strong case for interpreting a batch of texts in the *tertia pars*, it does not, on that account alone, point to the key-notion of Aquinas's soteriology.

Satisfaction: Required for the work of image-restoration

The notion of capital merit alone, however, cannot account for the efficacy of Christ's passion. "Once a certain hypothesis is granted ("ex aliqua suppositione facta"), there was no other way for the passion of Christ to bring about man's salvation," writes Aquinas. The work of image-perfection and image-restoration require merit and satisfaction, since the very fact that God permits sin establishes a certain temper in the history of salvation.

> From the moment of his conception, Christ merited eternal salvation for us. On our part, however, there were certain obstacles which prevented us from enjoying the result of his previously acquired merits. In order to remove these obstacles, then, it was necessary that Christ suffer (IIIa q. 48, a. 1, ad 2).

The hidden wisdom of God's plan, marked as it is by the permissive exercise of the divine will which permits sin, determines satisfaction as a necessary part of salvation. In a hypothetical other economy of salvation, some other mode could predominate. But in the actual order of salvation, the "Son of man must suffer many things, and be rejected by the elders and chief priests and scribes, and be killed, and on the third day be raised" (Lk 9:22).

Aquinas stresses that the incarnation embodies God's will to love us, "in accordance with the hidden plan of his judgments." Although the conceptualization of this important element in theology must escape the Scylla of universalism and the Charybdis of predestinationism, still God's actual salvific plan for reconciling all men and women includes his permitting sin. This does not mean that evil can mount a challenge against God's goodness, because "the devil was not so strong that he could harm men without God's permission." Nonetheless, evil does enjoy a limited power in the world. Aquinas insists, moreover, that "even now God allows the devil to try men's souls."[47] Hence God's permitting sin not only accounts for original sin (Aquinas's "chief" reason for Christ's passion) but also for subsequent sin in the world. Aquinas gives perspective to this confrontation of the power of evil with our desire to find happiness in God: "The remedy prepared by Christ's passion is always available to man. The fact that some prefer not to use this remedy in no way detracts from the efficacy of Christ's passion" (IIIa q. 49, a. 2, ad 3).

The Christian faith commemorates this victory which Christ wins by conquering sin and death. Gregory of Nyssa, for example, provides a celebrated and imaginative parable in *The Great Catechism*, c. 24. There he compares the devil to a ravenous fish who "gulps down the hook of the Godhead along with the bait of his flesh, and thus, life being introduced into a house of death, and light shining in the darkness, that which is diametrically opposed to light and life vanishes." In the *tertia pars*, Aquinas recognizes the profundity of the way in which the Christian triumphs over sin and death. In fact, when he speaks about the universal call to holiness, he stresses that divine grace always surpasses human weakness.

> Nothing, however, stands in the way of human nature's being lifted to something greater, even after sin. God permits evil that

he might draw forth some good. Thus the text in Romans reads: "Where wickedness abounded, grace abounded yet more," and in the blessing of the Paschal Candle: "O happy fault that merited so great a redeemer" (IIIa q. 1, a. 3, ad 3).

Christ the Redeemer, who makes satisfaction for sin, fulfills the divine promise that God will draw good out of evil. "But the free gift is not like the trespass. For if many died through one man's trespass, much more have the grace of God and the free gift in the grace of that one man Jesus Christ abounded for many" (Rom 5:15).

In another text, Aquinas directly associates the christological dimension of the "felix culpa" with Christ's satisfaction for sin. We find there besides corroboration for the thesis that satisfaction remain the key-notion for Aquinas's thematization of soteriology.

> Christ's passion delivered us from the debt of punishment in two ways. First of all, directly, for the passion of Christ was adequate, and more than adequate, to satisfy for the sins of all mankind. Once sufficient satisfaction has been made, the debt of punishment ceases. Second, indirectly, for Christ's passion is the cause of the forgiveness of sin, and sin is the basis for the debt of punishment (IIIa q. 49, a. 3).

The meaning of Christ's satisfaction for those who suffer in the world remains Aquinas's principal concern in the remainder of the *tertia pars*. The Church, for Aquinas, is the place where those who suffer find rest in Christ. "Come to me, all who labor and are heavy laden, and I will give you rest" (Mt 11:28). Hence the sacramental system in the Church incorporates the basic theology of satisfaction as Aquinas elaborates it in terms of Christ's victory over sin.

> In order to benefit from Christ's passion one must be likened to him. We are sacramentally conformed to him in baptism, for "we were buried with him by means of baptism into death." Hence no atoning punishment is imposed upon men at baptism, for they are then completely freed by the satisfaction offered by Christ. And since "Christ died once and for all for our sins," man cannot be conformed to Christ by being baptized a second time. It is therefore right that those who commit sin after baptism should be made to conform to the suffering Christ by experiencing some penalty or suffering in their own persons. This punishment, which is much less than man's sin deserves, does nevertheless suffice because Christ's satisfaction works along with it (IIIa q. 49, a. 3, ad 2).

Christian living, then, remains ordered toward reversing the effects of evil in the world. But the victory belongs to Christ.

Reconciliation: Effect of Christ's satisfaction

To sum up: the essentially cruciform pattern of Christian life itself harmonizes the themes of adoptive sonship and satisfactory suffering. The members of Christ's body actively united in faith with the eternal Son and Suffering Servant posses the integrity which Christ alone can provide. For in their own personal histories, members of the Church turns the "mysterium iniquitatis" into a happy fault for the development of the mystical body and for the worship of God's glory.

> Christ's satisfaction brings about its effect in us insofar as we are incorporated into him as members are into the head. But members should be conformed to their head. Hence just as Christ, who besides having grace in his soul also had a body that could suffer, attained through his passion to a glorious immortality, we who are his members are freed by his passion from the debt of any punishment whatsoever. But we must first have received into our souls "the spirit of adoption as sons" by which we are marked out for the inheritance of a glorious immortality, while yet retaining a body subject to suffering and death. Later, when we have "become like Christ through suffering and death," we will be led into eternal glory, according to the Apostle who says: "If we are sons, we are heirs also; heirs indeed of God and joint heirs with Christ, provided that we suffer with him, so that we may also be glorified with him" (IIIa q. 49, a. 3, ad 3).

In short, the work of satisfaction remains a work of reconciliation. "For in him all the fullness of God was pleased to dwell, and through him to reconcile to himself all things, whether on earth or in heaven, making peace by the blood of his cross" (Col 1:19).

God achieves his original purpose of communicating divine goodness to the world in a manner surpassing what would have been the case if Adam had not sinned. In fact, God's attitude towards us does not change. Why? Because "God loves in all men the nature which he has made; what he hates in man is the sins which men commit against him" (IIIa q. 49, a. 4, ad 1). The immutability of God's love forms the mainstay of Aquinas's soteriology. Unpersuaded of the need for a changing God to accommodate the erratic movement of human history, Aquinas prefers to locate the effect of the passion in the changeable creature instead of the transcendent God.

> When we say that Christ's passion reconciled us to God we do not mean that God has begun anew to love us, for it is written that "with age-old love I have loved you." Thanks to Christ's

passion the cause for hatred has been removed, both because sin has been wiped away and because compensation has been made in the form of a more agreeable offering (IIIa q. 49, a. 4, ad 4).

This points to an entirely different picture of vicarious satisfaction. God does not accept anything in exchange or relent on account of something which Christ does. If Christ substitutes for sinful man in the experience of his passion, he does so only to enable men and women themselves to experience again the compassion of God. It is not that God then resumes being compassionate; rather, the human person is then free to accept God's love. All in all, satisfaction changes us, not God.

As a result, we say that Christ's passion opened for us the gates of heaven. This metaphor refers, of course, to the removal of an obstacle in the achieving a final goal. Christ's passion removes both the obstacle of original sin and those sins which stem from it. The priesthood of Christ, however, figures in this satisfaction, since he offers to God a renewed humanity. Authentic worship of the Father transforms the human person, making him or her a sharer in the fruits of Christ's passion by faith, love, and the sacraments. Thomas develops this idea in the following text, which occurs towards the end of his treatise on the passion. In it we recognize Aquinas's preference for theological reflection which takes full account of the praxis of the Christian church.

A closed gate prevents entrance. Men were prevented by sin from entering the heavenly kingdom. Two kinds of sin prevent us from entering the heavenly kingdom. The first is the sin common to the whole human race, namely, that of our first parent, which deprived man of entry into the heavenly kingdom. Thus, after Adam's sin, "God placed the cherubim and the flaming sword which turned every way, to guard the way to the tree of life." Through Christ's passion, however, we are delivered not only from the sin of the entire human race both as regards the sin and the debt of punishment (for Christ paid the price of our ransom), but also from our own sins, provided we share in his passion by faith, love and the sacraments of faith. Thus through Christ's passion we find the door of the heavenly kingdom open. It was this that the Apostle had in mind when he wrote: "Christ as high priest of the good things to come entered once for all by virtue of his own blood into the Holies, having obtained eternal redemption" (IIIa q. 49, a. 5).

The sacramental reference brings this section of the study to a close. Aquinas extends the agency of the passion to the sacraments of the Church. These he calls separated instruments so as to compare them suitably to the united instrument of Christ's human nature. In particular, baptism and penance provide the means for the ordinary appropriation of Christ's benefits. But Aquinas also envisions a broader realization of the economy of salvation: "This mystery is a profound one, and I am saying that it refers to Christ and the Church" (Eph 6:32).

NOTES

1. *De Jacob et vita beata* I, c. 6, 21 (*PL* 14,607). St Ambrose (c.339-397), instrument of conversion for St Augustine, emphasized the importance of the passion in Christian soteriology. "Although the mysteries of the assumption of the flesh and the passion are equally admirable," he wrote, "the fullness of faith resides in the mystery of the passion" (*De Spiritu Sancto* 3, 17, 126 [*PL* 16:840B]). This emphasis subsequently distinguishes the Latin tradition from the Greek inclination to consider the very incarnation of the Word as, in fact, a divinization of human nature.

2. For example, in the Twelfth Book, (469-78), the Archangel Michael exclaims:

> "'O Goodness infinite, Goodness immense,
> That all this good of evil shall produce,
> And evil turn to good--more wonderful
> Than that which by creation first brought forth
> Light out of darkness! Full of doubt I stand,
> Whether I should repent me now of sin
> By me done or occasioned, or rejoice
> Much more that much more good thereof shall spring--
> To God more glory, more good will to men
> From God--and over wrath shall grace abound.'"

For a discussion of this passage, see Arthur O. Lovejoy, *Essays in the History of Ideas* (New York: G.P. Putnam's Sons, 1960), c, 14, "Milton and the Paradox of the Fortunate Fall," 277-95.

3. Edition used: *Summa theologiae*, Leonine edition, vols. 4-12 (Rome, 1888-1906). Latin-English bilingual edition by various editors/translators, under the general editorship of Thomas Gilby, O.P., in 60 vols. (New York: McGraw-Hill, 1964-76). Although I rely on these volumes for English texts of the *Summa theologiae*, I have at times modified the translations.

4. This position reflects Aquinas's general view concerning the origins of moral action: "Now the perfect correctness of reason in speculative matters depends upon the principles from which it argues; for example, science depends on and presupposes understanding, which is the habit of principles. In human acts, however, ends are what principles are in speculative matters, as stated in the *Ethics* [VII, 1151a16]. Consequently, prudence, which is right reason about things to be done, requires that a man be rightly disposed with regards to ends; and this depends on rightness of appetite." For further information on the place

of prudence in Aquinas's moral theory, see M. M. Labourdette, O.P., "Connaissance pratique et savoir moral," *Revue Thomiste* 48 (1948), 142-79.

5. See Ia-IIae q. 91, a. 2 where Aquinas locates the role of natural law in morality. His modest affirmations, it should be noted, do not at all support the negative criticisms made by those who decry "natural law thinking." For a good discussion of this important topic, see Benedict M. Ashley, O.P., *Theologies of the Body: Humanist and Christian* (Braintree, MA: The Pope John XXIII Medical-Moral Research and Education Center, 1985), especially, 372-96.

6. It remains difficult then to accept the position that Aquinas, in fact, endorses the view that one can rightly intend to do "ontic" or "pre-moral" evil for a proportionately greater or higher "ontic" or "pre-moral" good. In fact, Aquinas explicitly rejects the distinction. For further information on this current debate, see William E. May, "Aquinas and Janssens on the Moral Meaning of Human Acts," *The Thomist* 48 (1984), 566-606.

7. Aquinas's moral theology distances itself, then, from the perspectives of both casuistry and revisionism. For further discussion on this point, see T.C. O'Brien, *Effects of Sin, Stain and Guilt* (1a2ae. 86-89), Vol. 27 (New York: Mc-Graw-Hill, 1974), 101.

8. I think that this position adequately covers the traditional distinction between the pain of separation and the pain of sense. Even in this life, the creature who remains separated from God suffers also the disintegration of his or her personal qualities in which the body as an essential part of the composite participates.

9. As the *tertia pars* makes clear, the life of virtues, gifts and beatitudes actually constitutes a *sequela Christi*. See Colman E. O'Neill, O.P., *The One Mediator* (3a. 16-24), Vol. 50 (New York: McGraw-Hill, 1965), especially, xxi.

10. See *Summa theologiae* Ia q. 8, a. 3. This distinction forms the basis for the later doctrine of the divine indwelling, which Aquinas discusses as one feature of the missions of the blessed Trinity. See, especially, Ia q. 43, aa. 1-8.

11. See Colossians 1:15. The expression "vestigal image" points to the aptitudinal capacity for God which remains in the human creature even after sin. Augustine uses the phrase, for example, in *De libero arbitrio* II, c. 15, 41 (*CCSL* 29, 265): "Quomodo enim te uerteris, uestigiis quibusdam quae operibus suis impressit loquitur tibi et te in exteriora relabentem ipsis exteriorum formis intro revocat." Aquinas clarifies the distinction between image and vestige in *Summa theologiae* Ia q. 45, a. 7. For more information on the subject in Augustine, see *The Image of God* (Dubuque: Priory Press, 1963), especially, 220-31.

12. For further information on this subject, see Louis Richard, *The Mystery of the Redemption*, trans by J. Horn (Baltimore: Helicon, 1965), 178. For a detailed historical account, see Jean Rivière, *Le dogme de la Rédemption au début du Moyen Age* (Paris: J. Vrin, 1934).

13. Leo the Great (c. 390-461), a theologian Pope, confronted the Huns and Vandals during the decline of the Roman Empire in the West, while he also braved christological heterodoxy in the East. His letter to the bishop of Constantinople, *Tomus ad Flavianus*, contributed to the Chalcedonian formulation in 451. See especially, 3 (*DS* 293).

14. Pelagius, a monk of Irish extraction, lived in Rome from about 384 until 410. After the fall of Rome, he went to Africa where Augustine took strong exception to Pelagius's Christian mythology, especially as it pertained to original sin and the necessity of divine grace. He died in Palestine. His doctrine and followers consistently met with official anathemas, first at Carthage and Mileve in 416 and, later, at the 2nd Council of Orange (529).

15. The Piana edition inserts after the first sentence: "But a man admittedly can make satisfaction for sin." See *Scriptum* III d. 1, q. 1, a. 2, ad 4 for another place where the same argument appears in Aquinas's writings.

16. Thomas de Vio, Cardinal Cajetan (1469-1534), *Commentarium in Summa theologiae III* (Rome: Leonine Edition, 1903), q. 1, a. 2 [#6]: "Contra quartum dictum, scilicet quod 'omnis alia satisfactio efficax est ex satisfactione Christi,' occurrit ipsemet Auctor, in IV *Sent.*, dist. xv, qu. 1, art. 2, ad 1, dicens: 'Alii dicunt quod etiam quantum ad aversionem pro peccato satisfieri potest virtute meriti Christi, quod quodammodo infinitum fuit. Et in hoc idem redit quod prius dictum est' (scilicet quod non potest satisfacere secundum aequalitatem, sed secundum acceptationem divinam): 'quia per fidem Mediatoris gratia data est credentibus. Si tamen alio modo gratiam daret, sufficeret satisfactio per modum praedictum.' Ubi patet quod Auctor idem dat judicium de satisfactione mea, sive habeam gratiam per fidem Jesu Christi, sive aliunde haberem gratiam. Ac per hoc, non fit ex satisfactione Christi satisfaciens simpliciter, sed solum secundum acceptationem: cuius oppositum hic docere videntur. Et similiter non fit ex satisfactione Christi efficax: cuius oppositum expresse hic docet."

17. Anselm, *Cur Deus homo?* I, c. 21. For an interesting application of this principle to spirituality, see "St. Anselm, 'Satisfactio', and the 'Rule' of St. Benedict," *Revue Bénédictine* 97 (1987), 101-121.

18. Rupert of Deutz (c. 1075-1129 or 1130), a controversial monk during a turbulent period in western Europe, represents the early stages of interaction between the older monastic theology and the nascent

scholastic use of dialectic, marked, for example, by interest in the hypothetical.

19. For further discussion, see Eric Mascall, *The Importance of Being Human* (London: Oxford University Press, 1959), 92-93. Also, Jeremy Moiser, "Why Did the Son of God Become Man?," *The Thomist* 37 (1973), 288-305.

20. "Dogmatic theology should be so arranged that the biblical themes are presented first." See the *Decree on Priestly Formation, Optatam totius,* n. 1.6.

21. But see the reply of L. Malevez, "Nouveau Testament et théologie fonctionnelle," *Revue des Sciences Religieuses* 48 (1960), especially, 287.

22. For further information on the reception and binding force of the Chalcedonian definition, see Aloys Grillmeier, S.J., *Christ in Christian Tradition.* Volume Two, Part One, *From Chalcedon to Justinian I,* trans by Pauline Allen & John Cawte (Atlanta: John Knox Press, 1987), especially, 3-14.

23. Boethius (480-524), martyr for learning and orthodoxy, first translated Plato and Aristotle into Latin, but his *Consolatio Philosophiae* remains his most significant contribution to medieval culture. For further information on his contributions, see Etienne Gilson, *L'esprit de la philosophie médiévale* (Paris: J. Vrin, 1932), especially, c. 10, "Le personalisme chrétien." Gilson suggests, moreover, that the notion of person, even though developed largely by theologians after the Council of Chalcedon, represents a good example of Christian philosophy.

24. These two models of Christological interpretation enjoyed currency in the middle ages under the figure of "assumptus homo" and "habitus" theories. See Walter Principe, C.S.B., *The Theology of the Hypostatic Union in the Early Thirteenth Century* 4 vols. (Toronto: Pontifical Institute of Mediaeval Studies, 1963-1975).

25. For a modern treatment of the ontological constitution of the incarnate Son, see Charles Massabki, *L'Homme-Dieu Jésus-Christ* and *L'Offrande d'amour du Christ* (Prieuré Saint-Benoit, Saint-Lambert-des-Bois, 1982, 1979).

26. For further information see J.N.D. Kelly, *Early Christian Doctrines,* second edition (New York: Harper & Row, 1960), especially, 287-9. The author, however, considers more weighty the view that Athanasius did not modify his own christology at the time of the synod of 362.

27. Aquinas was acquainted with some of these heresies as he indicates in *De articulis fidei et ecclesiae sacramentis* I [606].

28. See the "Letter to Epictetus," 7. Athanasius has left his mark on all subsequent realist soteriology: "The Word of God became man in order

that we might be made god (theopoiethomen')" (*De incarnatione*, 54 [*PG* 255:192B]).

29. Christ's human knowledge also affects our salvation: "My teaching is not mine, but his who sent me" (Jn 7:15). Theologians point out that, since Christ possesses full knowledge of those things which he reveals about the Father, the source of this knowledge requires an adequate explanation. In addition, Christ's satisfaction also requires that he personally know "the many" for whom he offers up his life. "I am not praying for the world but for those whom thou hast given me, for they are mine; all mine are thine, and thine are mine, and I am glorified in them" (Jn 17:9,10).

30. First introduced by Origen, the concept of instrumental cause became a preferred way of speaking about the relationship of Christ's body to his divinity. Thus, Athanasius: "The proper works of the Logos himself, such as raising the dead and making the blind see and healing the woman with a hemorrhage, he accomplished through the instrumentality of his own body." See his *Orations against the Arians* III, 31.

31. See *Summa theologiae* III q. 15, a. 1, ad 1.

32. For example, in IIIa q. 48, a. 5, Aquinas writes that the blessed Trinity remains the "first and remote" cause of our salvation. The term physical distinguishes Christ's agency from those of a merely moral kind.

33. The *Oxford Latin Dictionary* (1971) lists the following meanings for "fundo, ere:" (1) to pour (fluids from a vessel), pour out; (3) to drench (with); (5) to send forth in a stream; (6) to cause to rush forth; to expend or pour out lavishly. But for "redundare:" (1) to pour over, to stream forth, to overflow. Aquinas uses traditional expressions of infusion for Christ's capital grace since they refer directly to the biblical notion of "pouring out." Thus in *Summa theologiae* Ia-IIae q. 113, a. 2: "Utrum ad remissionem culpae, quae est justificatio impii, requiratur gratiae infusio."

34. Augustine, *Enarrationes in Pslamos* 60, 3. In the same work, Augustine also provides the insight for Aquinas's ecclesiology, "quasi una persona." "Iam ergo non unus; sed ideo unus, quia Christus unus, cuius omnes membra sumus. Nam quis unus homo clamat a finibus terrae? Non clamat a finibus terrae, nisi hereditas illa, de qua dictum est ipsi Filio: 'Postula a me, et dabo tibi gentes hereditatem tuam, et possessionem tuam terminos terrae.' Haec ergo Christi possessio, haec Christi hereditas, hoc Christi corpus, haec una Christi ecclesia, haec unitas quae nos sumus, clamat a finibus terrae." *Ibid.*, 2.

35. Since they do not immediately relate to the passion of Christ, qq 27-38 which consider the mystery of Christ's coming into the world as well as qq. 39-45 on the mission of Christ in his life and public ministry have been omitted from this schema.

36. Adolph von Harnack, *History of Dogma*, trans W, M'Gilchrist (London: Williams & Norgate, 1899), 196: "When we review the exposition given by Thomas, we cannot escape the impression created by confusion ("multa, non multum").

37. For further information concerning these "méthodes d'investigation," see Lafont, *Structures*, 406-12.

38. See the Dogmatic Constitution, "Dei Filius," c.3 "De fide," (*DS* 3016) of Vatican Council I (1870).

39. See E. Schillebeeckx, O.P., *Theology and Revelation*, trans N.D. Smith, O.P. (New York: Sheed and Ward, 1967), 95.

40. Like Anselm, Aquinas also sets aside the patristic tradition that Christ paid a blood ransom to the devil. This theme is found in John Chrysostom and in other later eastern Fathers, for example, Gregory of Nyssa, *The Great Catechism*, trans P. Schaff and H. Wace (Grand Rapids: Eerdmans, 1976), especially, c.23. It also found strong advocates in the West, *viz.*, in Hilary, Ambrosiaster, and Augustine.

41. Still, Aulèn, *Christus Victor*, 150, maintains that Aquinas espouses what the author calls the Latin doctrine of redemption: "The actual atonement consists in the offering of satisfaction by Christ and God's acceptance of it; with this act men have nothing to do except insofar as Christ stands as their representative. Justification is a second act, in which God transfers or imputes to men the merits of Christ; here, again, there is no direct relation between Christ and men. Next, we have Sanctification, a third act with no organic connection with the preceding two." At best, this represents a caricature of Aquinas's actual position.

42. For further information on this controversial topic, see Jean Rivière, *Le dogme de la Rédemption* (Paris: Lecoffre, 1905), especially, 8. Also, the noted French orator, J.B. Bossuet (1627-1704), *Oeuvres oratoires*, ed J. Lebarq (Lille and Paris, 1890-1921), III, 382: "Dieu montre à son Fils ce visage (de la justice); il lui montre cet oeil enflammé; il le regarde de ce regard terrible qui porte le feu devant soi . . ." Again, the recalcitrant Jesuit, Louis Bourdaloue, S.J. (1632-1704), "Exhortation sur le crucifiement et la mort de Jésus-Christ," *Oeuvres complètes* (Besançon, 1823), IX, 161: "Sous cette lèpre de péché, la justice de Dieu l'envisage comme un objet digne de toutes ses vengeances. Voilà pourquoi elle s'arme contre lui, pourquoi elle le poursuit le glaive à la main, pourquoi elle prononce l'arret de sa mort."

43. The International Theological Commission, for example, observes that Aquinas formulated these models to account for the Christian belief that Christ's death accomplished the salvation of the world. At the same time, the Commission encourages theologians to develop the seminal insights provided by Aquinas. See *Select Questions on Christology* (1980), D.4.

44. Bernard Catão, *Salut et Rédemption chez S. Thomas d'Aquin* (Paris: Aubier, 1965), especially, 79-80: "car pour lui (S. Thomas) la satisfaction n'est pas la notion maîtresse, celle qui ferait comprendre en quoi consiste la valeur rédemptrice de la croix. Elle est simplement une bonne analogie, qui, entre autres, aide à comprendre pourquoi l'acte humain du Sauveur a été humiliation, souffrance et mort sur la croix." Although the author seeks to distance himself from exaggerated interpretations, especially those of the post-Vietnam War school of French theology, his position nonetheless fails to take account of the Aquinas's distinction between the motive and the end of the incarnation.

45. See *Summa theologiae* IIIa qq. 18, 19, especially q. 19, a. 1, ad 3: "operari est hypostasis subsistentis, sed secundum formam et naturam, a qua operatio speciem recipit. Et similiter in Christo oportet quod sint duae operationes specie differentes, secundum eius duas naturas: quaelibet tamen operationem est una numero in Christo, semel facta, sicut una ambulatio et una sanatio."

46. For further information on his position, see Lafont, *Structures*, 421-32, especially, 425: "Pour conclure ce thème du mérite capital, il faut souligner que c'est lui qui donne à l'activité concrète du Christ, à son 'acte extérieur' sa portée pour nous. Mais si la rectitude intérieure de la volonté du Christ donne à son acte toute sa porté méritoire, elle ne le constitue pas totalement pour autant. Concrètement considéré, celui-ci est satisfaction, sacrifice, rédemption. . . . Ces aspects complémentaires, dont la liste n'est pas exhaustive et qui d'ailleurs s'impliquent les uns les autres, sont successivement traités par Saint Thomas."

47. Even Christ was not spared this injury. Augustine, in the *De Trinitate*, XIII, c. 14 explains how Christ's justice nonetheless overcomes the devil's wiles. "Justitia Christi diabolus victus est: quia, cum in eo nihil morte dignum inveniret, occidit eum tamen; et utique justum est ut debitores quos tenebat, liberi dimittantur, in eum credentes quem sine ullo debito occidit."

CHAPTER VI

"A CERTAIN PARTICIPATION IN THE DIVINE NATURE"

In the Image of the Son

Adoptive Sonship as Model for the Union of Head and Members

We do not find a tract, "De ecclesia," in the *Summa theologiae*. This does not mean Aquinas declines to consider the Church as part of his theological synthesis. In fact, he shows great interest in ecclesiology, especially in pointing out what actually constitutes the Church of faith and sacraments. Still, he prefers to investigate the union which exists between Christ and his members in terms of the pattern natural to the incarnation itself, rather than in strictly juridical structures or in metaphorical models. Furthermore, because he accepts the Pauline intuition that the Church really is Christ, the "common nature assumed" and the instrumentality of Christ's human activities both contribute basic elements to a Thomistic ecclesiology. Aquinas's passages on the Church, in fact, duplicate the pattern found in the writings of St. Paul: "Christ Jesus himself being the cornerstone, in whom the whole structure is joined together and grows into a holy temple in the Lord; in whom you also are built into it for a dwelling place of God in the Spirit" (Eph 2:20-22). Texts such as this one govern Thomas's whole approach to membership in the Church.

In an especially astute move, he also incorporates the divine will, "the plan of the mystery hidden for ages in God who created all things" (Eph 2:9), into Christ's human subjectivity. Without speculating about other orders of salvation, Aquinas can pinpoint the mediation of divine wisdom to the Church as identical with Christ's own predestination. Once he has made his connection, moreover, he moves to situate the divine plan of salvation immediately in Christ's human actions, especially his death on the cross. As a result, Christ's own personal knowledge and love, "the unsearchable riches of Christ" (Eph 3:8), implement the consummation of God's loving design in a sinful world. Of course, Christ remains at once hypostatically united with divinity and genetically related to all other human beings, with the result that these same actions, in fact, also serve as efficient causes of his mystical body.

Although current theology does not use the term "physical" to signify the universal dimension of Christ's saving mission, we can neverthe_ less trace the theory that some kind of ontic communion exists between Christ and his members as far back as Irenaeus of Lyon and his theory of recapitulation. As its root "physis" suggests, "physical" points initially to a union based on common nature, but not, for that reason, an automatic incoporation of all rational creatures into Christ. Rather, the possession of an individual human nature establishes the threshold condition for direct and personal participation in the mystery of Christ. For Aquinas, Christ the Saviour realizes the perfection of the image of God in the order of grace and merit because he perfectly embodies that image in the order of the hypostatic union. Hence, Christ, in some way, really does include in himself, especially at the moment of his passion, all men and women destined by God for salvation. "He destined us in love to be his sons though Jesus Christ, according to the purpose of his will, to the praise of his glorious grace which he freely bestowed on us in the Beloved" (Eph 1:5,6). And in this way, Christ restores the fullness of the divine image to all creation.

The efficacy of Christ's passion and the subsequent union which it effects between himself and the members hinges, then, directly on the grace of union. For Christ alone remains Son by nature; we, on the other hand, obtain a share in this relation to God through grace. In other terms, Thomas's doctrine of the Church suggests the theme of adoptive sonship as St Paul describes it in Romans, "We know that the whole creation has been groaning in travail together until now; and not only the creation, but we ourselves, who have the first fruits of the Spirit, groan inwardly as we await for adoption as sons, the redemption of our bodies" (Rom 8:22,23). In adoptive sonship, the members of Christ abide in him, as "heirs of God and fellow heirs with Christ," just as Christ himself remains one with the Father and the Holy Spirit.

Since St Paul recognizes a relationship between the plan of creation and the realization of our status as God's adopted sons and daughters, Thomas points to a similar affinity which exists within the Trinity. Christ is both natural Son and eternal Logos. Thus, Aquinas can comment on themes similar to those raised by St Paul in Romans 8.

The Son's becoming incarnate was altogether appropriate, and first of all from the meaning of the union. Like is fittingly joined to the like. We can look to one sort of general affinity between the Son, the Word of God, and all creatures; the craftman's mental word, i.e., his idea, is a pattern for whatever he fashions; so too the Word, God's eternal conception, is the exemplar for all creation. Creatures are first established, though changeably, in their proper kinds by a sharing in that likeness; similarly it is fitting that creatures be restored to their eternal and changeless perfection through the Word's being united, not participatively, but in the person with the creature. The craftsman repairs his own work when it has been damaged on the same mental model he used in making it.

A second reason can be taken from the purpose of the union, the accomplishment of the predestination of those who are preordained for a heavenly inheritance. To this sons alone have a right; "If sons, heirs also." Appropriately, then, through him who is Son by nature men share by adoption in a likeness to his sonship: "Those whom he foreknew he predestined to share the image of his Son (IIIa q. 3, a. 8).

Thus one point remains sure: each adopted son or daughter participates in the unique sonship of the natural Son. As a result, each child of God, to the extent he or she remains united with Jesus, can manifest the goodness of the whole Trinity in creation. In like manner, Christ the incarnate Logos perfectly represents the wisdom and goodness of God in the order of created being.

The Sacraments of the Church: Instruments for Restoring the Image of God

The biblical theme of adoptive sonship supports Thomas's entire sacramental theology. In fact, he also calls the sacraments "instruments" of the humanity of Christ, as Christ's humanity itself instrumentally serves the divine Logos/Son. God, who accomplishes the concrete historical economy of salvation by the passion of his Son, also communicates with men and women through faith and sacraments. Although he grasped the full anthropological implications of divine agency through and in created realities, Aquinas nevertheless principally establishes the sacraments of the new law as instruments of the blessed Trinity.

The passion of Christ is the sufficient cause of man's salvation. Yet it does not follow on this account that the sacraments are not necessary for man's salvation, for they produce their effects in virtue of the passion of Christ, and it is the passion of Christ which is, in a certain manner, applied to men through the sacraments, as is borne out by the following saying of St Paul: "All of us who have been baptized into Christ Jesus were baptized into his death (IIIa q. 61, a. 1, ad 3).

The citation from Romans 6:3 signals an important feature of Aquinas's sacramental spirituality. He interprets the metaphorical reference to death as St Paul's way of insisting on the need for our configuration to Christ. The members of Christ's body should be configured ("configurentur") to Christ, affirms Aquinas, both by means of the image-restorative work which suffering effects and by that configuring which occurs in the sacraments.

From another perspective, adoptive sonship implies an eschato-logical reality, as the phrase, "And if children, then heirs also;

heirs of God and fellow heirs with Christ" (Rom 8:17) suggests. Although the New Testament plainly acknowledges a realized eschatology, still adoptive sonship does not consist so much in a state of being as in a tendency toward beatitude. Aquinas illumines this particular aspect of his doctrine in the context of explaining why Christian "praxis" refers to the Eucharist as viaticum. Christ's passion, in virtue of which every sacrament produces its effect, remains the sufficient cause of glory for his members. "Even so, we are not at once brought thereby into heaven, for beforehand we must, as St Paul states, 'suffer with him' that afterwards we may be 'glorified with him.' And so the sacrament does not immediately usher us in, but gives us the strength to journey to heaven. That is why it is called the viaticum" (IIIa q. 79, a. 2, ad 1). In any event, Thomas's sacramental theology forms warp and woof of his meditation on Christ and the Church. At the very stat of the *tertia pars,* he refers to the sacraments as those things "by which we attain salvation" ("quibus salutem consequimur"), for they mark the road we walk along with Christ.

Image-Restoration and the *Heilsgeschichte*

We can best display the harmony of Thomas's sacramental theology with the method and doctrine of the whole *Summa* by a presentation of selected texts in which he speaks explicitly about the notion of satisfaction. These texts represent each of the three major sections which comprise his systematics and concern the rational creature's origin in and movement toward God. In other terms, the following section provides a retrospect on the three *partes* of the *Summa theologiae.*

First, in the *prima pars* we discover how satisfaction brings into sharp relief both the original condition of the first parents, which required no sacramental mediation, and their helplessness after sin to make atonement. Second, in the *secunda pars,* we discover the relationship of image-perfection and image restoration examined from the different perspectives of the two dispensations. Finally, in the *tertia pars,* we again return to the efficacy of Christ's satisfaction and its relationship to the sacraments of the new alliance. The scientific method employed in the *Summa theologiae, does not allow Aquinas the opportunity to consider expressly what German theologians like to call the "Heilsgeschichte" viz.,* salvation history.[1] The following catena of texts, then, suggests what such a consideration might look like.

Satisfaction before and after the Coming of Christ

The Old Law

In discussing creation, Thomas considers the characteristics of the state of original justice in which the human creature came forth from the hand of God. For example, he speculates whether man was better able to merit in the state of original justice than after sin. He concludes that human deeds would have been more effective for meriting in the state of innocence than after sin, since grace would have been more plentiful then, "finding no hindrance to its entry in human nature" (Ia q. 95, a. 4). Consequently the meritorious deeds for which grace serves as principle and support would also have been greater. From another point of view, however, we stand in a better position to merit after original sin than before it. Although sin weakens human nature, there nonetheless exists a "proportional quantity" to merit calculated according to the capacity of the one performing the meritorious deed. So one who is enfeebled by sin can merit proportionally ("secundum quantitatem operis proportionalem") to a greater extent than one established in the state of original justice. Besides, if the deeds are penal, they also qualify as satisfaction for sin. Aquinas does not adopt a romantic view of our original state; rather, he looks for ways to apply one of his basic hermeneutical principles, namely, that whatever we receive in the Christian dispensation surpasses any other way God could have saved the world. In short, he consistently affirms the absolute primacy of Christ.

The sacramental system, then, belongs to the present order of salvation. Aquinas recognizes, moreover, a continuity between the sacraments of the new dispensation and those sacramental actions which God used to prepare the world for Christ. Like the passion of Christ which they instrumentally extend, the sacraments of the new law also perfect the figures of Israel's religious experience. In his discussion of the old law, for example, Thomas establishes the principle that "the reasons for the figurative sacrifices of the old law are to be drawn from the true sacrifice of Christ" (Ia-IIae q. 102, a. 3). So the sin-offering, especially when offered as a holocaust, prefigures the perfect satisfaction made by the immolation of Christ for all the people. In any event, as the 12th-century theologians intuited, healing and restoration after sin involve the sacraments. But the sacraments of the old law, though more numerous in kind, remained ineffective, since they were separated from Christ, source of the new law of grace.

The New Law

While Aquinas, like every Christian theologian, acknowledges the special importance of the work of grace, he also recognizes that image-perfection and image-restoration constitute two principal, yet distinct, features of the Christian life. In his treatment of grace, Thomas explains the relationship of grace, merit, and satisfaction in the attainment of our final goal of beatitude.

The state of man without grace may be thought of in two ways. The first is the state of intact nature, as it was in Adam before sin; the other is the state of spoiled nature, as it is in us before our restoration by grace. If, then, we have in mind man in the first of these states, there is only one ground on which he cannot merit eternal life by his purely natural gifts without grace. This is because man's merit depends on the divine preordination. Now in no case is a creature's act ordained by God to something surpassing the proportionate order of the power which is the principle and source of the act; for it is by an institution of divine providence that nothing should act beyond its own power. But eternal life is a good which surpasses the proportionate order of created nature, since it even surpasses its knowledge and desire, according to the text of I Corinthians: "Eye has not seen, nor ear heard, nor has it entered into the heart of man." Thus it is that no created nature is a sufficient principle and source of an act which merits eternal life, unless there is provided in addition a supernatural gift, and this is called grace.

But if we have in mind man under sin, over and above this, there is a second ground, owing to the impediment of sin. For since sin is an offence to God which excludes the sinner from eternal life . . . no one in the state of sin can merit eternal life without first being reconciled to God and having his sin forgiven, and this takes place through grace. For it is not life but death that is due to the sinner, according to the text of Romans: "The wages of sin is death (Ia-IIae q. 114, a. 2).

The distinction points directly at two dimensions of Christian life. First, nothing in our nature establishes a positive claim on God's love, which always remains transcendently free. Second, granted the impediment of sin, no one can merit anything from God "without being reconciled to him by making satisfaction." In short, Aquinas recognizes the primacy of the divine initiative at every step in our salvation.

In still another context, he considers the three traditional works of satisfaction, almsgiving, fasting, and prayer, as acts belonging to specific virtues. Since the life of virtue takes on new meaning in the Christian dispensation, Aquinas applies this to the standard works of satisfaction. Prayer as an act of religion forms a potential part of justice. Fasting as an act of moderation in food and drink remains allied with temperance. Almsgiving represents an act of mercy and thus belongs directly to charity. But one might object that almsgiving accomplishes satisfaction, and therefore should also be considered a work of justice. To be sure, Aquinas distinguishes an action as elicited by one virtue from the same action as commanded by another virtue, thereby answering the objection. But he also demonstrates how the three traditional penitential practices for sin embody the worship of God we call latria.

> There is no reason why an act which properly speaking belongs to the virtue which immediately elicits it should not also be attributed to another virtue, in the sense of being commanded by it and directed to that virtue's own end. And it is in this way that giving alms can be counted as a work of satisfaction, in the sense that our compassion for the wretched is directed towards satisfying for our sins. As well as this, the same act, when directed to appeasing God, assumes the character of sacrifice and so is commanded by the virtue of latria (IIa-IIae q. 32, a. 1, ad 2).

If Aquinas identifies satisfaction with latria, then we recognize the fundamental meaning assigned to penitential acts in Christian life: They are ordered to God's glory.

These texts represent those places in the *prima pars* and the *secunda pars* where Thomas speaks explicitly about satisfaction. Moreover, they include at least indirect references to the different epochs of the "Heilsgeschichte." First, Thomas points out the relative advantage which human nature as enfeebled by sin possesses with respect to pursuing our final goal of beatitude. Because of the satisfactory value associated with the laborious, Aquinas interprets our difficulty in performing good deeds as an advantage. Second, failing the perfect and efficacious mediation of Christ's satisfaction, our efforts at attaining eternal life remain thwarted. The rites of the old law serve essentially to prefigure the sacraments of the new law. Third, full image-restoration occurs only under the new law of grace founded upon the perfect merit and satisfaction of the Redeemer.

Since the satisfactory works of the members express the virtue of justice through its religious expression of latria, the sacrifice of Christ the Priest affirms the works of the members. The sacrifice of the cross does satisfy the divine justice precisely by giving God the worship, *viz.*, the works of satisfaction, that are his due. Satisfaction, however, remains a step toward restoration of all things in Christ. Because satisfaction brings the members who perform it into perfect union with Christ, such works also progressively accomplish image-restoration.

Now we turn to texts which appraise image-restoration and image-perfection during each moment of the "Heilsgeschichte." The first set of texts delineates the image of God at various stages, i.e., creation, fall, old law, new law, of human history. The second group of texts elucidates the role of the sacraments as separated instruments of Christ's saving action by comparing them with examples of sacramental representation prior to the establishment of the new dispensation.

The Image of God and Human History

Creation

While speculation about the state of original justice is not a major preoccupation for Aquinas, he nevertheless observes that the human person as he came forth from God is the most perfect human image of God. Aquinas succintly recapitulates the fundamental point contained in the Christian doctrine of creation: "There is found in Genesis 1:27 'God created man to his own image.'" (Ia q. 93, a. 1). And, conscious of what constitutes the distinctive feature of a human person, Thomas adds, "Now it is by the soul that man is after God's image" (Ia q. 93, a. 6). Although speculation about the state of innocence continues to distract even contemporary theologians, Aquinas observes due modesty about matters concerning which the scriptures give but a glimpse. Nevertheless, he gives full recognition to what Genesis straightforwardly affirms about the perfection of the divine creation. "And God saw everything that he had made, and behold it was very good" (Gen 1:31).

Fall

On the other hand, because the effects of original sin are now manifest in human beings, Aquinas recounts them unequivocally. Following Augustine, he considers the post-lapsarian image as reduced to a state of potentiality, a vestige of its original dynamism. This entails a state of enfeeblement and frustration. While fallen men and women retain a natural capacity to know and love God, they can actually do so only with difficulty and, even then, without the possibility of achieving that full union in knowledge and love to which the very "imago" itself draws them. First, then, Aquinas refers to the universal call to holiness as the single object of faith present in both dispensations, but he also signals the crucial difference which the birth of Christ makes for human activity and virtue.

> The unity of faith in the two covenants attests the unity of the end; for it has been said already that the object of the theological virtues, among which faith is included, is the last end. And yet the state of faith differs in the Old and in the New Law; for what they believed was going to happen, we believe has happened (Ia-IIae q. 107, a. 1, ad 1).

> All the differences which are proposed between the New Law and the Old rest on the difference between what is perfect and what is imperfect. For the precepts of any law are given in view of the active exercise of moral virtues. Now imperfect men, who do not yet have the stable habit of virtue, are drawn

to the exercise of the virtues in a different way from those who are perfect in virtue. For those who do not yet have the stable habit of virtue are drawn to the exercise of virtue by some extrinsic motive, e.g., the threat of penalties, or the promise of external rewards such as honour or riches and so on. And therefore the Old Law, which was given to the imperfect, i.e., to those who had not yet obtained spiritual grace, was called "the law of fear" inasmuch as it induced men to observe its precepts by the threat of various penalties; and it is said to contain various temporal promises. Those on the other hand who have moral virtue are drawn to the exercise of virtuous actions for the love of virtue, not on account of some external penalty or reward. And so the New Law, consisting primarily in spiritual grace itself implanted in men's hearts, is called "the law of love"; and it is said to contain spiritual and eternal promises which are the objects of virtue, especially charity. And so men are drawn to them intrinsically, not as to what is external to them but as to what is their very own (Ia-IIae q. 107, a. 1, ad 1).

To be sure, union with Christ constitutes the principal reality behind the moral life, but the practice of both virtues and the beatitudes specifies its practice in the ordinary course of human existence. Although sin leaves human nature crabbed and unproductive, it does not efface the "imago Dei." The sin of Adam inaugurates a long period in which God tutored the human race to prepare for Christ.

Old Law

Like St Paul, Aquinas understands the period of the old law as a time of preparation. It is ordered to bring us to a personal awareness of our enfeeblement and to recognition of our frustrated desire for God. Before Christ, we discern a period of signs and figures, mere shadows of the promised reality which are ineffective for achieving union with God. Still, because the "unity of faith in the two covenants" guarantees it, the old law, although imperfectly, nonetheless discloses God.

There is no doubt that the Old Law was good, for just as a doctrine is shown to be true from the fact that it is in conformity with right reason, so too a law is shown to be good from the fact that it is in conformity with reason. The Old Law was so conformed. The end to which divine law is directed is to bring man to the attainment of his goal of eternal happiness. Now any kind of sin--not only acts performed in the external sphere but internal ones too--constitutes an obstacle to this end. This is why that which is adequate for the completeness of human law, namely, the prohibiting of offences and the apportionment of penalties, is not adequate for the completeness of the divine law. This latter is required to make man totally equipped to share in eternal happiness--something which can be achieved only by the grace of the Holy Spirit, for it is by this that "charity is poured into our hearts," which fulfills the requirements of the law. For, "the grace of God is eternal life." Now the Old Law was not able to confer this grace; that was reserved to Christ. This is why we find it stated: "The law was given through Moses, grace and truth come through Jesus Christ." It is for this reason, then, that the Old Law is indeed good, but, incompletely so: "The law made nothing perfect" (Ia-IIae q. 98, a. 1).

Contemporary discussions concerning the specificity of Christian ethics sometimes misinterpret Aquinas's position on this matter. Although Gratian identified the natural law with the Old and New Testaments, Aquinas does not share this position.[2] Consequently, he does not advance the view that every precept of Christian morality already exists, materially speaking, in the precepts of right reason. The perfection which charity brings to the old law commandments actually makes up an entirely different human reality. Besides giving them an intrinsic orientation to eternal life, the grace and truth of Jesus Christ radically transform morals and human actions, making our lives so many expressions of divine charity in the world.

New Law

Indeed, the whole power of the new law dwells in the person of Jesus Christ, who through the Holy Spirit continues to sanctify the Church. The perfection of the godly image in each of us occurs only through Christ's capital grace. Although the old dispensation encompassed works of image-restoration, the new law of interiority alone definitively transforms the "imago Dei" into the perfection God ordains for it, a certain participation in divine love.

Now it is the grace of the Holy Spirit, given through faith in Christ, which is predominant in the law of the New Covenant and in which its whole power consists. So before all else the New Law is the very grace of the Holy Spirit, given to those who believe in Christ (Ia-IIae q. 106, a. 1).

The Gospel Law involves two things. Primarily, it is the very grace of the Holy Spirit given inwardly. And in this respect the New Law does justify. As Augustine says: "There"--in the Old Covenant--"a law was set up externally, with which the unjust might be threatened; here"--in the New Covenant--"it is given

> internally, so that they may be justified by it." The other secondary aspect of the Gospel Law is found in the testimonies of the faith and the commandments which order human attachments and human actions. In this respect the New Law does not justify. So Paul says: "The letter kills, but the spirit gives life.

> Thus even the Gospel letter kills unless the healing grace of faith is present within (Ia-IIae q. 106, a. 2).

Lived out in accordance with the dynamics of the new law, faith and morals possess the power to effect salvation. Thomas's vision of the Christian life so stresses interiority that the difference grace makes can never be explained simply in terms of an extrinsic analysis, such as rewards and punishments. For Aquinas, charity remains the heart of the Christian life: "grace moves towards eternal life, but the development of this movement occurs by growth in charity" (Ia-IIae, q. 114, a. 8).

The perfection of the godly image results in the reconciliation of the world to God. If God finds appeasement in Christ's satisfaction, this happens only because the hidden plan of his wisdom to unite all things to himself in Christ reveals itself in the Church at worship. To be sure, Aquinas unequivocally distances himself from the harsh rhetoric of substitutional satisfaction theories. Why? Because for him, those explanations of Christ's victory represent distortions of the authentic Gospel.

> What God seeks from our good works is not profit but glory, that is, the manifestation of his own goodness; this is what he seeks from his own works too. The reverence we show him is of advantage not to him but to us. And so we merit something from God, not as though he gained any advantage from our works but inasmuch as we work with a view to his glory (Ia-IIae q. 114, a. 1, ad 2).

This conforms to Aquinas's general theory concerning final causality in God. In short, God loves us not because we are good, but because he is. In this way, the divine goodness, concretely realized in the restoration and perfection of the godly image, remains the end of everything.[3]

Aspects of Sacramental Mediation
throughout the *Heilsgeschichte*

Although only the sacraments of the new law effect what they signify ("efficiunt quod significunt"), Aquinas nevertheless considers other sorts of sacramental efficacy which God manifests in creation. In each phase of the "Heilsgeschichte," the value which he assigns to the different sacramental systems always remains determined by their relationship to Christ. To put it differently, Aquinas estimates sacramental mediation in the various circumstances of redemption on the basis of their capacity to move us toward beatitude.

State of original justice

In the state of original justice, sacraments had no role to play. The unsullied divine image in the first parents was perfectly ordered toward its perfection so that their communion with God required no form of created mediation. Even so, this prerogative of image-perfection in the state of original justice constitutes a freely-bestowed grace for the creature. God gave the grace directly, however, without using the instrumentality of anything created.

> In the state of innocence man had need of grace, although he did not need to attain to this grace through any visible signs but rather did so in a spiritual and invisible manner (IIIa q. 61, a. 2, ad 1).

As visible signs of invisible grace, the sacraments consequently were inappropriate. Nor did Adam yet require a remedy for sin. Once sin entered the world, however, we became destined to form a church of faith and sacraments, which Christ also makes a church of glory.

Original sin

First, original sin destroyed the "habitus" of original justice in the human race. The race became enfeebled and incapacitated. For fallen man the movement towards God is difficult; and the aids which God confers in the sacramental signs of the old law, although numerous, can only point to the Redeemer.

> The state of the human race after sin and before Christ can be considered under two aspects, first from the point of view of the essential meaning of faith, and in relation to this it has always remained the same in the sense that it has always been through faith in the future coming of Christ that men have been justified.

> But we can consider the state of the human race under a different aspect, that namely of the greater or lesser intensity of sinfulness, and also of explicit knowledge of Christ prevailing within it. For as the years passed sin began to gain an increasing hold upon man in virtue of the fact that as human reason was darkened by sin the precepts of the natural law

were no longer adequate to enable him to live aright, making it necessary to define the precepts in the form of a written law, and together with these to institute certain sacraments of faith. It was also necessary that as the years passed the knowledge of faith should become increasingly explicit. For, as Gregory says, with the passing of the years knowledge about God grew and increased. Hence it was also necessary under the Old Law to define certain specific sacraments of the faith which men had concerning the Christ who was to come. And in fact these sacraments are related to those which existed before the Law as that which is determinate is related to that which is indeterminate. For prior to the Law it was not specifically laid down for man which sacraments he should use, as it was laid down by the Law. This was necessary both because of the obscuring of the natural law and in order that the signs in which the faith was expressed might be more specific (IIIa q. 61, a. 3, ad 2).

While Aquinas insistently reminds us of the unity of the two covenants, he nonetheless accurately describes what life without access to the incarnate Son means. Optimistic anthropologies tend to elide the difference between fallen and restored human nature, but Aquinas rejects this fundamentally anti-Christian perspective. As the New Testament makes clear, Christ alone is our integrity.

Old dispensation

To the extent that they indicated the perfection of the law to be accomplished by Christ, the sacraments of the old law served a useful and good purpose. Aquinas even speculates on the unity of faith in Christ which united the old and new dispensations, and asks whether it might not in some way account for the justification of the Old Testament saints. In fact, he once even considered circumcision as the practical equivalent of baptism. As the rite directed Israel toward the future redeemer, he reasoned, can it not serve as a sign of justifying faith? But in the *Summa*, he alters his position.

We must say that in circumcision grace was bestowed, with all the effects of grace, but not in the same way as in baptism. In baptism grace is conferred by the power of the sacrament itself which it has insofar as it is an instrument of the already realized passion of Christ. Circumcision, on the other hand, conferred grace insofar as it was a sign of faith in the coming passion of Christ in such a way that a man who accepted circumcision made profession of such a faith, an adult for himself and someone else for an infant. For this reason Saint Paul also says that "Abraham received the sign of circumcision, the seal of his justification by faith," because justification came from the faith signified and not from its sign, circumcision. Further, because it operates as an instrument of the power of the passion of Christ, baptism, but not circumcision, imprints a character which incorporates a person into Christ and bestows grace more abundantly than circumcision; a reality already present is more effective than a mere hope (IIIa q. 70, a. 4).

Even if the institutes of the old law represent faith in the passion of Christ by which we are now justified, "it is clear that the sacraments of the old law did not contain within themselves any power by which they could actively contribute to the conferring of justifying grace" (IIIa q. 62, a. 6). Instead, Aquinas explains as follows how the rites of the old law played a role in the justification of the Old Testament saints:

> The fathers of old were justified by faith in the passion of Christ as we ourselves are. For the sacraments of the old law constituted a special kind of protestation of that faith inasmuch as they pointed to the passion of Christ and its effects (IIIa q. 62, a. 6).

But, as the descent into Hell reminds us, even the great saints of the old law had to wait for Christ in order for their justification to be perfected and completed.

New law of grace

Sacraments and image-restoration

On the other hand, the sacraments of the new law possess full power to bring about our salvation. Aquinas recognizes the definitive character of the Christian dispensation in a way which reminds us of St Paul: "For I am sure that neither death, nor life, nor angels, nor principalities, nor things present, nor things to come, nor powers, nor height, nor depth, nor anything else in all creation, will be able to separate us from the love of God in Christ Jesus our Lord" (Rom 8:38,39). The sacraments remain foremost instruments for extending the benefits of Christ's passion to us. Granted that they exercise a special causality when celebrated within the Church and by her ministers, the seven sacraments bring about image-perfection and image-restoration in the believer.

> Just as the fathers of old were saved through faith in the Christ who was to come, so we too are saved through faith in the Christ who has already been born and suffered. Now sacraments are the sort of signs in which the faith by which man is justified is explicitly attested, and it is right to have

different signs for what belongs to the past, the present, or the future. For, as Augustine says, the same reality is proclaimed in one way when it is still to be achieved and in another when it has already been so. So too the very words "passurus," "destined to suffer," and "passus," "having suffered," sound different to our ears. Hence it is right that in addition to the sacraments of the Old Law which foretold realities that lay in the future there are certain other sacraments in the New Law to stand for realities which have taken place in Christ in the past (IIIa q. 61, a. 4).

Of course, Aquinas's theology precedes the Reformation controversies over the efficacy of the sacraments. Nevertheless we do find in his theory a right balance between the functions of theological faith and the "ex opere operato" aspect of a sacrament. For Aquinas, in short, the sacraments are signs which effect a real change.

Instruments of grace

For this reason, Aquinas chooses to use the same analogy for the sacraments which he employed when speaking about the hypostatic union. The sacraments of the new law are instruments of freely-given grace. But in order to distinguish them from personal actions of Christ himself, Aquinas qualifies the sacraments as separated instruments. Since Aristotelian philosophy rejects motion at a distance, we can appreciate that Aquinas clearly intends to push our thinking toward some other explanation than that suggested by a merely physical or mechanical model.

Now it belongs to God alone to produce grace in this way as its principal cause. For grace is nothing else than a certain shared similitude to the divine nature. This is confirmed by the passage in II Peter which runs: "He has given us most great and precious promises, that by these you may be made partakers of the divine nature."

An instrumental cause, on the other hand, acts not in virtue of its own form, but solely in virtue of the impetus imparted to it by the principal agent. Hence the effect has a likeness not to the instrument but rather to that principal agent, as a bed does not resemble the axe which carves it but rather the design in the mind of the carpenter. And this is the way in which the sacraments of the new law cause grace. For it is by divine institution that they are conferred upon man for the precise purpose of causing grace in and through them (IIIa q. 62, a. 1).

Since Aquinas introduces the distinction between conjoined and separated instruments, he must account for its suitability. In the following text, however, he simply makes it clear that the center of the sacramental system remains the person of Jesus Christ. A full account of the analogy of separated instrument indispensably points to Christ as the source of sacramental life in the Church.[4]

> Now there are two kinds of instruments, one a separate instrument such as a staff, the other a united instrument conjoined to the principal agent such as a hand. And it is by the conjoined instrument that the separate instrument is moved as a staff is moved by the hand. Moreover the principal efficient cause of grace is God himself, and the humanity of Christ stands to him in the relation of a conjoined instrument, whereas a sacrament stands in the relation of a separate one. Thus it is right that the power to bestow salvation should flow from the divinity of Christ through his humanity into the actual sacraments (IIIa q. 62, a. 5).

Contemporary theology emphasizes the affinities between sacraments and worship in the Church. For Aquinas, liturgical rites constituted only the "sacramentum tantum," a single part of the full sacred reality. Nevertheless, he does recognize the profound connection between sacraments and the virtue of religion as the ground for the rituals of the Christian faith.

Expressions of worship

Sacramental grace possesses a twofold significance for Aquinas. First, and especially in baptism and penance, it points to the work of satisfaction. To put it differently, the sacraments effect image-restoration. Second, it perfects the soul for the worship of God. In other words, sacraments also accomplish image-perfection. Granted, in the Eucharist satisfaction holds a secondary place, still the sacraments remain both instruments of Christ's passion and at the same time effective causes of our transformation. A particular theology is at work here. Just as the doctrine of the real presence stands at the heart of Eucharistic theology, so Aquinas establishes the sacraments as essential features of Christian life and conversion. In both, a real transformation in faith takes place. In the Eucharist we call this transubstantiation, but for Christian life we call it metanoia and justification.

Since the virtue of religion can direct the satisfactory works of the members to its own finality, a sacrament establishes the locus where the members of Christ become a pleasing sacrifice of worship offered to God in Christ's passion.

Furthermore sacramental grace seems to be designed chiefly to produce two effects: First, it removes the defects of past sins inasmuch as the guilt of these endures even though the sinful acts are transitory. Second, sacramental grace is designed to perfect the soul in all that pertains to the worship of God in terms of the religion of the Christian life. Now from the arguments set forth above it is manifest that Christ delivered us from our sins chiefly through his passion, and that not merely by way of efficient causality or merit, but by way of satisfaction as well. Similarly through his passion he also inaugurated the rites of the Christian religion by "offering himself as an oblation and sacrifice to God." From this it is manifest that in a special way the sacraments of the Church derive their power from the passion of Christ and that it is through the reception of the sacraments that the power flowing from this becomes, in a certain way, conjoined to us. This is signified by the fact that from the side of Christ hanging on the Cross there flowed water and blood, the first of which pertains to baptism and the second to the Eucharist, these two being the greatest of the sacraments (IIIa q. 62. a. 5).

The sacraments, then, derive their power from the passion of Christ, but they lead to the glory of his resurrection. "It is fitting," writes Thomas, "that the power to bestow salvation ("virtus salutifera") should flow from the divinity of Christ through his humanity into the actual sacraments" (IIIa q. 62, a. 5). In the sacraments of the Church, Christian faith finds its incarnation daily, for, as Leo the Great remarks: "Our Redeemer's presence has passed into the sacraments."[5]

In the Church of Faith and Sacraments

Aquinas considers only four sacraments in the *tertia pars*. His experience in St. Nicolas's Chapel, at the Dominican church in Naples, put a halt to his writing career before he finished the treatise on penance. By a curious coincidence, Thomas put down his pen just at the moment when he would have treated satisfaction within this context. According to the earliest oral traditions, his brethren judged that this turn of events represented a divine approbation of his work completed up to that time. Still, we possess enough of his writings on the sacraments to recognize their distinctive contribution to the history of theology. Since the focus of our investigation, however, concerns satisfaction, we explicitly address the sacraments of baptism and penance.

The Sacrament of Baptism:
Incorporation into Christ as Adopted Children

The transformative power of Christian faith and sacrament controls Aquinas's treatise on baptism. Admittedly, Thomas borrows heavily from the Pauline metaphor of adoptive sonship in order to develop this treatise. Trinitarian theology consequently gives coherence to his discussion of baptism, even though the leitmotiv of the *tertia pars* itself requires that the sacraments lead us back to God. In the *Summa*, the images of God and adoptive sonship constitute the thematic expressions of the "exitus-reditus," which Aquinas uses to establish the trinitarian dimensions of the human creature. In fact, only as a result of the divine indwelling can the member of Christ's body achieve a certain shared similitude in the divine nature itself. St Paul dramatizes this transformation by comparing it to life and death. Aquinas makes this perspective his own.

> As Saint Paul says: "All of us who have been baptized into Christ Jesus were baptized into his death." And later he concludes: "So you also must consider yourselves dead to sin and alive to God in Christ Jesus our Lord." It is evident from this that by baptism a man dies to the old life of sin and begins to live the newness of grace. But every sin pertains to the former old life. It follows then that every sin is taken away by baptism (IIIa q. 69, a. 1).

While it is true that sanctifying grace gives a stable participation in the divine nature, it is no less true that grace provides a divine source of activity, giving a dynamic impetus toward God. Seen in this light, adoptive filiation in the Son falls into place in the schema of the whole *Summa theologiae*, deriving therefrom its theological intelligibility.

As Aquinas repeatedly points out, however, this adoption is something which must be progressively realized in the members of Christ in virtue of his mediation. Thomas elaborates his teaching on the effects of baptism so as to explain how this continuing transformation takes place. The sacramental washing of baptism itself suggests the twofold effect of a physical washing has on the body, namely, elimination of bodily stain and bodily refreshment. Aquinas not only relates the special effect of baptism, the full remission of punishment for sin, to the sufferings of Christ the head, but also interprets the nature of this relationship from a personalist perspective. Christ supplies spiritual refreshment to the soul. Even the actual effects of satisfaction, that is, the work of self-reformation, serve this purpose, to configure the believer to Christ.

> Since the one baptized, inasmuch as he becomes a member of Christ, participates in the pain of the passion of Christ just as if

he himself suffered that pain, his sins are thus set in order by the pain of Christ's passion (IIIa q. 69, a. 2, ad 1).

Because baptism unites the member with the perfectly-formed image of the suffering Christ, it establishes something definitive in the member. Theologians dispute over the meaning of the character which baptism leaves in the one who receives it.   Excluding more or less poetic or fantastic explanations, it becomes clear that baptism leaves the member permanently disposed to live by faith in the Son of God.   The disposition remains active as long as the bond of charity exists between head and member.

Nevertheless, despite its emphatic instrumentality, baptism still leaves room for growth in the spiritual life.   Several reasons explain this traditional teaching of the Church.   First, although the newly-baptized members are free from sin's debt of penalty, they nevertheless encounter those who, because of their own post-baptismal sins, still struggle with sin's defects.   In other words, the Christian still lives in the world.   Second, although baptism removes the debt of punishment, it does not remove the effects of sin, which continue to impair the psychological and moral capacities even of the baptized.   In other words, the Christian still suffers the relics of the old self.   Like St Paul, Thomas explains this particular ordination of divine providence as reasonable in light of the untoward consequences which would otherwise result.   If, for example, baptism actually effected a premature exaltation of the members' bodies (by which Aquinas includes the right ordering of sense appetites, memory, and imagination) as well as the purification of their souls, Christian life would take a very different shape.   But God did not ordain such an abrupt sanctification of human history.   Instead he chose the way of the Lord Jesus.   God allows whatever inclinations to sin baptism leaves in us so that our individual spiritual training ("spirituale exercitium") will develop.   This sort of spiritual devotion, as the saints remind us, brings sweetness and delight.   In other words, God intends our weaknesses for no other purpose than to draw us more closely to himself in Christ.   All in all, God's love for the creature, manifested especially in the passion of Christ, moves us to live by faith and to perform the spiritual works set forth in the Gospels.

Aquinas's sacramental doctrine points to the imitation of Christ. Thus, as a paramount reason why baptism does not entirely remove the penalties of the present life, he cites the "sequela Christi."   In the following text, in fact, he describes the lingering effects of our old nature as marking the first stage in a process by which members grows are configured to Christ.   In his analysis, we can see the parallel he draws between the life of the believer and Christ's own experience.

Because by baptism a man is incorporated into Christ and becomes one of his members, it is therefore fitting that what took place in the head should also take place in the member incorporated with the head. But Christ, although from the first moment of his conception he was full of grace and truth, nevertheless had a body subject to suffering which through suffering and death was raised to a life of glory. So also a Christian in baptism acquires grace in his soul and yet has a body subject to suffering in which he may be able to suffer for Christ; but he will finally be raised to a life without suffering. In this regard, St Paul says: "He who raised Christ Jesus from the dead will give life to your mortal bodies also through his Spirit which dwells in you." Later he adds: "Heirs indeed of God and fellow heirs with Christ, provided we suffer with him in order that we may also be glorified with him (IIIa q. 69, a. 3).

Aquinas's view of baptism points to the catechetical instruction Paul gives in Romans 7, which encourages Christians to regard their personal struggles as so many means to serve the law of Christ.

Christ provides the exemplar, the model for human fulfillment. Where he has trod, there we must follow. But this following does not constitute a long day's journey into the unknown or an unguided search for a hidden God. Instead, we stand between God and God; therefore our lives form so many reticulations of his creative impulse, so many embodiments of a Father's love. Thus the saints serve as the best instructors in the Christian life, since they most perfectly embody the model. For example, we have the saying of Teresa of Avila (herself taught by Thomists in a "siglo d'oro") which recapitulates Aquinas's basic message about baptism: "To be on the way to heaven is heaven itself."[6] Even so, we encounter a mystery when we ask why sufferings continue to affect even a sinless baptized person. The answer surely involves the underlying mystery of the Christian faith, namely, that the sinless Christ suffered for our sins.

In this context, the mention of suffering in Christ and his members no longer primarily evokes punishment for sin. Rather, according to the true ways of divine wisdom and justice, suffering is an element in the recapitulation of the entire created order in Christ. Incorporation into Christ, then, means both "illuminatio" and "fecundatio" for the member; and these sharply contrast with the darkness and sterility characteristic of the vestigial image left in us by sin.

By baptism a person is reborn in the life of the spirit which is proper to the faithful of Christ, as St Paul says: "The life I now live in the flesh I live by faith in the Son of God." But there is no life if the members are not united to the head from which they receive feeling and motion. Thus it is necessary that a person be incorporated by baptism into Christ as a member of him. But as feeling and motion flow from the natural head to the members, so from the spiritual head, which is Christ, there flow to his members spiritual feeling, which is the knowledge of truth, and spiritual motion, which results from the impulse of grace. Thus John says: "We have beheld him full of grace and truth, and of his fullness we have all received." It follows that the baptized are enlightened by Christ in the knowledge of truth and made fruitful by him in the fruitfulness of good works by the infusion of grace (IIIa q. 69, a. 5).

Aquinas adopts a strong sacramental position, one which gives the divine agency its full measure of created realization in the signs and words of the seven sacraments.

"Baptism causes the opening of the gates of heaven," he writes, "because the obstacle to that opening is removed by the passion of Christ" (IIIa q. 69, a. 7, ad 1). Just as satisfaction serves as a key-notion of the passion itself, so it also unlocks the door to baptism's power. Thomas's sacramental theology makes the sacraments participations in the satisfactory character of Christ's passion. As a result, Christ's satisfaction opens the gates of heaven and admits those who even before Christ "had charity and the grace of the Holy Spirit" (IIIa q. 49, a. 5, ad 1) along with all those made perfect in Christ as a promise of beatitude.

The Sacrament of Penance:
Spiritual Medicine for Prodigals

Like the other sacraments, penance manifests God's wisdom and providence for the member of Christ. Moreover, it plays a vital role in the life of the Church, since it provides a remedy for sins committed after baptism. Two underlying factors account for such sins. First, divine grace, even when it operates in final causality, does not detroy human freedom. Second, concupiscence, which affects even the post-baptismal condition of the human person, makes it difficult to live a steady life of virtue. Aquinas, therefore, describes penance as a medicine because it provides a sacramental remedy for prodigal children, who turn away from God by sinning. It restores that dignity of soul in which adoptive sonship, as he explains, principally consists.

Through sin a man loses before God a double dignity. The first and principal one is that by which "he is numbered among the children of God" through grace. This dignity is recovered through repentance, as is indicated when the father commanded the restoration of the "best robe, ring and shoes" to his prodigal son (IIIa q. 89, a. 3).

As this suggests, Aquinas's theology of penance is centered in the New Testament parables of forgiveness.

Although they form part of a single divine providence, the specific purposes of baptism and penance differ. Thomas approaches this difference by making a comparison between the number of times that a person can receive each sacrament.

> Baptism has its power from Christ's passion as a kind of spiritual rebirth from the spiritual death of a previous life. Moreover, "it is appointed unto men once to die" and to be born once. And, therefore, man ought to be baptized but once. But penance has its power from Christ's passion as a spiritual medicine, which can frequently be repeated (IIIa q. 84, a. 10, ad 5).

The efficacy of penance, then, derives from the passion of Christ, but its necessity (unlike baptism's) is a conditional, namely, on the supposition that one has committed a mortal sin.[7] Although recent theology suggests different ways to distinguish one sin from another, Aquinas maintains that mortal sin, the prime analogue for every sin, simply destroys the bond of charity and friendship which the creature enjoys with God. Consequently, his idea of the "res et sacramentum," the abiding reality of this sacrament, takes account both of the repentant sinner's new choice to turn back to God and the power which the sacrament instrumentally communicates in the Church.

> A thing is necessary for salvation in two ways, first, absolutely; second, conditionally. That is absolutely necessary without which no one can obtain salvation; examples are the grace of Christ, and the sacrament of baptism through which one is born again in Christ. The sacrament of penance, in turn, is necessary conditionally: indeed, it is needed, not by all, but by those in sin.

> Now as James says: "Sin, when it is completed, begets death." And therefore it is necessary for the salvation of the sinner that his sin be taken away. This, indeed, cannot take place without the sacrament of penance, in which the power of Christ's passion works through the absolution of the priest, together with the action of the penitent who cooperates with grace for the destruction of sin. As St Augustine says: "He who has created you without yourself will not make you just without yourself." So then it is clear that the sacrament of penance is necessary for salvation after sin just as bodily medicine is needed should a man have fallen seriously ill (IIIa q. 85, a. 5).

One advantage of Aquinas's sacramental theory in comparison with more contemporary efforts to explain how the sacraments work is its ability to integrate diverse theological principles. Since the disintegration of theology as "sacra doctrina," one finds the sacraments taught, for example in most university centers of theology, from the perspective of liturgy, or ecclesiology, or communications skills, or even counselling. But an adequate theory of sacramental efficacy remains out of reach unless one takes into account such realities as the missions of the blessed Trinity, the satisfaction of Christ, and the created grace and freedom of the human person, as well as issues raised by philosophy and anthropology such as symbol, meaning, celebration and so forth. Only "sacra doctrina" establishes the right context in which to interpret these indispensable signs of the Christian faith.

Since the interior effect ("res tantum") of penance involves the reconciliation of a repentant sinner with God, it properly belongs to the new law of grace. Furthermore, the power to forgive sins, or what theologians subsequently called the power of the keys, pertains to Christ as the priest of the new alliance. Thus, when she mediates Christ's mercy toward sinners, the hierarchical Church can appeal both to the power of jurisdiction as well as to the power of order in the sacrament of penance. Aquinas distinguishes the virtue of penitence from those actions which constitute the sacrament of penance. Still, Christ's suffering during his passion can also arouse in us the natural impulse to express sorrow for our culpable fault, thereby informing our penitence with the grace of the sacrament. Aquinas relies upon the New Testament account of the sacrament's institution to explain the place penance holds in the life of the believer.

> From natural reason man is prompted to repent of the evils which he has done. It is of divine institution, however, that a man should do penance in this or that way. Hence, in the beginning of his own preaching, our Lord commanded men not only to repent but also "to do penance," signifying definite kinds of acts required for this sacrament. But he determined that which belongs to the office of the ministers when he said to Peter: "And I will give to you the keys of the kingdom of heaven," etc. Then he manifested the efficacy of this sacrament and the origin of its power after the resurrection, when he said, "It behoved . . . that penance and remission of sins be preached in his name unto all nations." He prefaced this by speaking of his passion and resurrection; for, by reason of the name of the suffering and risen Christ, this sacrament had its effectiveness for the forgiveness of sins. And so it is clear that this sacrament was properly instituted in the New Law (IIIa q. 85, a. 5).

Reconciliation, as the earliest controversies over this matter illustrate, always involves membership in the worshipping community. But despite what some contend, it is not sufficient to define the effects of penance simply in terms of re-admission to the Eucharist. The sacramentality of penance, as Aquinas makes clear, means that but it also means image-perfection in the forgiven sinner.

Hence, satisfactory acts remain the ordinary way in which we "cooperate" with the sacramental grace of penance. When the priest imposes a penance or satisfaction in the sacrament, he stipulates the first step of a process which continues throughout the life of the penitent. From a certain perspective, the Church is full of forgiven sinners, and the sacrament of penance always makes room for more. On the other hand, God's providence is not limited to operating in this way. The all-sufficient satisfaction of Christ's passion can also bring about an immediate healing in anyone.

> God heals the whole man completely. Sometimes he does this all at once, as he restored the mother-in-law of Peter to perfect health, so that "rising up she ministered to him." But sometimes he does this little by little, as was said of the blind man whose sight was restored. So also spiritually, sometimes he converts the heart of man with such great force that in an instant he attains perfect spiritual health, with not only pardon for sin but also with the eradication of all sin's remnants, as was the case with Mary Magdalene. Sometimes, however, he first forgives sin through operating grace; and afterwards, through cooperating grace, he takes away sin's after-effects little by little (IIIa q. 86, a. 5, ad 1).

While no one receives justification apart from a free choice to accept it, the initial moment of justification nonetheless remains an operative grace. Ordinarily, we choose to perform satisfaction, but God can also restore our capacities for the practice of virtue and for the following of the beatitudes even before we complete our penance. Thus, the Church points to the infused virtues as part of the spiritual endowment justification generates.

In the ordinary way of divine providence, however, the living out of divine grace operates similarly for the prodigal as for the newly-incorporated member. For both, grace remains the principle of charity. According to a traditional division, moreover, we can speak of "operating grace" ("gratia operans") and "co-operating grace" ("gratia co-operans"). On this basis, Thomas distinguishes two moments in the justification of a sinner: first, divine grace removes the debt of eternal punishment; second, grace empowers satisfaction for the temporal punishment.

> Grace in man is operating with regard to his justification and co-operating with regard to his living rightly. Therefore, pardon for sin and guilt of eternal punishment is the work of operating grace; but the release of the burden of temporal punishment, that of co-operating grace, in the sense, namely, that with the

> help of divine grace a person is absolved from the debt of
> temporal punishment also because of bearing suffering patiently.
> Therefore, just as the effect of operating grace comes before the
> effect of co-operating grace, so also the remission of sin and of
> eternal punishment comes before the full release from temporal
> punishment.   Each is from grace, but the first is from grace
> alone, the other from grace and free will (IIIa q. 86, a. 4, ad 2).

These two moments of the single act of justification correspond to
image-perfection and image-restoration respectively.   Just as sin
destroys personal well-being and human fulfillment, the sacramental
economy of salvation restores the person to happiness and a complete
life.   And satisfaction heals the disorders that arise from a disordered
attachment to some created good.

A personalist interpretation of satisfaction also finds support in
Thomas's description of the integral parts of penance.   These are the
actions which make up the complete sacrament of reconciliation:
"contritio cordis, confessio oris, satisfactio operis."   In this context,
Aquinas defines satisfaction in its full evangelical sense.   "For here in
penance not only is the restoration of the balance of justice sought, as
in retributive justice, but above all ("magis") the reconciliation of
friendship" (IIIa q. 90, a. 2).   Thus, we can conceive image-restoration
according to a threefold process of development.   Although Thomas
describes these steps while discussing the virtue of penitence, they also
describe the major moments in the ordinary course of a personal
salvation history.

> This change of heart is threefold.   The first is by rebirth to a
> new life.   This is the concern of the repentance preceding
> baptism.   The second is by reforming after a life that has been
> ruined by sin.   This is the objective of repentance for mortal
> sins committed after baptism.   The third change is towards
> living a more holy life.   This engages the repentance for venial
> sins, which are pardoned through any fervent act of charity (IIIa
> q. 90, a. 4).

In the final analysis, God wants only perfection for us, since man
remains the only creature God has willed for himself.

Even when ennobled by sacramental grace, the virtue of penitence
remains attached to the cardinal virtue of justice.   Although not a
theological virtue, penitence nevertheless returns something owed to
God.   As a part of commutative justice, it governs relations between
non-equals, namely, between the creature and God, in matters
concerning the "justum," or the right thing to do.   Aquinas assigns
penitence to the class of virtues associated with justice "because the
penitent grieves over sin committed as it is an offense against God and
because he has the purpose of amendment" (IIIa q. 85, a. 3).   This

explains why every work of satisfaction embodies a fulfillment of justice. But Aquinas realizes that the justice at work in something like penitence rests on principles which only the New Testament can provide, since only Christ reveals the personal forgiveness of the heavenly Father available to every person. Penitence accordingly requires the theological virtues lest it stray from its evangelical foundation. Moreover, it can transform the whole of the Christian life, since every virtue can form part of what we owe to God as satisfaction.

> Although penitence is directly a species of justice, nevertheless in a fashion it includes what belongs to all virtues. For inasmuch as it is a kind of justice governing man's relationship with God it must join with the theological virtues which have God for their object. Hence penance is associated with faith in Christ's passion through which we are justified from sins, with hope of pardon and with hatred of sin which belongs to charity.

> Inasmuch as it is a moral virtue it shares in prudence which directs all moral virtues. From its very nature, being a kind of justice, its concern is not only with what belongs directly to justice, but also with what belongs to temperance and to fortitude, namely, inasmuch as the pleasurable things for temperance to deal with or the frightening things for fortitude to moderate become matters required in justice. In this way, both to abstain from delights according to temperance and to sustain hardships according to fortitude, belong to justice (IIIa q. 85, a. 3).

According to this explanation, the virtue of justice surpasses anything which philosophers have to say on the subject. Aquinas resolves the whole of the Christian life, suggested by his reference to the theological and cardinal virtues, into a new and elevated kind of justice, one which has much more to do with the New Testament's understanding of justification than with Aristotle's notion of "dikaiosunē."

The Satisfaction of Divine Justice: Restoration of all Things in Christ

For Aquinas, Christ's satisfaction holds a central place in the Church's life of faith and sacraments. Christ preeminently exercises the priestly office in the new covenant. Configured to the person of Christ in baptism, the member of his body joins in the pleasing sacrifice which Christ himself offers to the Father. As something due to God satisfaction constitutes an act of worship on the part of the creature. In this sense, satisfaction pleases God. By the same token, satisfaction, though by nature penal, also renders a sacrifice of praise. This happens, however, only when the unity established between Christ and his members makes of the whole body a single oblation to the Lord. All in all, Thomas's theology of satisfaction moves beyond penal satisfaction and redemption, represented especially in the sacraments of baptism and penance, and points to the celebration of the Eucharist in the Christian community.

In the *Summa theologiae*, Aquinas makes explicit the association of satisfaction with the Eucharist. To be sure, Christ did not primarily institute the Eucharist for the remission of sins. Instead the sacrament of unity and charity serves the member's spiritual nourishment through sacramental union with Christ himself and caritative union with his members. For this reason, the Church must celebrate the Eucharist in faith. Although charity and sin remain incompatible, however, Thomas does attribute to the blessed Eucharist a concomitant principal effect which approaches satisfaction. For instance, he acknowledges that those who share in the Eucharist receive a partial remission of sin proportionate to the fervor, devotion, and faith with which it is received.

On the other hand, when we consider the Eucharist as a sacrifice, then the sacrament renders satisfaction for sin in a more direct fashion.

> Considered as a sacrifice, however, it has the power of rendering satisfaction. In this the affection of the offerer is counted more than the size of the offering, as our Lord said of the widow who offered two coins that "she has put in more than all." Although the offering of the Eucharist suffices of its own quantity to satisfy for all punishment, nevertheless, it renders satisfaction for those for whom it is offered, and also for those who offer it, according to the amount of their devotion, and not for the whole penalty (IIIa q. 79, a. 5).

Aquinas stresses that only a part and not the whole of the punishment due to sin is pardoned in the Eucharist. But he explains this sheerly in terms of defect in our devotion, not because of something lacking to Christ's power.

Understandably enough, the theology of redemption always retains an element of the juridical in its structure. This perspective appears more pronounced in Thomas's earlier works. Like Anselm and his *Cur Deus homo?*, Aquinas sought a counter for the enormous effects of sin in a remedy of far greater magnitude. Thus, he developed arguments of fittingness based on the fact that the price of our redemption was paid by an incarnate God. Despite the radical change of theological perspective evident in the *Summa*, even in Aquinas's final writings there still remain references to satisfaction which evoke Aristotelian justice. Are these references to be considered as so many leftovers from an earlier theological mentality which Thomas simply failed to integrate into the new and superior synthesis of the *Summa*? I think not.

Granted the centrality of priestly latria in Aquinas's definitive theology of satisfaction, we can easily incorporate strands from the justice tradition in his later works into a synthesis. Aquinas's theology of redemption forms part of a larger theological scheme which discovers its focus and motivating power in the notion of divine final causality. Since the divine attributes belong to the unity of the divine nature, even the Old Testament revelation concerning the wrath of God can fit nicely into this ecumenical picture. Indeed, in the final analysis, Thomas forges an understanding of God's justice which, as it remains identical with the divine nature itself, therefore must also fully manifest the divine goodness. God reveals himself as one who calls all men and women to a certain participation in his divine life.

Finally, the godly image finds its perfect restoration in forgiveness and satisfaction. The notion of commutative justice allows Aquinas to develop this position with full attention to the need for adequate human analogies to interpret the Gospel, since commutative justice applies to just relations within families.

> It is this sort of being that enters into penitence, and it is thus that the penitent turns to God, with the purpose of amendment, . . . as the son to his father according to Luke: "Father, I have sinned against heaven, and before you" (IIIa q. 85, a. 3).

The New Testament discloses a God who demonstrates no interest in acting according to the norms of vindicative justice. On the contrary, the Father of mercies and the God of all consolation acts towards his prodigal children more like a human father concerned to reunite a separated family. Through the means of sacramental satisfaction, the power of Christ's passion brings each one of us into that divine communion of love, which, like St Peter, Aquinas calls a certain participation in the divine nature.

NOTES

1. Since the "return to the sources" movement began at the turn of the last century, theologians have taken an interest in the "history of salvation" approach. Vatican Council II endorsed this approach to theology, while at the same time it urged the "tutelage of St Thomas" for efforts as speculative reason in theology. See *Optatam totius* 16.

2. For further information on the role of law and custom in the new dispensation, see John P. McIntyre, S.J., "Customary Law in the *Corpus Juris Canonici*," unpublished doctoral dissertation, The Catholic University of America, Washington, D.C., 1989, especially, p. 124ff.

3. See his remarks in *Summa theoloigae* Ia q. 44, a. 4: "Sed primo agenti, qui est agens tantum, non convenit agere propter acquisitionem alicuius finis; sed intendit solum communicare suam perfectionem, quae est eius bonitatis. Et unaquaequae creatura intendit consequi suam perfectionem, quae est similitudo perfectionis et bonitas divinae. Sic ergo divina bonitas est finis omnium rerum." See also, q. 19, a. 5.

4. For an excellent contemporary theology of sacraments, which takes full account of Aquinas's doctrine, see, Colman E. O'Neill, O.P., *Sacramental Realism* (Wilmington: Michael Glazier, Inc., 1983).

5. See his Sermon 2, "On the Ascension," c. 11 (*PL* 54:398). Furthermore, this general perspective on the presence of Christ in creation coheres with a certain Franciscan stress on the purpose of the Incarnation. Indeed, St Francis himself bore witness to the reality of Christ's presence among us by his gentle reverence for the created order as well as by his firm insistence that his friars welcome everyone with the peace of Christ (*Pax et bonum*).

6. "Por eso, hermanas mías, alto a pedir al Señor, que pues en alguna manera podemos gozar del cielo en la tierra." Teresa of Avila, *Castillo Interior* V, 1, 2 in *Obras de Santa Teresa de Jesus*, ed Silverio de Santa Teresa (Burgos: El Monte Carmelo, 1922), 587.

7. In fact Aquinas argues that one's personal act of sorrow for sins forms part of the "matter" of the sacrament of penance, even comparing our personal acts of conversion to the waters of baptism. See *Summa theologiae* IIIa q. 86, a. 4, ad 3.

CONCLUSION

The present study has been an exercise in historical theology. In such an exercise, careful attention must be paid to both terms of the phrase "historical theology." If this work has succeeded in illuminating the historical fact of development in St Thomas's soteriological teaching on Christ's satisfaction, its purpose has not been simply to ascertain and interpret a body of historical data. Rather, beyond rendering judgments of historical fact, I have been mindful of a larger and properly theological aim: to make valuable and distinctive elements of St Thomas's teaching available to contemporary discussion of Christ's saving work.

Materially speaking, the study has traced an arc of development from a juridically construed understanding of Christ's satisfactory work in St Thomas's *Scriptum super Sententias* to a thoroughly personalist understanding established in the *Summa theologiae*. Indeed, as Chapter Two argued, based on a survey of Aquinas's biblical commentaries, a personalist inspiration was never utterly absent from St Thomas's reflection on Christ's saving work. However, this inspiration does not for the most part determine the account of satisfaction which he renders in his earliest work of theological synthesis, the *Scriptum*. There, as indicated in Chapter Three, the Aristotelian understanding of virtue and the definitions of Anselm and pseudo-Augustine prevail, with the result that the notion of satisfaction is largely construed as an act of penitence. Only after St Thomas freed himself from the limitations of theological method and of the "Auctoritates" of Peter Lombard in works of original systematization such as the *Summa contra gentiles* did personalist categories (and above all, the pivotal role of the surpassing charity informing Christ's human will) begin to emerge. This trajectory remains closely associated with a broader theological understanding of justice as it figures in the account he gives of satisfaction. For alongside the Aristotelian model is set an "evangelical" understanding of justice, one which St Thomas never fully succeeded in relating to the Aristotelian model. Both share the ratio of "rectus ordo" or "rectitudo," but the latter more clearly indicates that the performance of the just deed proceeds on a prior divine initiative and that it consists formally in the subordination of the human person and his destiny to God in love. It is this same evangelical justice which constitutes the inner motive of Christ's satisfactory work and to whose restoration he directs that work. What seems an emerging trend in St Thomas's first original works of synthesis is consolidated in his account of Christ's satisfactory work in the *Summa theologiae*, as examined in some detail in Chapter Five. This determines the several ways in which satisfaction has a personal relevance to individual destiny and communal salvation-history, as suggested in Chapter Six.

Beyond the historical ascertainment of the fact of development in St Thomas's satisfaction-model, however, I am convinced that this development constitutes a significant enrichment of the soteriological tradition and a precious legacy for the ongoing work of theological revision as well. This enrichment consists preeminently in a systematic employment of a style of thinking that may rightly be called "personalist" while also exhibiting the rudiments of a sense of human historicity. The results of the present study suggest that St Thomas's overall theological vision as expressed in the *Summa theologiae* can illuminate certain issues of moment for contemporary soteriology so that, if the term "satisfaction" cannot be restored to current usage, then certainly the substance of St Thomas's understanding of satisfaction can and should be.

In the first place, the central elements of the explanation which St Thomas employed in his account of Christ's satisfactory work are also at the heart of the whole enterprise of theology as he understood and practiced it in the *Summa theologiae*; they provide that enterprise with remarkable systematic unity. For, as I noted earlier in this work, it is to the account in the *tertia pars* of salvation-history as enacted in Christ that St Thomas's theological exercise is directed. That account can legitimately be read as illuminating what comes before it, as it were, completing what is partial there.

In St Thomas's view, the divine reality is distinguished as sheer subsistent "esse," which equals identically subsistent understanding and loving. The persons of the Father, the Son, and the Holy Spirit communing in the divine nature are both distinguished and constituted by relations of mutual opposition within acts of knowing and loving. Yet we forfeit some of the richness and originality of St Thomas's trinitarian theology if their communion is regarded as being only at the ontic level, at the level of the intelligibility of the common divine nature. For their communion is personal as well, insofar as each of the subsistent relations constitutive of the persons is also a subject of the notional acts of knowledge and love. The three persons communing in the divine nature do so in that nature as distinct subjects within an identical consciousness and love.

By divine condescension, human reality has been created in order to enter into communion with the fellowship of the divine persons--a destiny that remains strictly supernatural. The open-endedness of the human intellect and of human love institutes, as it were, the negative condition for the achievement of this supernatural destiny. In its capacity for communion this basic human constitution aptitudinally images the personal communion of Father, Son and Holy Spirit in knowledge and love. What originates only as a kind of trajectory impressed upon human nature finds its termination and fulfillment in the gracious conferral of resources proportionate to a supernatural destiny of communion: habitual grace and the theological virtues. By the former, the human person is transformed so as to share in the divine nature; by the latter, a share in the divine knowing and loving is conferred. Thus, the merely aptitudinal imaging of the three divine persons found in human nature itself becomes an actual imaging of the three divine persons as regards both their communion in the divine nature and their personal communion in knowledge and love. The image of the three divine persons is actualized in precisely those dimensions of consciousness and free self-determination through love that also constitute the ratio of human historicity.

When St Thomas places basic human constitution in the context of history, he enters upon his account of salvation-history--the history of the original conferral, loss through sin, and restoration of the actual imaging of the personal communion of the Father, the Son, and the Holy Spirit. To Adam personally were given habitual grace and supernatural endowments of knowledge and love; to human nature as it existed in Adam was accorded the gift of original justice, consisting in an integration of human energies as focused upon God. The sin of Adam resulted in the loss of the resources for supernatural communion with the divine persons (and thus, for actually imaging their communion in fellowship with them) while also incurring objective guilt and proportionate punishment for human nature as generated by Adam. To this fault of nature, individuals have added personal moral fault accompanied by its own guilt and debt of punishment. Thus, in St Thomas's view, the human need for salvation requires both that sin and its attendant guilt and punishment be dealt with as the cloture of a destiny of personal communion and that those supernatural endowments in whose acts the perfect imaging of fellowship of and with the Trinity consist be restored.

Co-present in the divine intelligence with the tragedy of human history is its merciful remedy. Before all time the human history of Jesus Christ as head and salvific focus of historical humanity has been predestined; in that human history and destiny all human histories have been actively saved. The termination of that election of Christ's human history in the plenitude of grace and of all supernatural gifts makes Christ historical head of humankind. Christ's is to be the first human history, the first consistent deployment of supernatural knowing and loving to perfectly image divine personal communion within God. The endowment bestowed upon human nature in Adam on the supposition of his personal obedience to God becomes in an excelling mode a gift made to that nature insofar as it is assumed by the Word and rendered obedient through his human freedom. He who in the depths of the divine reality is the perfect image expressed by the Father and who together with the Father breathes forth personal love as the bond of fellowship, replicates this divine communion within the medium of his humanity and his human history for our sakes.

In St Thomas's view, it is a particular expression of divine love and justice to show mercy, and this condescension accounts for the incarnation and actively shapes all that transpires in the human intellect and will of Christ. To the human will of Christ God communicates the fullness of supernatural love as a capital endowment, such that his love for the Father should be both abounding love for us and the love of the Father on behalf of the members of his body. Thus rectified by charity, the human will of Christ fulfills the divine justice--that is, performs the substance of Adam's original establishment in justice: a complete submission and subjection of all human energies and interests to God. This "evangelical" justice, suffused by excelling charity, forms the inner core of Christ's salvific work under its satisfactory aspects. For, in this attitude of subjection and obedience, Christ ratifies the Father's salvific plan within the ambit of his human will and the free self-disposal of his human history and destiny. What is salvifically determinative and satisfactory about Christ's human destiny, therefore, is not simply the physical event of his passion, the exaction of a penalty of death, but the inner attitudes of love, obedience, and self-disposal in the Father's favor that animate Christ's suffering. The perfect mesh of the Father's loving initiative to save humankind and of Christ's human response is a crucial feature of Christ's satisfactory work, according to St Thomas. For in that communion of loves our own imaging communion with the Trinity is restored.

Of course, Aquinas's account of Christ's salvific work in its satisfactory character addresses more than the achievement of this sort of personal communion between head and members and of the whole body through its head with triune fellowship. It equally confronts the historical situation of such communion and that which has rendered it historically impossible: the reality of human sin, as a concrete determinant of universal human history. The "economy" of sin is by no means an ultimate nor is it even on a par with the economy of salvation in St Thomas's view. Indeed, inasmuch as human moral fault lacks due order and is characterized by deficient causality and unintelligibility, its historical shape is parasitic upon God's governance of his creation. Likewise, medicinal punishment as an effect of human moral fault shows that God's loving intentions retain the upper hand in guiding human history to its true destiny. It is the incarnation of the Word, radically, and Christ's consequent disposal of his historical freedom in loving response to the Father which show that what is uppermost and triumphant remains the Father's love. In that perfect response to the Father's saving will, Christ has freely and lovingly chosen solidarity with human history as a history of suffering (imposed as a punishment). In virtue of Christ's solidarity with suffering humanity, penal suffering becomes "once and for all" truly restorative and rectifies human willing. For, in truth, Christ "learned obedience through suffering," inasmuch as the full range of Christ's subjection of himself to the Father's saving will includes accepting the experience of suffering as the historical locale for obedient and loving acceptance of that will. The supernatural gifts which the body have from their head are such as to effect a personal solidarity with him in the historically unavoidable situation of human suffering. The grace and charity which Christ's members have from and in him are the grace and the love of his cross. These conform Christ's body to Christ's own obedience and love. This conformity urges Christ's members to "make up what is lacking in the sufferings of Christ"--that is, to supply their own free ratification of the experience of the Cross as the definitive historical shape of communion with the Father and the Holy Spirit in and through their head.

APPENDIX

St Anselm's *Cur Deus homo?*

The name of Anselm of Canterbury remains as closely linked to the doctrine of redemption as that of Athanasius to the dogma of the Trinity or that of Augustine to the teaching on grace. F.-R. Hasse expresses this judgment in his *De ontologico Anselmi pro existentia Dei argumento*, which, although written in the middle of the 19th-century, remains an important study on the archbishop of Canterbury.[1] St Anselm (c.1033-1109) was born in Aosta, the son of a Lombard landowner, and is the author of several theological treatises. *Cur Deus homo?* ranks among his more important works. Composed towards the end of the 11th century, it holds a significant place in the history of atonement theology. Indeed, Anselm's brief meditation on the purpose of the incarnation brought the notion of satisfaction into full theological currency, establishing it as a permanent feature of subsequent soteriological discussion. Thus, as one contemporary historian has remarked, after Anselm no treatment of the redemption could avoid taking some position with regard to the central thesis of *Cur Deus homo?*.[2]

St Anselm has also been called the "Father of Scholasticism." Indeed, his insistence on a rational methodology for theology foreshadows the singular achievement of the 13th-century theologians, even though the latter recognized the need to transform his "rationes necessariae" into arguments of fittingness. Most theologians agree that St Anselm's monastic discipline, especially devotion to "lectio divina," in fact led him to posit "necessary reasons" for the free decisions of the divine will. His theology, then, reflects more what Aquinas will later describe as the gifts of the Holy Spirit, especially understanding and knowledge, that is, affective knowledge of the truths of faith, than an unwarranted intrusion of human reason into divine mystery. On the other hand, some biblical themes and certain elements of the patristic tradition escape Anselm's particular method of theological reflection on Christ's saving work. For example, the prevalence of commercial metaphors and feudal images in the *Cur Deus homo?* reflect his uneven approach to soteriology. For this reason, his critics even characterize his essay on the atonement as a "théologie de comptoir."[3]

Anselm's work nevertheless does make a positive contribution to the development of Christian soteriology. Above all, his *Cur Deus homo?* eliminated the "rights of the devil" theory as a dominant soteriological theme, although until then the myth had controlled much of theological discussion on the redemption in the West.[4] In brief, the "rights of the devil" theory advanced the view that the devil, as a result of the original sin, enjoyed certain rights over fallen man. From this perspective, theology looks at the death of Christ as a ransom paid to the devil. Since the devil had to surrender captives whom he had won fair and square, this mythological explanation, promoted by an uncritical reading of certain New Testament metaphors, actually interprets salvation as a sort of exchange required by some form of cosmic justice. St Anselm explicitly rejects this theory and emphatically shifts the emphasis in soteriology to the absolute rights of God. Since he portrays God as the unparalleled master of creation, *Cur Deus homo?* also eliminates a cryptic dualism which can only distort Christian soteriology. In any event, Anselm does succeed in making atonement theology conform more to the New Testament accounts and less to the imagination of ancient folklore.

Furthermore, Anselm's theological method represents an advance in theology. Indeed, his starting-point, "neque enim quaero intelligere ut credam, sed credo ut intelligam," still provides a charter for Christian theologians.[5]   Among the many who have sought to interpret this principle, E. Gilson makes the following remark.[6]

> The order to be observed in the search for truth is therefore the following: first, to believe the mysteries of faith before discussing them through reason; next, to endeavor to understand what one believes. Not to put faith first is presumption; not to appeal to reason next is negligence. Both of those faults must therefore be avoided.

Of course, to seek understanding of the "necessity" involved in any mystery of the faith means one thing for St Anselm and something else for a rationalist. The history of christology, for example, provides a good illustration of how theology must avoid the Scylla of myth and the Charybdis of rationalization. At Chalcedon the Church steered a steady course between two extremes: easy mythological explanations of Christ, for example, when it rejected the "Heavenly Man" of Apollinaris of Laodicea, and neat rationalizations, for example, when it rejected the "Christ prosopon" of Nestorius. St Anselm was a man of faith. As a monk, he devoted time to prayerful meditation on the Word of God, and this brought him to behold a coherent vision of God's work in the world. Undoubtedly, this is what he called divine "necessity."

The Argument for Satisfaction

At the beginning of *Cur Deus homo?*, Anselm describes two kinds of necessity: one diminishes or even removes the voluntary character of an action, while the other makes an action all the more voluntary. Anselm intends to explore the latter kind of necessity as it operates in the incarnation. Thus, even if God could only effect a completion of the whole human project through grace, it nevertheless remains something necessary for the divine goodness to accomplish. He writes, "Yet we may say, although the whole work which God does for man is of grace, that it still remains necessary for God on account of his unchangeable goodness to complete the work which he has begun" (II, 5). The immutability of the divine goodness explains why God could not allow the whole of humankind to remain locked out of the possibility of attaining its end. On the other hand, sin serves to frustrate this divine necessity.

For St Anselm, sin constitutes a theft, since it steals from God something which belongs to him. To put it differently, sin affronts God, since by it man fails to do God the honor which he requires from every creature. But nothing could be less tolerable in the order of things ("ordo universitatis") than creatures who take away from the Creator his due honor. Of course, we recognize in the "ordo universitatis" Anselm's peculiar perspective on the created order and, especially, on God's place in that hierarchy. Because of the divine governance, Anselm envisions peace and harmony as the ordinary state of affairs in the world. Only sin can destroy that harmony. This provides a fuller definition of sin, one that respects its relational character, namely, our failing to respect the order of things established by God.

While St Anselm does not allow the possibility that God could tolerate the disorder of sin, nonetheless sin springs out of human freedom. He recognizes only two alternatives as responses to this misuse of freedom, namely, that "the honor taken away must be repaid, or punishment must follow" (I, 13). By this, he wishes to avoid the misconception that the divine love, although transcendent, can remain indifferent toward sins. Therefore, only two courses remain open to the sinner: freely to acquit himself of sin or unwillingly to suffer retribution. "It is impossible for God to lose his honor; for either the sinner pays his debt of his own accord, or, if he refuses, God takes it from him" (I, 14). The conservation of the "ordo universitatis" remains uppermost in St Anselm's mind. There is another factor, however, introduced into the argument at this point: what man has taken from God by sinning, i.e., his honor, he is unable to pay back, "for a sinner cannot justify a sinner" (I, 23).

Why is it impossible for a sinner to make satisfaction to God? Because everything that we might offer to God, namely, penance, contrition, humility, abstinence, work, obedience, mercy and so forth, already belong to him. But for St Anselm, one can only satisfy by offering a work of supererogation, i.e., "something greater than the amount of that obligation which should have restrained one from committing the sin" (I, 11). This definition forms the basis for Anselm's conception of satisfaction. By the same token, it creates an impasse. For since in the case of original sin, God's honor should have kept us from sinning at all, how can we even imagine something greater than his honor as a means towards satisfaction? Although this disorder has robbed God of his honor, the creature certainly remains unable to repair by himself the total disorder which sin has introduced into the order of the universe. Nor can we satisfy, since to offer something greater than the offense, we must offer to God something greater than the entire created order. In St Anselm's phrase, "greater than all the universe besides God" (II, 6).

Still the responsibility for making satisfaction falls to us, because one who possessed human nature sinned. Only God can produce the "something greater" required to make satisfaction, but only man ought to furnish it. For such a satisfaction "which none but God can make and none but man ought to make," argues St Anselm, "it is necessary for the God-man to make it" (II,6). Thus he concludes his argument: "necesse est fieri per Christum," that is, "only Christ can accomplish our salvation" (I, 25). The infallible character of God's plan for bringing us to beatitude finds its means in Jesus Christ. So even though sin exists, God necessarily, but freely, accomplishes that which he had intended from the beginning, namely, to unite us to himself.

Although St Anselm treats other themes in the course of *Cur Deus homo?*, we should inquire about the effect of Christ's death and satisfaction. Anselm explains, "If he allowed himself to be slain for the sake of justice, did he not give his life for the honor of God?" (II,18). Frequently associated with Anselm's theory, the notion of a substitute victim who satisfies divine vindicative justice dimly emerges at this point in the explanation. In any event, we remain the beneficiaries of the arrangement. And although the explanation suggests to some a barter or exchange, St Anselm nevertheless tries to account for the universality of Christ's satisfaction. He asks: "To whom else should the Son have more suitably ceded the fruits and the recompense that his death was worth than to those for whose salvation he came? Could God have refused him this request since he--being innocent--could have no need of any such recompense?" (II,19). Although St Anselm himself stops here, his genius provides direction and inspiration for theologies of the atonement.

NOTES

1. F.-R. Hasse, *De ontologico Anselmi pro existentia Dei argumento* (Bonn: Leçon de maîtrise de la Faculté de Théologie Evangélique, 1849). For further information on Anselm's life and work, see R.W. Southern, *Saint Anselm and his Biographer. A Study of Monastic Life and Thought* (Cambridge: University Press, 1966), especially, 77-121.

2. René Roques, *Pourquoi Dieu s'est fait homme*, French translation of *Cur Deus homo?* (Paris: Editions du Cerf, 1963), 182.

3. For a good treatment of modern opinion on the *Cur Deus Homo?*, see J. McIntyre, *St Anselm and his Critics: a reinterpretation of the Cur Deus homo?* (Edinburgh, 1954). For a broader assessment of his theology, see *Actes du Congrès international du IXe centenaire de l'arrivée d'Anselme au Bec* (Paris: J. Vrin, 1959).

4. For a detailed historical study of this aspect of patristic soteriology, see Jean Rivière, "Le droit du démon sur les pécheurs avant Saint Augustin," *Recherches de théologie ancienne et médiévale* 3 (1931), 113-39. Rivière also considers the subject in medieval theology, see "Réveil de la théorie du rachat au cours du moyen âge," *Revue des sciences religieuses* 13 (1933), 353-92.

5. We find the formula in *Proslogium*, c. 1. But Anselm also refers to the celebrated principle of theological hermeneutics in *Cur Deus homo?* I, 2.

6. See Etienne Gilson, *History of Christian Philosophy in the Middle Ages* (New York: Random House, 1955), 129.

INDEX

Adenulf of Anagni 13
Alexander of Hales 1, 70
Ambrose, St 57, 116
Anselm, St xvi, 2, 53-58, 61, 62, 67-71, 73, 75-78, 81, 88, 91, 97,
      103, 120, 128, 130, 134, 148, 153, 159, 200, 203, 208-211
Apollinaris 209
Aristotle 3, 10, 17, 54-56, 94, 132, 199
Arius 137
Athanasius, St 137, 138, 208
Augustine, St 1, 2, 44, 53, 62, 85-87, 105, 109, 120, 125-128, 136,
      137, 142, 145, 148, 155, 181, 183, 188, 195, 208
Aulèn, G. xvii
Bernard of Clairvaux, St 2
Bernard Gui 1
Boethius 133
Boso 76, 77
Cantor of Antioch 6
Capreolus 52
Catão, B. 159
Cerfaux, L. 35
Chalcedon xvi, 19, 128, 132-134, 136, 209
Chenu, M.-D. 5, 6, 9-11, 33, 40, 67, 101, 103
Cicero 105
Damascene, St John 15, 124, 128, 140, 141
Dodd, C. H. 34
Erasmus 28
Flavian of Constantinople 128
Francis of Assisi, St 202
Fulgentius of Ruspe 85
Gennadius 53 (also see *pseudo-Augustine*)
Gérard d'Abbeville 12, 14
Gilson, E. 209
Glossa ordinaria 88
Gregory the Great, St 8, 39, 63, 105, 186
Gregory of Nyssa, St 162
Hasse, F. R. 208
Hilary of Poitiers, St 101
Hill, E. 27
Hugh of St-Victor 10
Ivo of Chartres 2
Jerome, St 2, 45
John of Vercelli, Bl. 12
King of Cyprus 41
Lafont, G. 19, 161